DEAD RIGHT THERE
BOOK 2: THE DETECTIVE YEARS

More Memories and Confessions of a Former Military and Texas Lawman, Private Investigator and Bodyguard

By W. Hock Hochheim

High Home Endeavors
Copyright 2010-2026
All rights reserved.

Other Titles by W. Hock Hochheim

Fightin' Words
Dead Right There
Don't Even Think About It!
Rust In Pieces
Gunther 1: Gunther! Law West of Medieval
Gunther 2: Riders of the Khyber Pass
Gunther 3: Guns of the China Alamo
Gunther 4: Last of the Gunslingers
Gunther 5: Rio Grande Black Magic
Gunther 6: The Horse Killers
Impact Weapon Combatives
Knife Combatives
Training Mission Series 1-5
The Great Escapes of Pancho Villa
Kellog 1: Kill Them Back
Kellog 2: Face the Muzak
Kellog 3: Takedown the Take
Renegade General 1: Swellen's Reckoning
Renegade General 2: Swellen's Orphans
Confrontations: Who, What, Where, When, How, Why
Migraine: Who, What, Where, When, How and Why

Disclaimer: This book is a memoir. It contains information about real events as Hock experienced them during his long career in the military and in law enforcement. In some cases, names, places, timelines and personal descriptions have been changed to protect the privacy of others. As Hock so often states, if the information is positive and you think he's talking about you, then he is. If it's negative, then he's absolutely referring to someone else entirely.

TABLE OF CONTENTS

Prologue: The Night We Caught the Wrong Armed Robbers.
An Army Detective Story. 7
Chapter 1: Lynch and His Hunch 19
Chapter 2: The Albino Caper 27
Chapter 3: The Greatest Shot I've Ever Seen 69
Chapter 4: "And Hock, You Take the Back!" 85
Chapter 5: Shadows and Glass 91
Chapter 7: A Murdering Cop I Knew. 97
Chapter 8: Libby, Bozo and Sidney 105
Chapter 9 A Barbershop in Waco 113
Chapter 10: Fear and Loathing of the Killer,
    Henry Lee Lucas 119
Chapter 11: Jailbreak! Psycho Martin Crebbs 139
Chapter 12: You Can't Hide Your Lying Eyes 169
Chapter 13: The Face Mask Murders 181
Chapter 14: Hacking the Hammer 215
Chapter 15: The Dead Baby 225
Chapter 16: True Detective - Murder, Mayhem,
    and Killer Potboilers 231
Chapter 17: Showdown at Jacksberg Lumber
    Yard 259
Chapter 18: I Caught the Hitman 277
Chapter 19: Benny Parkey. Adios Amigo 283
Chapter 20: The "Hockford Files." Private
    Investigator the Last Murder Case 289
Chapter 21: Back to Lynch's Hunch 305

Prologue: The Night We Caught the Wrong Armed Robbers. An Army Detective Story.

Before I start with the twisted Texas tales, I must remind you that before Texas, I was an investigator in the U.S. Army, part of the MPI – Military Police Investigation unit. It wasn't a money promotion jumping up from the MP patrol division to MPI detective division, but you had to be identified as having some "snap" to be selected.

We were the grunt detectives in a big-city-sized American Army base. Inside the MPI was also the M.D.D.S. The Marijuana and Dangerous Drug Section, where we worked also. Back in the 1970s, sadly, marijuana had received nothing short of heroin status.

Back then, Army CID, the Criminal Investigation Division, was staffed by officers, and warrant officers and was like the FBI where we were. To us. If major things started popping, we would report the details to them, and they almost always told us, basically, "Ok. Keep us posted."

We were kind of the grunt first line, responding detectives. Here is quick Army detective story setting the stage for the rest of the book.

The 1970s...
Payday at a major military base was always a big event, at least it was back when I was in the Army decades ago because it was a cash, check-cashing and carry world back then. And what you could cash and carry could be swindled, sexed-drugged and rock n' rolled, or strong-armed, or weapon-robbed.

For a Military Police officer (MP), paydays meant drug deals, parties, hookers, wrecks, fights, drunks, and robberies; and once in a while it was worse, like rape, aggravated assault, or murder. For an MPI agent we were on surveillances, stand-by, dispatched to, and-or had to investigate these crimes.

Drug dealers, hookers, dice games, card sharks, and stolen-property buyers and sellers would drive in from states all around us and setup shop in motels, hotels, and parking lots. They also grazed the strip joints and bars for business. It seemed like scumbags treated our paydays as if they were a monthly business convention or some kind of damned flea market.

Not only would those thugs trade for the weekend, but they would also organize longer-term criminal rings of all sorts with questionable soldiers. All year long, we'd lose military weapons, gear, and supplies to those networks on a black-market style operation. In return we got an influx of drugs, drugged soldiers, beaten and-or murder victims, addicts, counterfeit money, and other sludges.

Our U.S. base was a large city all unto itself connected to an even bigger civilian city. The PM (Provost Marshal or the "High Sheriff") took every payday seriously; and especially with the occasional one landing on a Friday kicking off a three-day binge, he really put on the dog. Well dogs yes, he sent the K-9s out, too, but a lot more. We had helicopters up with searchlights and extra squad-car patrols, and we plainclothes MPIs (Military Police Investigations) were sent out on various jobs.

When I was in Military Police Investigations (MPI), the General Investigations section, we were facing one of those upcoming three-day stints. But just a few weeks before the payday mayhem, we had been plagued with a small robbery gang that worked around the enlisted-men hangouts, the bars, the clubs, and restaurants, etcetera, on base. They would surround a victim and rob him. Those guys would secure single-edged, razor blades between the fingers of their open hands with tape and slap the faces of their victims in the process. The victims got slapped around and gave up their money.

But only later would some of the victims learn of their facial wounds and go to the hospital. Unless they were first shown the razor blades to comply. Otherwise, victims just thought they were being slapped around.

Odd, because surely the robbers thought they were scaring the hell out of their victims with those razor blades even if unshown. Yet in the dark, the victims didn't see the blades nor succinctly feel them during the robbery! They had, however, seen the thin red lines on their faces right after the act. And the blood. Several of us would get called out to work on these cases.

We nicknamed them the "Razor Blade Robbers," but it wasn't that gang that initiated our three-day, payday, stakeout weekend. It was the "Golf Course Robbers."

G.I.s would get their monthly stipend and would hit the main city strip where all the music, girls, booze and drug action took place. They'd get tanked up and many would eventually walk back to their barracks on base. Late. For hundreds of these troops, that often meant a long staggering walk northwest across a dark military, 18-hole golf course just off the main gate. Traps more than sand traps, criminals would emerge robbing them holding guns, knives or knocking them on the head with a club. But the golf course robberies persisted oblivious to paydays.

The robbers started picking up to weekends and some weekdays. Troops would take these walks every night and sometimes get robbed by a group of two or three guys. The last victim had been stabbed multiple times and almost died in what was a classic escalation of gratuitous violence.

With the near-death stabbing, CID had to step in but had no leads. The Provost Marshal decided that on the upcoming long payday and three-day weekend, our entire Military Police Investigations unit would stake out that golf course.

So, an OP (Operation) had been organized by our fearless leaders. The entire AO (area of operation) for the stakeout included the main gate, "Main Gate Highway," and west of there the entire golf course. The golf course was then surrounded by a major hospital to the north, a housing addition, and a bit further northwest a densely populated barracks area. To the east of Main Gate Highway, and not our concern these nights, was a large military airport surrounded by a tall, barbed wire fence. Mostly used by helicopters. The whole op would be run by an MPI segreant on the roof of the aforementioned hospital. Each night we would rotate positions. I was hiding behind different trees and bushes, well aware that robbers might hide beside us too. Such was the point!

If we saw suspicious jerks crossing the course and hiding out, we were to wait until possible victims walked by, and catch them in the act! We were hiding with and from the hiders, so it was a bit tricky. Rules of engagement? Simple. Shoot them if you had to. Ten-four on that.

We would sleep by day and report in at night. We all had Vietnam-era Starlight Scopes, which were aplenty, sans the M-16s. That primitive, heavy, long, thick, pipe-like canisters were the first real night vision devices the Army used. It felt very, very heavy when it rested atop your M-16 weighing in at 6 pounds. It functioned on enhancing any available light by some 60,000 times and dark green images of about four times normal vision size. God help you if you pointed it at a regular bright light like a streetlight! It would burn a painful beam like a laser-spike deep into your brain! We just held them up like a telescope, sans the M-16, to look through.

See atop the weapon.

We'd dressed in clothing as dark as possible with black watch (skull) caps and brought our snub-nosed .38 pistols, flashlights, cuffs, binoculars, portable radios, and earpieces. As the first night fully set in, we jogged out to our assigned spots in the AO.

Nothing happened the first night. The second night, I started off in the rotation of a good position up on the roof of the Army hospital. The multi-level, multi-story roof offered an excellent view of the golf course and then the north side of the city beyond the main gate. For a few hours I scanned the landscape with binoculars and a Starlight scope being careful not to tip-slip into a city light and freak-fry my eyeballs.

Then we shifted locales. I went down to the course, and someone else took that bird's-eye vantage point. I found myself sitting on the ground back up against a tree in a small section of trees on the course.

On our isolated radio frequency, my friend and fellow MPI agent Hitch suddenly broke the silence and said, "118 to 100." (I have completely forgotten our MPI call signs, so these are substitutes; but 100 was an MPI supervisor on the hospital roof.) Hitch (118) called the MPI supervisor.

Hitch had hunkered down in a small construction ditch on the east-side shoulder off the Main Gate Highway with his back to the airport, facing the golf course. Hitch reported...

"118 to 100 ... I think I see some men running across the airport behind me."

Huh? I pushed the little earpiece, much like a cheap one from an a.m. radio, deeper into my ear to hear all this.

"Ten-four, 118," the voice of 100 replied calmly. This was of little concern at the moment. It wasn't uncommon for some knucklehead soldiers to trespass across restricted areas like airport runways for shortcuts across the base to the main gate. But one of the MPI supervisors on the rooftop started changing radio channels to see if anything else had been going on since we were on an isolated channel.

"100 to 118, where are they now?" a now desperate-sounding sergeant's voice asked Hitch.

"Running straight up behind me," Hitch answered.

"All positions on or near Main Gate Highway respond to 118's position. Those are armed robbers approaching 118 from the airport," 100 commanded. "They just committed a robbery of the far side of the airport, at their NCO club."

"What?" I thought. Our golf course armed robbers? No. Our radios had but a few channels; and we had switched on the one frequency for this assignment; else we would have known that all hell was breaking loose to the east of us on the other side of the terminal.

Just outside the airport at an NCO club near the terminal, the infamous Razor Blade Robbers had cornered, slapped, cut up, and robbed an artillery sergeant, who fought back. The struggle slowed the robbers down and caused a lot of noisy attention in the parking lot. Witnesses called in the crime. Patrol units responded, cutting off their avenues of escape. So, the three bad guys had jumped a security fence (barbed-wire and all) and had desperately dashed west across the airport to escape. Heading our way!

I jumped up as did two or three other agents who had been stretched out on the course near the Highway. I stopped for a second, looking down ... the heavy damn Starlight scope! Should I just leave it here? YEAH! I started out at a dead run for Hitch.

As I got clear of some trees and closer, I was able to actually spot the three figures running over the airstrip and under the small revolving construction beacon where Hitch had been burrowed down. The men had indeed been running straight at him! If I could see them, then they could see me; so, I tried to get into an even lower-profile combat run with a slightly wider angle.

The closer I got, the lower I tried to get. The bad guys hit the fence and started over it. Another crouched-over MPI agent approached north from the south. I was coming in from the north. When all three of the suspects hit the ground on this side of the airport fence, Hitch could wait no longer. He stood up, lit them up with his flashlight, pointed his revolver, and shouted,

"Freeze! Police!"

The bad guys fidgeted; all three had been juking in different directions. Then they turned and stutter-stepped to the north and saw me running in, my gun up in a single hand. They stuttered the same to the south and then saw the other agent. Gun up.

Hitch closed in on them, cussed them, and ordered,

"Grab some fence, you sons-a-bitches!"

Three guys. Three of us. Not bad at all. But we didn't know if they were armed, other than razor blades? They looked at our pistols, turned, and grabbed the fence.

We cuffed them and did a quick search. Patrol squad cars screamed down Main Gate Highway and screeched their brakes to stop by our waving flashlights. The patrolmen took the trio in because we had to return straight back to our original positions on the golf course and to our original task.

Back at my little grove of trees, I was happy to see the expensive Starlight Scope still on the ground right where I left it. They would have skinned me alive if I'd lost that thing.

After our stakeout that night, we would have paperwork to do at headquarters (Remember, there was no "overtime" in the Army, you were just ... in the Army.).

These three men were soldiers from our base, not the usual civilian gypsy-payday entrepreneurs. I cannot recall exactly how the bad guys kept the razor blades between their fingers. But they dropped them on the run on the airstrip. Best I can remember they did it with duct tape. We never caught the Golf Course Robbers. Perhaps they read the news that were out there. But in Monday's local newspapers, the headline read,

"Military Police in Stakeout Catch Armed Robbers."

But little did the public know...we'd caught the *wrong* damn robbers!

These days there is much attention paid to military police investigators. The whole NCIS series. (I only liked the "Tony-Ziva" era-days of the original, oh and the Gibbs-Origin series version is growing on me).

And of course, there's the Reacher books. Life is not quite like NCIS and the whole Reacher thing is a fairy tale by a British author who knows zero about the US Army military police. I really like the Amazon TV series though, but I just can't stand the books.

As *this* book continues, I may drop back to some partial Army MPI memories, and even Army and patrol days if relevant.

```
Police Detective Notebook...
```

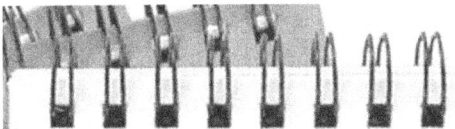

> "Down these mean streets a man must go who is not himself mean, who is neither tarnished nor afraid. The detective must be a complete man and a common man, and yet an unusual man. He must be, to use a rather weathered phrase, a man of honor by instinct, by inevitability, without thought of it, and certainly, without saying it. He must be the best man in his world and a good enough man for any world."
>
> — Raymond Chandler

Chapter 1: Lynch and His Hunch
Texas...1970s

Police Chief Hugh Lynch

I fully embraced the role of patrol officer in the 1970s. Army and Texas. Those stories are all in my "Don't Even Think About It" memoirs book, "Book 1" of this series. And even though I'd been an investigator in the Army, once back in Texas, I had settled back well into a patrol car.

Yes, I was bored some of the time in patrol. Cops were bored everywhere around the world at times. But our city back then had a kind of a wilder, cowboy, anything-can-happen edge that just seemed to keep things interesting. Our city sat atop Dallas and Fort Worth, the Metroplex they call it, with a teeming population even back then. And in those years the two cities were both in the top five crime capitals in the USA. This mess regularly spilled over to our neck of the woods.

In the late 1970s it did not go unnoticed by the Detective Division that I had worked general investigations and narcotics in the Army. Especially noticed by one CID Sgt. Howard Kelly. Kelly was pushing for a serious war on drugs; and though I had never sat and talked with him about it, I'd just seen him about a hundred times on calls as he was always helping we patrol officers with backups, crime scenes, etc. He went on a whisper campaign in my favor.

The CID section was really the go-to backbone of the agency back then. Detectives were the SWAT team and the go-to problem-solvers. Everything just got handed over to the detectives when they arrived.

CID seemed also like a tight-knit fraternity of good ol' boys who knew each other closely. Oh, not just Texans mind you; there was a detective in there from England. Of course, he was called "Limey." With the arrival of COPS, Community-Oriented Policing many years later, the operational priority went back to the patrol division as the spinal cord of the P.D.

One afternoon in 1980, I was booking a person in the jail, and Police Chief Hugh Lynch came by and stood beside me.

"Whatcha' got there, Hock?"

"Arrest warrant out of Dallas."

He looked over the papers on the tall counter and then looked up at my profile and got right to the point.

"You want to be a detective?" he asked me right out of the blue as they say, with that infamous giant cigar between his teeth.

Boom. Huh? What? Well, at that point, I never really gave it much thought. I was happy where I was running the streets. I also knew well the complicated hassle a detective's life could be.

"Ahhh, yeah," I mean what else could I say? To the Chief! He just winked, smiled, nodded, and walked away.

There was of course an official process to become a detective. First, it was a lateral transfer. No official monetary promotion. But people coveted that job. Admin took letters, applications and interviews when a CID position opened.

Within a month, a detective quit and moved off. The CID opening was announced. I saw Howard Kelly in the hallway, and he smiled at me from under a big white Stetson and said-

"Reckon you are putting in a letter for CID if an opening comes up?"

"Ah, I am."

"You'd better," and he strutted on past me.

I did submit such a letter. And I showed up for my assigned CID interview with Sgt. Kelly and two other detective supervisors that I can no longer remember who they were. Howard Kelly led the questioning and steered the interview toward my time in the Army Military Police general investigations. They all knew I had graduated from the Military Police Investigation School and had worked numerous cases. The results of all the letters and interviews ended up in a pow-wow in the Chief's office.

Within a week, there was a letter posted on the main bulletin board of my transfer to the Criminal

Investigation Division. In the end, it was Lynch's choice, and I gather he knew all along.

I got part of an annual $500 clothing allowance since some of the year had elapsed. And I appeared on the morning of the designated date, as a new detective, but I wasn't really new-new.

I was first assigned to a Detective Willy Skeens (an alias) for training. Bad start. Like I said. I was not exactly new to the investigation "thing," but such a period was mandatory, and I still had to be trained as a formal process. I still knew enough to spot that this guy Skeens was nearly a total waste of time and energy. I think he was "on the spectrum" as the saying goes. Possibly even, dare I say something of an idiot savant? Brilliant is some ways. But it was just for a few weeks. I could tough that out

As I sat next to Skeens in the morning meetings, the CID Lieutenant would assign crime reports to investigate. The LT. would hand Skeens his crimes. As soon as the LT. left the room, Skeens would mumble a few curses at him and throw the reports right into the trash can! Granted, these were not triple murders but low-running crimes. But still!

I'd had an Army CID sergeant tell me once years earlier that –"If you would work an auto burglary as fiercely as a homicide, you would solve a lot more crimes."

That simple advice really stuck with me. Now Skeens (and eventually me) was responsible for follow-up investigation reports on all of these throw-aways. First contact with complainants had to be made in three days. The first contact was important for citizens. If you wanted to get into trouble with CID admin, ignore the 3-day, first contact rule and have a complainant call the P.D. screaming – "Where's my detective!" after 3 days. Yet, into the trash these Skeen cases went!

Granted, Skeens and I were kind of friends. Yes. But he was a mess. He would spend most of his day playing pinball games in hotel lobbies and convenience stores. Me being there, ruined this. That got worse as new computer games appeared.

Of course, Skeens would rise to become a lieutenant in our department. I mean he had serious obsessive-like skills like in computers. But that, my friends… was life on the force and government work and probably any job I guess. Peter Principal test-takers get promoted.

I was cut loose from that albatross after a long two-week period. Skeens was a *heavy* smoker, and he has since passed away from heart attacks I am told.

My first solo case was an armed robbery. A man was kidnapped, taken out to the country at night at gunpoint, beaten, robbed, and stripped of his clothes. The next day I drove this guy out to find the country crime scene in the daylight and we looked around. There I was in suit, tie, and gun again searching for some evidence. It struck me right then and there that I was a working detective once again like in the Army. It was really what I was supposed to be, what I was meant to be. It felt like all was right with the universe.

Investigations became an addiction for me. It wasn't a good addiction for me either. It cost me parts of my personality, hell, it became my personality. Cost me parts of my normal human happiness, and its lifestyle cost me my family. It cost me all this.

My decisions. My choices. My fault. Me. But now, decades later, I still remember that moment, that feeling that morning. I guess it was sort of like a hit of heroin. Sort of.

And decades later, I still miss it every day. Not the small cases. Not the boring cases. Not the admin interferences. But the felonies. The big ones, and the idea that every day might bring more of them. I didn't take the job to be a missionary or a social worker. To "serve." I just wanted to catch criminals.

All the do-good trappings of police work offered plenty of cover for someone like me. Deer hunters and duck hunters didn't get out of their beds at 4 a.m. just because they believed so strongly in conservation. Conservation is a side issue. A cover. An excuse for hunting. Hunters want to hunt.

I really wanted to catch criminals. Being a detective put me more on course or on the trail. All I did was solve crimes for almost two decades. And at the end of each rainbow…was a criminal. Giving me good cases to work was like giving me dope. Give me more…

Police Detective Notebook...

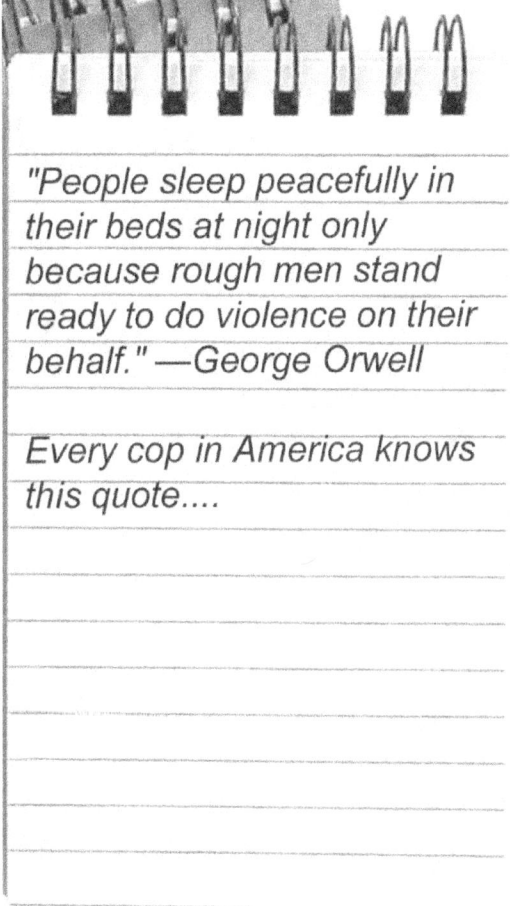

"People sleep peacefully in their beds at night only because rough men stand ready to do violence on their behalf." —George Orwell

Every cop in America knows this quote....

Chapter 2: The Albino Caper
1972 in Stony Point, Texas...

Before the Army. I was on a Harley with a girl on the back, whose name I now forget, but I do recall she had longer hair than I did. But not by much. She had cajoled me into this ride out into the countryside to meet with…a psychic.

Those that know me, know I am a natural-born skeptic. I was so skeptical even way back then. Nowadays, I am so skeptical, I am skeptical of my skepticism. But the girl was persuasive and, as a younger man, I was easily persuaded by such girls, long hair and all. Which, you take heed all you young men reading this, these surface predilections alone not always such a good thing.

A psychic, we'll call her here "Della Hawkins," entertained her customers right there at her rural, Stony Point house by manifesting predictions and problem-solving on demand. The two-story house was set on a rocky and sparsely treed rise of land northeast of Dallas. The immediate grounds and long front porch were chock full of odd artifacts and bizarre lawn goodies. Statues, globes, gnomes, cones, wind chimes, benches, cheap plug-in fountains. Years of collecting that even a tasteless punk like me could discern "no taste" when I saw it.

We parked and walked into the front room of the house, crammed with the same kind of, well...shit. You couldn't see the walls or the floor for the collection of antiques and non-antique junk! Stuff peppered everywhere! Weird looking voodoo, magic stuff, interspersed with Christian crosses, pagan symbols and checkered with Jesus statues. I didn't mind all that diversity, but jeez lady...pick a plan for Armageddon and run with it, will ya'?

Such peppering was a personality flaw to me but, after all, this was a popular psychic and a little weird by nature don't you think?

Popular? I could discern through this massive wall of photos. Della with Elvis. With Nixon. Several governors of Texas. Johnny Cash. The wall of big names sitting or standing next to Della was quite impressive! The girl with the long hair clung on my arm, her boot heels chaffing with excitement as we perused the collection of celebrity photos.

A wooden door opened and another excited woman, giddy-voiced and all teeth, emerged beside theeee' Della Hawkins. I guess the giddy girl got some good, giddy, psychic news? Della was a short, stocky, white, women with dyed, bright white/blonde hair brushed back and magic-marker eyebrows. Della filled out a flowing, smock-ish gown.

"Next," she said in a bored sigh, like a tired old doctor. The announcement cue. Enter into her twilight zone. We took a seat before a large oriental desk in yet another insanely cluttered room. She introduced herself.

"I am Madame Della Hawkins," she started. "I can help people and predict the future." So on and so on. "We will start with $10 dollars."

Now the running gig was you got a "reading" for $10 and you also had to produce a quarter coin from your pocket. You see, the metal in the coin was a touchstone for her to hold and get mystical vibes and galactic mojo from. You've heard of the metal vibe schtick before with "readers"? Right? Oh, and by the way, the "Madame" keeps the quarter too! Now it's 10 bucks and 25 cents and back then such bought a lot of Lone Star beer and barbecue, plus a few nights at Casey's Campground. Gas was 38 cents a gallon, and a skinny feller like me could go a long way on a Harley for a buck's worth of petrol.

But I coughed it up as entertainment for this long-haired, cute gal I was with. An integral step was rubbing the coin and her hands in Jerkins Lotion (a fourth dimensional conductor?).

She asked me a few basic questions. I replied with my, back then thick, "Archie Bunker" New York style, Yankee accent. She looked me over, and I had Yankee transient written all over me. All the while, she dipped and re-dipped the quarter in Jurgens (also a disinfectant?)

And she rubbed the coin in her hands, the pitch is to impress you with some secret observations, then hook you into her amazingness, then predict something-er-other' that you will believe and maybe come back again with another $10.25. And soon! I hate to be such a killjoy, but bubba? That is how your psychic cookie crumbles!

So, after the hand rub in the astrologic, "Nebula" outer-dimension, lotion, next came the swami part. She told me ...

"You have just taken a trip. You will take another trip."

And I would take another trip. Out of there. And that was about it. Since it was my quarter, the girl received no advice, but to maybe stay the hell away from me? We left. Bye!

I quickly came to realize that the cute, long-haired girl was just interested in seeing if I would stay in Texas with her and what my "prospects" were. I could have told her from the source. I considered myself utterly prospect-less. But some women need to get outside confirmation from a Voodoo/Christian shaman to make these life-changing decisions.

After a short time, I never saw the cute, long-haired girl again. The predicted, pending trip I presume? In fact, though, this wasn't the only time that female psychics jacked with my so-called love life. These sad and strange stories should appear in another kind of book. *Fifty Shades of Psychic.* But, through time this princess left for good,

I would indeed see the Grand Madame Della Hawkins again, despite my wishes! She never warned me though, that, "our paths would cross again – with blood and violent crime! Some psychic, huh? A couple of Vegas-Mafia thugs damn near beat her and her husband to death while stealing her gold bullion. And I had to catch them!

Some 15 years later, the 1980s...

One Friday night, as a police detective I was summoned, code red, to a private house in our city. Armed robbery. Attempted murder. I had just arrested a burglar with an arrest warrant and was busy booking him into the city jail, when I got the phone call from the front desk that I was needed ASAP across town to this crime scene. I'd wanted to interrogate the burglary suspect, but this new duty called instead. Direct from my favorite sergeant, Howard Kelly. (Those familiar with the NCIS TV show, Kelly was my Jethro Gibbs.) I quickly locked up the burglar. One never catches up in this business.

 I walked upstairs to the front desk to get more info from the patrol lieutenant Russel Trapp. Trapp told me that an elderly couple was almost beaten to death with baseball bats and robbed at gunpoint. Gold bullion was stolen.

 When I arrived at this very busy crime scene, patrol and detective supervisors were standing by for the detective, as in me, to pass the whole mess off to. Me. Oh, lucky me. But you know what? I lived for this stuff.

 Where's a good psychic when you need one? This should be easy, right? The victim such a renown soothsayer?

It was quite a crime scene. The house was a mess, and by a mess I mean a real mess. Not only had the "Madame Hoarder" maintained her massive collection of exotic and weird stuff, much of it was busted up and strewn all over the place. And the house was full of uniformed patrolmen and EMTs, traipsing around to no good end, in my opinion. Even several of the county sheriff's office investigators were there. Which was unusual.

Back then, common "cop shops" were at the cusp of new, crime scene advancements-requirements. Pre-cusp, maybe? But cuspy or not, mandates for pristine crime scenes for evidence collection had not really, fully integrated successfully across America yet. Should have. But just hadn't. One of the common crime scene problems back then was how to diplomatically keep all unnecessary personnel (that means supervisors for one, and "blue" rubberneckers) out of crimes scenes.

I spotted Sgt. Howard Kelly (he did need to be there) in the kitchen and he called me over.

"Hock, do you know Tom and Della Hawkins?" he asked.

"Know of them," I answered, not wanting to slow the conversation down with my silly story from my past.

"Della is a psychic. Famous, world famous," Howard told me.

"She has rich clients from all over the world."

A county sheriff detective walked up with a big grin, replete in a white, snap button shirt, bolo tie, western hat and vest, and a Texas Ranger-like gun belt. He nosed right into our conversation..

"Tonight," Howard continued, "two men in masks got into the house, jumped Ted and Della. Beat 'em. Tied them up and beat them some more. One had a ball bat. Wrapped them up with masking tape and duct tape. They got them to admit where all their money and gold was."

"Jewelry?" I asked, as in gold.

"No. Bullion," Howard answered. "Bars of gold."

"Where are the Hawkins now?"

"They are at the hospital. Tom is damn near dead. Della's in a little better shape," Kelly said. "I saw them when I got here. Roughed up, bruised-beaten. She said that the robbers were a team from Las Vegas, connected with the mob."

"How she know that?" I asked.

"We'll have to find out," Kelly said.

"Investigator Lt. Dale Winston," a county detective interrupted us, shaking my hand. He knew Howard Kelly.

"Della was a big supporter of the Sheriff, and if there is anything we can do?" he said. (Supporter is code-word for campaign contributions.)

I nodded to him. I'd seen him around, but we'd never officially met until this moment.

"Russell Lewis is in the bedroom now," Howard Kelly continued with a thumb pointed over his shoulder. Russell was our crime scene guy.

I walked that way of the thumb, followed closely by Dale Winston and his partner, another county detective I did not know and was not introduced to. Russell was bathed in the flashing, white lights of a photo session. The room was also a mess, and I saw a mummy's amount of duct tape on the floor. I knelt down and knocked the tape around with my writing pen.

"You know, Russell, I just read in a police journal the other day that a case was made somewhere in Missouri by getting fingerprints off of duct tape. The sticky side."

He hadn't heard that yet. There were new advancements in fingerprint detection back then, using glue, or super glue, fumes. If you put your evidence inside a sealed case (usually a fish tank) with open super-glue and "hide and watch." The fumes produce hands-free, dust-free fingerprints. The discovery was made by mistake by some small-town cop. By mistake! How that sort of oddball, set-up occurred for such a discovery, I don't recall.

Rescuers had manhandled and cut the tape off the victims but try we must anyway. They often wear medical gloves at scenes. Hit and miss back then.

"You think a suspect may have touched something else around here?" Russell replied sarcastically, shaking his head at the mess. Any part of the huge house, and hoarded items could have been touched by the bad guys or the near dozen of EMTs, cops and detectives parading around.

"I guess I'd better get to the hospital and interview the Hawkins," I told him. "They may tell us something, and then we might isolate a few more printable places."

"Off to the hospital," I told Howard Kelly as I passed him in the hall. I saw another evening shift detective, Jack Breasley, there now. A dozen? Make that 13 traipsers. Poor Russell.

"I'll go with ya'," Howard Kelly said.

"Me too," Lt. Winston counted himself in. Dale insisted on riding with me, and I was subjected to a 15-minute dissertation on how police agencies should work together and be all kinds of real extra, friendly unison. Mutual cooperation lecture. I was about 35 and he was maybe 50. So, I needed this lecture? Where was all this professional-amigo talk going?

The one-way conversation ended at the hospital, where nurses told us both Della and Tom were placed in separate rooms, as Tom, in his 80s, was in horrible condition. Near death. While he was "still around," I figured I'd better talk with him, pronto.

When I got there, I also found a man in the room who identified himself as Tom's son. Tom was as still as a corpse. Eyes closed. His face and arms were visible above the bed covers, and though treated and bandaged, I could see the seriousness of the wounds on an old gentleman like this.

I badged the son and bent down to Tom's face, "Tom?"

"Yup?" he mumbled; his eyes still closed.

"Tom, I'm Hock, a detective with the city police department."

"Hi, Hock."

"I gotta' ask you a few questions."

"I know you do."

And in a low, gasp whisper, Tom told me the story, helped by his son, and it went like this, the quick, cheat-sheet version:

Condensed episode 1: Della Hawkins had an employee a number of years earlier, more like a maid or an assistant, named Dotty Wren. Dotty and Della were close. Dotty married a guy from up north named Carl Wren, and the marriage was trouble from the start. Carl Wren had been married many times before and stayed in trouble with the law.

By that I mean serious trouble. Arrested for scams, robberies and muscle for debt collectors. The mafia in Vegas was mentioned. Eventually Dotty divorced Carl, but not after much cost and emotional heartache. Della and Tom had met Carl Wren several times through Carl's short marriage with Dotty.

Condensed episode 2: Three weeks earlier, in a total surprise and after 14 years, Carl Wren showed up at the Hawkins' house for a social visit! Carl claimed he had lots of business deals in the work, and he really needed Della's psychic advice. Carl came in alone, but Tom said he looked out the window and saw a man waited inside a parked car outside.

"I didn't see him, but Della said she saw him out there," Tom whispered. "A figure of a man. I'll tell ya' what Carl really wanted on that first trip. To case our house, the summa-bitch. Della talked with him that night. Hell, I can't stand the summa-bitch. Do you know he robs and beats people up for the mafia in Las Vegas? That's what Dotty eventually told us." (Thus, the baseball bats).

Condensed episode 3: So, after that first casual (casing) visit, Della set another appointment for Carl Wren. A second consultation. And when the doorbell rang, Tom answered the front door and saw a strange car out on the street. Then two men in masks jumped in the doorway and hit him. He fell. They kicked him, hit him with a baseball bat and one ran through the house looking for Della.

"I heard his voice and one of them sounded like Carl Wren to me." Della said. "Sounded like Carl. It wasn't… it was Carl for sure. Just a…sounded like.

Was Carl about the same size and shape as a robber?" I asked.

"I guess," Tom said. (I guess, wasn't an "ID" in court. Far from it.)

"What kind of car was on the street?"

"It was a four-door sedan. It wasn't the same car Carl had the first time he visited."

"Different cars," I repeated. Rentals, probably. I noticed that Lt. Dale was beside me taking notes. He was taking this friendly agency thing pretty far.

"Tom, you get some rest," I said. "I'm gonna' talk to Della."

I (and Dale) walked out and down the hall to Della's room, where Kelly was, and Della was sitting up in bed, bruised, but much better than Tom.

"I'll tell you who did this! That robbin' bastard Carl Wren and his son!" she yelled.

"His son?" I asked.

"They came to my house two weeks ago. His albino son was sitting in the car outside waiting for him. He never came inside that night, that thieving little fucker. He used to steal things from me when he was a kid, whenever his step-mother was over working at my house."

"Al... bino?" I said.

"That's right. White-skinned freak, curly, white hair like a Brillo pad. Who are you?" So much for her psychic powers.

"That's Hock, Della," Kelly introduced. "He's gonna' be working the case."

"And we'll help, Della!" Lt. Dale quickly chimed up, like a pet schoolboy. It was becoming apparent to me that Della was a big contributor to the sherif, the sheriff wanted a hand deep in on the case for bragging rights.

"Hock's solved a number of big crimes for us," Kelly added, obviously a little peeved too at Lt. Dale's outside proclamation of help and to shore up confidence in her eyes.

"When the...albino son was in the car, waiting? What kind of car was that?" I asked Della.

"A white mustang."

A white albino in a white mustang...how about that?

Howard Kelly and I planned to pow-wow later back at the police station, minus the new shadow I had inherited. That is Lt. Dale "Shadow" Winston.

I left the hospital, but I still had to drive back to the Hawkins house and drop Dale off at his car. I tried to concentrate on the armed robbery during the drive, but I couldn't because Dale would not shut up about the theories of agency cooperation, and so forth.

Of course, we detectives worked with the S.O. constantly, but it was obvious he wanted to cement a working, side-by-side partnership in this case. Politics. I was kind of a loner working cases.

Once back at the Hawkins' "museum," it was sealed up and I dropped Dale off by his car and his abandoned partner. A partner who had obviously observed every single thing Russell Lewis had done, by the way. Whatever. I didn't care. I just noticed these things.

"We'll work on some leads," Lt. Dale had the gall to shout to me as they left!

What? What leads? If he had leads? I'd sure like to know them. What happened to this cooperation thing?

"See ya' tomorrow!" he finished up as he got into his car.

Tomorrow? My…my…new…partner.

The score card so far in this cast of characters:
- Della Hawkins, victim and psychic extraordinaire.
- Tom Hawkins, victim and psychic husband.
- Dotty Wren, former, longtime maid and assistant to Della.
- Carl Wren, Vegas hoodlum who married Dotty.
- "Albino" Wren, son of Carl, soon to be identified as the Ronald…the albino.
- Lt. Dale, ordered to over-assist me by his Sheriff for political reasons.
- Larry Brearley, another detective on our squad.
- Sgt. Howard Kelly, you know him already.
- Russell Lewis, crime scene man extraordinaire.
- Yours truly, international man of mystery.

I got to the station and met up with Kelly and Russell at the CID offices. Kelly had some NCIC (National Crime Information Center) teletypes in his hand.

"I have a gut feeling these guys might have used a rental car tonight for this," I said. "They sound like travelers. I mean who else do they know around here, but there his…"

"…Dotty Wren," Kelly finished for me. He lifted the NCIC papers he held. He'd run her name on the police computer.

"She lives in north Dallas. She drives a Ford mustang. Betcha' its white. (The car used in the first Della visit.)

"We need to bust our asses down there right now. I have them (dispatchers) searching on Carl Wren's name now, but we might have to make some phone calls to Vegas and the FBI in the morning."

That "we" of course, meant "me," by the way. I would be expected to work a day and evening shift the next day, or…so. And more. No extra pay of course. Maybe, probably some comp time. And that was no problem at all, as I live for this shit.

"What can I do?" Larry Brearley asked, walking into the detective bay.

"Can you check the rental car companies and see if they rented a car to a Carl Wren or an Albino…Wren?" I asked him. "And what if they are flying to Vegas out of Love Field or DFW airport?"

"I'm on it," Brearley said. Back in the early 1980s, there weren't that many car rental business branches around, and even fewer in our city. And when the police called them back then, they didn't freak out with all kinds of privacy concerns and demand search warrants. They fell over backwards wo help us! They just coughed up any and all information willingly, on anything we asked. After all, "We was the PO-lice."

The rental car people would help, but the airlines information would be different bucket of monkeys to wrestle. Back then, they did not have immediate information on hand of who was flying where. You pretty much had to call the desk worker at the very flight gate of some airlines to see who bought tickets and who checked it. Then, some airlines recorded the info, processed it, but only held that information for a short period of time. So, unless there were some extenuating circumstances, the window of opportunity to easily collect names and destinations was short.

The last resort was asking them to perform a hideous search of paper trails, which they hated to do for a half-clue, guess or assumption. You pretty much had to ask the FBI to ask them to do it. Another job for me the next morning. I knew just who to call.

Kelly and I jumped into his private pickup truck, foregoing our easily identifiable, detective cars, and we high-tailed it down the interstate and then to a major, looping road around the city of Dallas. All we had for a radio was Kelly's CB radio on his truck dashboard and a police handset radio with the effective range of a cheap water pistol. We were effectively disconnected from any authorities except for CB truckin' "good buddies" like "Lightening Rod Jack" or any other "handle" we might get on a channel. Imagine...

"Breaker, Breaker good buddy...hate to break up your convoy, Rubber Ducky, but can you call the Dallas Police department and send us some Smokies? We are about to die out here in a gunfight!"

We found Dotty Wren's apartment complex right off the loop. Sure enough, the white Mustang was on the lot. Howard backed off and away from it, and I wandered up to the Mustang with a flashlight, keeping an eye on Dotty's 3rd story, apartment windows. I looked inside the car and saw nothing suspicious. The hood was cold.

"See anything?" Kelly asked as I climbed back into his tricked-out Chevy truck.

"Nope. Clean."

We drove back out of the complex and parked in a strip center parking lot across the street, at a vantage point where we could see both Dotty's apartment door, the Mustang and a goodly amount of parking lot.

"Let's sit on this for a while and see what happens. After a bit, then we'll hit that apartment," he said.

(Another Note: Little did we know that very night, in the shopping center right behind us, a disgruntled "Persian" male stomped out of a disco, went to his car, got a machine gun, and re-entered the disco. He shot half a dozen people. Survivors jumped him. All the while we sat there down the street, oblivious. We didn't know something was up until we saw the many responding police units and ambulances drive past us. And still, we didn't get the whole story until we read the Dallas newspapers the next day! This mass shooting was back in the 1980s!)

Hours later, I stood by the apartment door with my .45 in my hand, held down beside my thigh. In my left hand was my badge. Howard stood on the other side of the door. The lights were out in Dotty Wren's apartment for a good 30 minutes by then. It's always good to get after felons late at night while they are asleep, or in their Ho Chi Min flip-flops and Mickey Mouse pajamas. (Army joke.)

I rapped on the door with my left hand, several sets worth, and louder each time.

"Dotty!" I called out.

Mumbling. The door opened a crack, just enough to see a woman's eye. It scanned my badge.

"Police," I said in a whisper and barged in, gun up. The door knocked her back, and Howard followed, his gun up.

"Looking for Carl," I said over my shoulder, dashing for the bedroom. Clean. Bathroom. Clean. The apartment was small and a quick search. No Carl. No albino.

Dotty stood there in her nightgown.

"Seen Carl lately?" Kelly asked, holstering his .45.

"Carl..." she muttered, shaking her head. "Yes. What has he done?"

"We think he and his son beat up and robbed Della and Tom Hawkins tonight?"

Dotty sat down on a chair. She looked genuinely sad as well as shocked.

"Oh my God. How bad?"

"Bad," Kelly said. "They are in the hospital. Tom might not make it. One of them had a baseball bat."

"Oh no," she said. "He and Ronald have been around here. Dallas. They stayed here for a few days. In from Vegas. He said they needed things to 'cool off,' there in Vegas."

"Ronald an albino?" I asked.

We sat down.

"Yes, he is not my son, but I raised him for a while. He's Carl's son from another marriage."

We filled her in. Dotty said that her ex-husband Carl and stepson arrived on her doorstep about four weeks earlier, full of plans and business schemes. She reluctantly let them stay with her for a brief time, even let them borrow her car. She said that they also rented cars when Dotty needed hers. She swore she LOVED Della and would never do anything to hurt her, promising to report to Della's hospital room the next day.

I asked her for her recent telephone bills. She retrieved them from the kitchen, and I noted that there were some phone calls to Las Vegas. I wrote them in my small pocket notebook. The very latest calls were coming on the next pending bill. I made a mental note to try and get intel on those phone numbers ASAP from "Ma Bell" (the old nickname for the phone company).

Otherwise, no luggage left. No left-over possessions. She gave us birthdays and other important ID info. Both had been in jail in Nevada and Carl in Virginia and New Jersey. Ronald's real mother lived somewhere in Dallas, but the ex-wife mom despised Carl, and Dotty was sure the mother would have nothing to do with Carl. Her son? Yes.

"Where's the mother live?"

"She's here in Dallas. She works at Zampetios."

Howard Kelly and I exchanged glances. Zampetios was a known Dallas, mob hang-out, with customers as Italian mob as a Texas mob could get, with some Italians too.

Dotty thought that Carl knew Della collected gold bullion for many years just from their general conversations. She received a lot of gold pieces in her "profession" from customers (including Elvis Presley) and would regularly smelt it all into bars when she could. Then she and Tom would also buy more bars of gold too.

She told us that Carl and Ronald were always in trouble, but she guessed they were in some kind of new trouble for robbing people in Las Vegas too. They owed his bosses money and they needed money. And she said she was, "…worried that they were wanted by the law and the police would eventually come after me."

"Well, we're not after you. We just need you to help us," I said.

Howard nodded with a "Yup."

There was a lot to do and a lot more to learn. I asked Dotty to stop by the police station the next afternoon after seeing Della, and I would take a written statement on all this and more, upon which she promised to appear. She was, after all, involved and had to officially clear her name with a signed statement.

When we got back to headquarters, it was nearly 3 a.m. We never went in. We called it a night. Howard just dropped me off by my detective car, and we went our separate ways. Once at home, I tiptoed down the bedroom hallway, avoiding all the creaks and groans of the wooden floor, as I was an expert on their precise positions and tenor, so as to not awaken my wife. I collapsed in bed and passed out.

The next morning foggy-headed and baggy-eyed, I showed up about 10 a.m. and the TV and radio news was abuzz about the Persian with the machine gun shooting up the Dallas disco the night before. THAT alone was depressing because we were so close and yet missed it, along with our suspects.

But Good Golly Miss Molly! It was like Christmas morning at my desk when I got in at about 10 a.m., all thanks to Detective Santa-Larry-Brearley-Claus. I sat and read his reports and looked over the Polaroids he took. He'd hit a grand slam while Howard and I were sitting in the dark watching the Mustang.

After we'd left for Dallas, Brearley called all the car rental businesses in town and found one that remembered renting a four-door Dodge to an albino. The albino must have used false identification because the user name was Charles Huxley. Brearley had the idea that the robbery duo must have had another car to first bring the albino to the rental shop. He figured they'd dumped the rented robbery car after the robbery and left the city in the original car.

Armed with this hunch, Brearley and another detective, Ron Nimsom, started driving the city streets looking at parked cars on the streets and businesses between the Hawkins house and the interstate. He asked for help from the patrol cars. Thousands of streets to look over. And he found the Dodge!

He found it! And all within a few hours. Ironically, the car was parked not far from the car rental business on the Ramada Inn Parking lot. Brearley impounded the car.

And things got better still. As I was consuming my station house coffee, Russell Lewis was hard at work collecting some trash items from this rental car, fingerprinting them and the car.

You know what? It's gotta' suck to be an albino criminal for all the obvious identification reasons. A dispatcher handed me his criminal history; it was quite lengthy. His overall description matched the second masked suspect's.

But wait, it gets even better. Breasley also called Love Field and DFW airports and made a run at the airline records and lists of names of people flying to Las Vegas that night. They said they would investigate. My phone rang and the airport police were on the line with the information. On the list? A Carl Wren flew to Vegas about two hours after the robbery. Not Ronald Wren, the son, or his alias like Charles Huxley, though. Just Carl alone. Probably with a suitcase full of...gold bullion?

Howard Kelly got in about 1 p.m. and I bombarded him with all this fantastic news, and the touchdown pass Jack Brearley threw for us.

Carl Wren had left the state. Hmmmm. Flight, as in what we legal-beagles call "interstate flight." I sat back in my chair and smiled. This case was still all circumstantial, mind you. I still had to place these two as the two masked men who actually committed the robbery. But Wren fleeing from the state at that timely post-robbery moment helped.

A nail in the proverbial coffin. And it might qualify for a federal, interstate flight charge. Interstate flight meant I could get the FBI involved in the hunt, and have 10s, if not 100 agents working on the arrest, as well as inadvertently facilitating the case with intel, incidental to the hunt. But we'd need a local Texas arrest warrant first. Solid probable cause. Plus, our district attorney (not me) would have to make the flight investigation request in the form of an official letter to the SAC (Special Agent in Charge) of the Dallas office.

Ohhh, the FBI. We had lots of fun nicknames for the FBI. "F.B.-One." Or, "Friendly, But Ignorant." But it's usually a pleasure working with most of the agents. I had, however, no love lost with some of their professional profilers who had a penchant when consulted on a violent crime, to give you nothing much to work with at all, generic junk, but then when *you* cleared the case, they back-wormed their way into it with speeches, credits and even books for "their successful investigation and help" resumes. "I had a case once…" It comes out as "one case I worked on" in speeches and books. No. *I* had a case once, *you* just read the reports. Yeah. It's a tricky relationship.

Many of the regular FBI field agents were well-meaning lawyers and accountants but with very little street grit, street time, and creds. Director J. Edgar Hoover hired really clean-cut, "milk-drinking," professionals who super-understood the law and deep bookkeeping, as is the nature of much of their white-collar crime work. But it soon became apparent that a certain…well… street savvy and toughness was missing.

Then smartly, the FBI then began hiring a small percentage of non-college grad, former police detectives, to kind of "man-up" the ranks, peppering them through the field offices. One such agent in Dallas was a Grayson Caine.

Caine was an ex-big city patrolman and long-time detective from the Detroit, and he was part of that city's new FBI SWAT team. He was recruited in this "get-vet/get-tough" FBI hiring program era. We'd worked some cases together before, and after teaming with Grayson Caine it was hard to settle for any other

FBI agent in our region when the pushin' came to shovin' (and shootin').

Caine could kick an ass and pull a gun in a New York minute. In short, I really liked Grayson Caine, and we all hoped he would never be transferred to another city. Caine even wore a freaking, trench coat. He already had to wear a pork pie, fedora hat. FBI rules. He was federal, Mike Hammer.

If I got Grayson involved early in this, he could cut through red tape like a G-Man laser beam. If it all panned out, then we'd get the interstate flight case up and running. I called our D.A. (a close friend and collaborator, Jerry Cobb, asking to request Caine with his request for a interstate fugitive help. Then I called Caine up and I read off that litany of nouns.

"Armed robbery. Attempted murder. Vegas. The Mafia. Interstate fugitives. Gold bullion. I needed multi-state records, fingerprints, documents from airlines, Vegas Organized Crime Unit Intel and I needed them all, and FAST!"

After each one Caine said, "Yeah, yeah," louder and louder. He also lived for this shit. He was ready to go and just needed a Texas warrant and that written, signed request for help from our DA.

I marched into Russell Lewis' museum of crime in the stone room basement of the police headquarters. He was busy as usual, processing and moving evidence around. All the evidence of the Hawkins robbery case surrounded him.

"You know the fingerprint-on-tape idea you mentioned?" he said to me over his lab-smocked shoulder. "Look here. I got something."

Back to this fingerprint in a fishtank discovery...previously I'd been to a Texas Attorney General Police Investigation Symposium in Austin. A forensic expert had introduced a fingerprint collection method accidentally discovered. Super glue. An enclosed tank, like a fish tank, with evidence inside it, exposed to super glue fumes, and heretofore fingerprints on difficult objects...arose.

Accidentally discovered? Yes. There were a few accidental experiments but most significant was The use of superglue for forensics was also discovered unintentionally in Japan, in 1977, in what was called a laboratory mishap. Fuseo Matsumura, a hair and fiber expert at the Saga Prefecture Crime Laboratory, was using superglue to mount microscope slides.

He noticed that fingerprints were developing along the edges of the slides where the glue had fumed. He shared this with a colleague, Masato Soba, who formally developed the "cyanoacrylate fuming" technique.

Interestingly, there is also a popular "forensic lore" that the technique was discovered in the USA when a police officer left a tube of superglue on a patrol car dashboard in the sun; the tube burst, and the resulting fumes revealed every fingerprint inside the car!

When I returned from the symposium, I told Russell about the fish tank, superglue trick. He immediately got a tank and glue for his lab. He'd stuck the cut duct tape once binding the victims in the tank, along with a McDonalds Styrofoam coffee cup collected from the back seat of the rental car.

Sure enough, Russell had lifted fingerprints from the masking tape, the sticky side!

"Wow! Workable?"

"There's enough points there for a match up," Russell said. "It was tricky. I had to shape the tape. Fold it. Unfold it."

Prints from the crime scene. Cool. Fingerprints with identification "points" consist of bifurcations, ending ridges, dots, ridges and islands. A single rolled fingerprint may have as many as 100 or more identification points that can be used for ID purposes. Fingerprint class is now DIS-missed!

"Get this," he continued, "rolling around loose on the back floorboard of the rental car was a McDonald's coffee cup. Look what I found."

He had the cardboard cup upside down and tottering on a pencil. I could see the developed fingerprint on the cup.

I pictured Carl or Ronald mindlessly tossing the empty cup over their shoulder into the back seat. You might think this was careless, or stupid, but they probably assumed we would never connect the random, rental car to the specific crime. What's a loose, used coffee cup in the back of a fleet of rental cars? And frankly, prior to me hearing the breaking news about the first masking-tape, fingerprint lifting, almost no one had done it before. Russell Lewis could well have been the second or third forensics guy to actually do this process.

"Ha! Different than on the tape?" I asked.

"Different print. And look at this," he handed me a sales receipt.

"From the back floorboard too. No prints on it though."

I looked at the receipt. It was from one of our K-Mart stores. Several items were purchased. An item from the "sports category" and one listed as "household." I took the slip and laid it on Russell's copy machine. Enlarged the setting. Hit the print button. A giant version scrolled out.

"I'll bet the sports deal is a ball bat and the household deal is tape," I said. "I got Grayson Caine of the FBI in on this, this afternoon. He is going to get the Wren father and son fingerprints overnighted to us from their prior arrests.

You could get faxed fingerprint cards pretty easily back then, but they usually weren't any good for comparison. Couldn't trust the quality. You needed a real good copy of a fingerprint card to work with, and that almost always meant multi-day, land mail time and then "personnel" lag-time. By personnel lag-time I mean as in someone finding the cards, pulling the cards, super-quality, copying the cards and land-mailing them out.

How many, many times I've had to call and hassle some dunderhead, civilian clerk somewhere to get prints in the mail to us. Two ways to speed that process up and put the fear of God in the lazy and the uncaring? The other? Texas Rangers and the FBI could scare us up the prints.

"Going to K-Mart?" Russell asked as I left.

"Aaaa-ttention K-Mart Shoppers!" I shouted as I turned for the hallway." (That's an old joke) Have you seen an albino?" (That part wasn't in the commercials.)

At K-Mart I sat in the manager's office and showed her my gigantor' version of the sales receipt. She consulted with several thick books of folded, continuous printout sheets. All products now have these new scan, codey-box...things! (Remember this was the 80s.) This new scanning-picture-box-thingamajigs that recorded each item purchased was just amazing. How did they do it? Those blocky lines wrapping around a can of soup, beer or a round hammer handle? And whatever you bought was also typed right on the receipt!

"This number here is a baseball bat. This other number is duct tape," the manager told me. "This number here is the cash register and here is the time of purchase. Let's go up there and see who's working now."

"Let's," I added.

We weaved our way through the store to the cash registers.

After a conference with some of the cashiers, she managed to determine who was working the register at the time of the transaction. A hefty woman with her hair erected up into a frozen whirlwind, looked at the copy of the receipt and then fanned herself with the paper. She squinted at me and asked, "Was this guy an albino?"

As I said before, it must suck to be an albino criminal. But I didn't say that. Instead, I pretended to be a professional and said, "Yes, ma'am I will come back tomorrow or the day after with a photo-line-up, and we'll see if you can pick the man out."

I knew it would be hard to get a photo line-up of

Five or six albinos together, but I would have to try. That's why I get paid the big bucks.

"Much thanks, folks."

But seriously, given the totality of building circumstances, the witness alone mentioning the word "albino" alone did help build the case for probable cause warrants. Arriving fingerprint cards would cinch the saddle.

Back at the police station, Dotty Wren was waiting for me in the CID lobby. We sat at my desk, and I spent about two hours getting a detailed statement. Times. Places. Motives. Whereabouts.

One new lead developed. Dotty recalled, "Ronald's real, blood mom still works at Zampetios. She has for about 20 years. Carl wouldn't dare darken the door of the ex-wife's place, afraid that she would have him killed or something if he showed up. But Ronald? He's there all the time," she said.

"He is?" I asked. "You think he's still going there?"

"Yeah! He eats there for free. I know he went there many nights just this last month since they've been back. See his mom. But really to eat for free. She…tolerates him."

After Dotty left, I called the FBI switchboard to get Grayson Caine, with this Ronald and Zampetio news. The Feds always like to hear about organized crime. They tracked Caine down, and he got on the phone.

"Okay," Grayson said, "I have some news. We have confirmed Ronald Wren has an aggravated robbery warrant from Philadelphia. If he goes to this restaurant a lot? I'm going to start watching it tonight, Hock."

Which I thought was fast and great.

"Well, I am stuck up here on evening shift tonight. But I'll get down there with you tomorrow night then."

"Okay, you and I will set a stakeout tomorrow night, and maybe I can squeeze some more agents on this too. I think I can get a week's stakeout on this, especially after what I found out from Vegas."

"Whatcha' find out about Vegas?"

"These are some bad boys, Hock. And they are playing around with the Vegas mob. The Vegas office needs an informant, and either Carl or Ronald could be it. I am supposed to find out more tomorrow in a conference call and will fill you in tomorrow night."

We hung up. He was on though for tonight! I sure did like working with Grayson Caine.

That first night passed. No Ronald. Grayson called me at home about midnight, to say the well was dry.

The next night Grayson and I, with another agent, watched the restaurant's front doors. We sat in a dark, hidey-hole, parking spot up a treed street from the restaurant. We could easily see every person walking in and out of the eatery.

Caine filled me in on the Wren clan history he'd gathered from his colleagues in Vegas –

"The Vegas office says that Carl Wren was working as a collection man for some gamblers. The gamblers were 'connected' to Chicago," he said. "Wren collected some money one time, and he asked some poor loser for more than the official debt, and Wren kept the difference. Somehow this word got back to Wren's bosses. The gamblers suspected Wren might have done this a few times to their "clients." They presented Wren with a bill. A bill that included a punishment penalty with interest."

"With interest. So, Wren needed a robbery to pay them off, and with gold bars to boot," I said.

"His kid is a punk. A loose cannon. A chip off the old Dad's block. He has helped the dad beat up a few people in Vegas. Very violent. No charges filed there because they were mob debts. But he robbed an old man in a Philadelphia hotel as part of a high-dollar robbery. Beat him bad with a bat. It was well planned. He had an accomplice. We could assume it was his father."

"You know," I said, "it must really suck for Ronald..."

"...to be an albino?" Caine finished for me.

"Yeah."

That night passed. No Ronald.

The next night I was again stuck working inside my city working on another case. Grayson Caine and a few agents were in place watching the "mafia" restaurant.

About 8:30 p.m. The police dispatcher contacted me by radio that I had an important phone call. Station bound, I got to the front desk LT. He gave me the message. I called.

"He's here," Grayson told me.

"Damn!" I cussed. I was in the wrong place at the right time.

"He just walked into the restaurant. We spotted his car and, well Hock, we'd rather arrest him outside and after his dinner than rush him while he is inside and make a big scene inside the 'Don Corleone' Pizzeria crowd. No one must know he's been picked up in case we turn him."

That was my cue. I had time.

"I can be down there in 30 minutes. If he comes out? Take him down. If not? See ya' in 30 minutes!"

I raced down the stairs, across the lot and slid into my Dodge Diplomat, busted through town, and broke the sound barrier on the interstate. Then, across north Dallas, pounding the wheel at every silly red light. I pulled up behind Grayson's car on that treed street in about 40 minutes or so. I probably had a nosebleed.

In the Fed car, we kicked over a plan or two, but this wasn't the D-Day Invasion. It's just that the punk could be armed. Grayson had called for two more agents from downtown, and they were already in place at either end of the street. Within 20 minutes after I got there, the doors of Zampetio's opened and for the first time, I laid eyes on our albino prey. He was wearing a thick jacket, which could conceal knives and guns.

"Subject's coming out," Grayson spoke into his car mike.

But Ronald stopped on the walkway! He reached into his pocket and turned for a pay phone booth, not his car. He got in the booth and started using the phone.

We all started down the street on foot, but I bolted for the booth with Grayson right behind me. We ran up to his rear side, and he never saw us. I pulled my .45 out, and with my left hand shoved the phone booth collapsible door hard. It opened, knocking him aside.

Ronald was shocked. I pointed my gun right at his head, elevating his shock level to awe.

Grayson had his gun out in one hand, his badge in the other. The kid was all giant-eyed looking at us. Grayson said in a steadfast, serious calm...

"FBI. If you pull so much as a toothpick out of your pocket, we'll blow your brains all over this fucking phone booth."

Silence for a few seconds.

"We heard you were a real bad boy. Well...be bad now," Caine said. Caine wished. Me too.

Ronald dropped the phone and lifted his hands. Palms up. All the other agents converged, and Ronald Wren, AKA Charles Huxley the Albino was heretofore under arrest. (This is why I always like working with Grayson Caine. And we were far from being done.)

Downtown Dallas in deep night is empty. Like a ghost town. A science fiction movie. Our sedans ripped through the empty streets in a caravan, my gold sedan standing out among the line of black Fed cars. We stopped at a secluded back door of the Federal Building and walked our suspect inside and upstairs to the FBI floor.

Over the next few hours, we sat around and talked with Ronald Wren. Smoked and joked. He had coffee, snacks and cigarettes. I got a few color Polaroids of Ronald. I got a written confession of the Hawkins robbery. No promises made, just a show of cooperation to make things easier on him later. But what was really cooking there that night for the FBI was the birth of an insider informant on various organized crime felonies from Las Vegas to Chicago. Maybe?

It's going to really suck to be an albino in the witness protection program.

Grayson followed me out with a hand on my shoulder and said, "We'll keep you posted. Next, we'll get the dad. Get me a warrant and we'll request a fugitive apprehension warrant."

"You bet," I said.

It was about 3 a.m. and I coasted on I35 to the ol' hacienda.

WBAP radio had the Bill Mack, the Midnight Trucker show on, playing country and western songs. But the warbling took a distant second to the thoughts of my next steps in the case. I would use this new confession to get a warrant on Daddy Carl Wren. The eventual fingerprints and K-Mart identification were now loose ends that would just firm up the case.

I zipped on north with the windows down and caught that cool, night breeze with a great rush of satisfaction, as I wondered where in the world Carl Wren was. It was my job to find him.

The next day I came in at 1 p.m. (2 hours early) to begin my paperwork chase. Howard Kelly told me that both Tom and Della were released from the hospital and were back at their house. He told me that later we would drive over to the Hawkins house and give them some updates on our progress. See how they were doing. No sooner did I sit down at my desk than in walked Sheriff's Office Investigator Lt. Dale Winston and his partner. They sat in my guest chairs. Dale opened a file folder,

"Got something for ya'," Dale said with a smirky smile. "Here's your man."

He laid the file down and spun it right side up for me. It was a file on albino Ronald Wren. A mug shot and miscellaneous arrest records from out of state, were stapled into it.

"Yeah. I ah…Dale…I arrested him in Dallas last night." I told him.

He sat there sort of shocked. He exchanged glances with his equally shocked partner. We sat there and looked at each other. I think maybe he wanted a copy of the arrest report, or a confession. Honestly, I just didn't know what he expected. Did he think I was lost, or stuck and that I needed him to show up with this file?

"Oh, Gooood!" he said. "Tell ya' anything?"

"He confessed," I answered.

"Gooood."

"The Feds took the confession. I don't have a copy yet," I said.

"Well, okay. Do you need this?" he said while standing up and gesturing toward the file.

"Oh…no, Dale. Actually. Thanks, but I have …a big file already…. On him…ahhh, here."

I tapped a much bigger folder to my right.

"Well, if you need any help, give us a holler," he said.

"You bet," I said.

I can only assume he was ordered by the sheriff to solve the case, and he was obligated to do something, anything. I would bet he reported back the Sheriff that "we" (he and I) made an arrest.

Howard Kelly shouted at me, and we left for the Hawkins' house for a follow-up.

This was the first of a number of follow-ups, house visits/sit-downs with Hawkins and honestly, I found them all to be a bit uncomfortable. Mostly because Della, like Deputy Winston, insisted on also "helping me" but with her psychic abilities. These times didn't cost me 10 bucks and a quarter, like my first "biker visit ages ago." She would often go on and on about the locations of the gold bars. She "felt" they were here, or there. She "knew" they were there, and I was supposed to jump right up, disregard all laws, break and barge into some abstract locations and find the bars.

She told me she saw Carl Wren in Canada. Next, Italy. If she was so damn good, why didn't she predict her own robbery before it happened and who the suspects were.

Ever see those psychic shows on TV at night? The "readers?" The host gets a message from dead Uncle Ralph and tells his family, "Thanks for all the pizzas," or "Go ahead and buy that new house. Grandpa Johnny would be proud." The family bursts out in tears.

What a connection? What a WASTED connection! Why aren't we constantly solving some murders with this magic connection? Skip the pizza? Why isn't a ghost telling the host who killed John Kennedy and Jimmy Hoffa? Why aren't we channeling dead girls left on the roadside to tell us their grisly stories and describe their assailants? WHY!

They say these hosts are like magicians who trick-work the crowd methodically to hone in info. I don't know but my conversations with Della Hawkins weren't going anywhere.

Then I got an idea. "Della, you know who has the time to look into that? Lt. Dale at the Sheriff's Office. I am so busy, but he has promised to help me and you in any way that he could. You need to go see him about where the gold bars are. Ask him here for a visit. Give him all these gold bar clues."

Kelly gave me an evil eye, but he laughed about it later in the car. (She did start bothering Lt. Dale, but alas – after a period when Dale found no bars, frustrated, she started bugging me again.)

The next few days, cluttered with other pending and new cases, I chiseled away on the loose ends and report writing. I got the cases filed, arrest warrants and FBI interstate requests done. I walked downstairs to the dispatchers and asked that Carl Wren be listed on the NCIC as a wanted man for aggravated robbery. There was nothing left but the ugly, tedious business of chasing a guy across the United States…by proxy. I called the police stations of all the local areas we knew Carl would visit. Grayson Caine alerted the FBI Fugitive Task Force (my best bet in finding him), and I started cold calling any and all relatives, friends and associates, anyone…to get a tip or a handle on where this som-bitch might be.

Almost a whole year passed, and then I got a phone call one afternoon.

"My name is Troopah' Emory of the Pennsylvania State Police," he told me. "I have some news. I worked a traffic accident on the highway this morning. A woman named Linda Patterson was driving. She hit a car on the turnpike. I had to collect, you know…the information, and there was a guy in the passenger seat of her car.

I got his name for the report you know, as a passenger-witness. Birthday. The usual. Finished the report. Well, so, this afternoon I am closing out my paperwork and running the VIN and names on the computah' and I got a 'wants and warrants' hit on the passenger in Linda's car! And I let the guy get away hours ago! I mean, it was just a traffic wreck. He was just a passenger."

"What's his name?" I asked anxiously.

"Carl Wren."

And a fantastic sense of miraculous elation passed through me. I collected all the information and asked for a copy of the accident reports to be faxed to me. Linda Patterson lived in central PA, in what appeared to be a house, by the nature of the address. Carl gave another address. False, I'll bet. I called FBI Grayson Caine who then forwarded it all to the Scranton FBI office. But I didn't stop there. I called some of the local police agencies, and one local patrol sergeant told me,

"Yeah, I know that neighborhood. Nice. Tony Pobelski lives there. Yeah! Tony is a state police investigator. He lives right there. I'll bet he can keep an eye out and watch for that guy."

Wow! I made several more calls through the state police system and got Investigator Tony Pobelski at one of the police barracks.

"I know this Linda Patterson," Investigator Pobelski said. "She's a real 'lookah'. A babe. I know this house. There is a new guy liven' with her now. Flashy. Black, dyed, hair all greased back. He has a red convertible. Car's always there at night."

THAT was surely Mister Carl Wren. I faxed him photos and the case info. He called back.

"That's him! I will catch this motherfucker for you. I see him all the time. He's just down the street from me."

Within 48 hours I heard back from a breathless Tony Pobelski,

"I saw him this morning by his car in Linda's driveway. I stopped, got out, and walked up to him. He froze at first, then dropped the grocery bag he held in his hands, and the motherfucker turned and ran into the woods and up the mountain…"

"Up the…mountain…?" I interrupted.

"Yeah. We live by mountains. It's a big fuckin' mountain right behind us."

"Did you get him?"

"No. We have instigated a massive manhunt on the mountain. Dogs. Helicopters. We've got the state police and local police out. FBI. TV news. Everything."

This was turning into a Humphrey Bogart movie! You know what flashed through my mind though don't you? CAN I GET UP THERE? Can I possibly get up there and be a part of this?

"He can't last long," Pobelski said, instantly killing my dream of a mountain manhunt.

"He has no jacket on and it's really cold here at night. And the mountain is half-covered in snow. We'll catch him before you fly up here and land. We'll get him, or he'll freeze to death. "

"I'll settle for either way." I told him. "Keep me posted."

I sat back and imagined Vegas hotshot Carl Wren struggling through the snow on a PA mountain. The barking dogs. The thrush of chopper blades. Like the Rambo movie only Carl ain't Rambo. I walked into Howard Kelly's office, sat in a chair and told him the delightful news. We both laughed out loud.

I was real lucky to find Tony Pobelski. Good thing Linda was a "lookah,'" else Tony might have "overlookah-ed'" his fugitive neighbor. Detectives can make their own luck sometimes. But luck counts.

Many years later, on an episode of the Sopranos on HBO, Soprano was visiting a fellow mobster, and the police raided the house. He escaped out back and into the snow and woods and for the better part of the episode, He struggled to get home through the woodsy parts of New Jersey. When I saw that episode, I immediately thought back to when Carl Wren struggled to escape on that Pennsylvania mountain.

Unlike Tony Soprano, Carl Wren was found nearly dead on the mountain after about 2 days of searching. Long story short, we extradited him back to Texas. Once in my clutches, no bail, we convicted both Carl and his son in another year later in a trial. Still with the convictions, both had a kind of over-riding deal with the Feds concerning the mob, I am not at liberty to discuss. It was important for them to be convicted in open court. All the dangerous parties to the deal are long dead now anyway.

The gold bullion? Las Vegas Organized Crime office told me that there was loose talk of gold bullion on their streets. A payoff of some kind. They did hear talk that the gold bars were immediately melted down, reshaped and sold. Gone. Della Hawkins did not predict any of this. I guess she didn't have a quarter to rub Galaxy lotion on.

Yet for the next few years, Della Hawkins would call me occasionally and just pester me about her psychic feelings about where a bar or two of the gold was, and how I needed to run or fly to those locations. I tried to be polite. I would listen and again try to explain why I couldn't kick in a stranger's front door in the Bahamas without a warrant and get her gold brick back, based just on her voodoo word. I would remind her to contact Lt. Dale at the Sheriff's Office with these clues.

In those conversations, I would also casually add each time,

"Hey, I'm taking a big trip! Can you guess where?"

She never knew what I was talking about. I guess my accent had changed. And she never said that my dead Uncle Freddy thanked me for all the pizzas. I bought that guy a lot of pizzas! The ingrate!

Still, I am grateful for the great case to work on. It was quite a rodeo ride. The Madame took a lot of customers for a ride. In fact, there was a lot "taking-took" rides going on in this case...

- The Vegas gamblers were "took" by Carl who raised the debt price and kept the money.
- Carl got "took" by the mob who found out about the price fixing and Carl's skim.
- Tom and Della were "took" by Carl and Ronald. Gold bars. Cash. Jewels. Carl and Raymond got taken down by me.
- The Feds took down some mobsters, thanks to Carl and Raymond. One of them "took" a deal to talk.

- Then Della's husband Tom got "took," dying of old age first, a few short years later, accelerated by his baseball bat injuries. Then the big "they" from above, the wisp, dead folks that Della consulted with, took Della too.
- Tony Pobelski took a trip to Texas to testify. We took the brother out to some real barbecue and some country and western bars.
- Lt. Dale and apparently the Sheriff took a breather from the case, as they lost interest during the year-long, out-of-state hunt for Carl Wren. The topic never came up between me and Dale again. We wound up working on a few things through the years, like a big, attempted jailbreak (see a later story.)
- Graham Caine. This took time out of his bust days, being the coolest old school FBI agent ever. He retired and then passed away.
- Me? This took time. I'm out a lot of time, worry, sweat and 10 bucks and 25 cents if you count that initial visit.

Frankly, I think we all got taken-snookered by some con game. I can't tell when the con started and I don't know when it all will end. And...it must really suck to be an albino criminal.

Old newspaper photo of Howard Kelly and me, circa mid-1980s.

Police Detective Notebook...

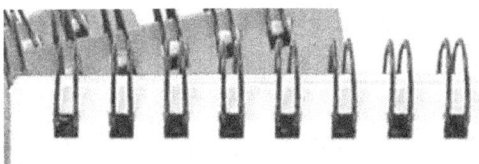

""Never jump to a conclusion at a crime scene. Study it, remain open and absorb. There are patterns, yes, but verify.
The worst detectives I've ever seen, jump to conclusions and were too stubborn by their very nature to admit their conclusions were wrong." - Hock

Chapter 3: The Greatest Shot I've Ever "Seen!"
It was gruesome. Memories of pain fade, but not those of parents much. Out of respect for the surviving parents, I will pass on revealing the details of this child murder here, the death, rape and mutilation of a very young girl. Suffice to say that we'll just start the story here, when this freshly, arrested child killer was first incarcerated in our county jail, so that I might focus on the tale of the greatest shot I have ever "seen," or more specifically, ever investigated, and one that has all the elements of a helleva', Texican lawman tale.

It was the 1980s. The day after the arrest of the brutal killer, Reilly Rice. He was in the county jail and due for his very first visit to a judge for his judicial warnings, what is often called a preliminary arraignment. In our old, county jail building, just up the street from our once city police headquarters, one such presiding judge had a court and offices on the first floor. This made such procedures a handy process, as the jails themselves were all upstairs. (This is the same jail of the prior jailbreak story I mentioned that will come up later in this book.)

Getting that first day in person, mandatory visit in court could be geographically challenging in some jurisdictions nowadays. This type of appearance is often done by close circuit TV! Not so, years ago.

Judges can be power mad, quirky or cantankerous. You've seen this on TV, movies and in the last two decades. Some actually talk and act like those characters. On this fateful day a traveling judge was in chambers, and he was a liberal one that demanded all prisoners who entered his court must be free of shackles. I guess he hadn't had his nose broken yet. But something dramatic was about to happen that would at least make him think about that loose idea.

Whatever the process was for assigning jailers to suspects for their court trip downstairs... what... Rotation? Dice game? Short straw? Chance? Whatever method, an overweight, out-of-shape jailer named Barry Bale got the chore of marching Reilly Rice downstairs to the judge's chamber for this un-handcuffing, pre-lim visit.

Enter Ranger Texas Weldon Luca, was in on the arrest. At that very appearance time that afternoon, Weldon walked into the Sheriff's Office on the first floor. He was there to collect paperwork on the case to send to his Dallas Ranger Company office and then on to Austin.

Lucas was dressed in his usual work clothes of a classic Ranger, western boots, pants and matching vest, embroidered gun belt and classic, engraved, model 1911, .45 caliber handgun. The famous Ranger badge adorned his vest like it had on the Rangers for a 100-plus years. Lucas was a regular sight to every police agency in the region, and I can't think of a police officer that didn't know him, or know of him, certainly we detectives all did.

Appointed by the Texas governor, Rangerin' was a great job coveted by almost all, and Lucas was one of the troops that had considerable experience in investigation before pinning on that legendary badge. He'd been a state highway patrolman, as all Rangers start out, and then worked auto theft, narcotics and organized crime. Many Rangers are appointed without such stout backgrounds and are a bit behind the curve in investigation skills. (I sadly recall one Ranger being "made" that had worked only as a patrolman and then for too many years in a office-desk section called "Weights and Measures." Weights and Measures involved weighing and overseeing trucks on the highway. Jobs like this offer zero qualifications for an investigative position, but sometimes politics did get in the way with appointments.) Very few applicants had Weldon's extensive investigative background.

Reilly Rice was due in court. Since it was a child murder case, a local Dallas television station sent a news van up to the court to film the proceedings. The reporter and cameraman positioned themselves in the hall for the 6 and 11 o'clock news shot of Reilly Rice walking into the courtroom. No cameras were allowed inside. A reporter would enter and take notes.

A hurried representative of the DA's office showed up, but not much legalese would be crunched in this first visit. Jailer Bales took suspect Reilly down in the elevator. He walked Rice past the camera crew and into the court. He took off the handcuffs, as required. The TV crew got their "perp shot," and walked out of the building to their van. Weldon Lucas was talking with some deputies in the lobby of the SO just down the hall.

And then, all hell broke loose.

Me? I was working in our detective bay, closing out the day, when that all hell broke loose. There were also some other investigators there. I can't remember who bellowed out the announcement across the room.

"Reilly Rice just escaped from the jail. Eastbound on foot."

What? And we were off, stampeding down the stairs, hit the street and ran to the SO just a block away.

Oddly, there were quite a number of prisoners through the years who'd escaped from the Sheriff's Office right out the back doors, usually too near and during the book-in process, or some transfer process. The bad guys could see the irresistible green of City Center Park out the glass back doors and windows and they bolted. They were always caught.

We ran, all of us passed on the option of getting into our cars and driving there, thinking we would be quickly searching the surrounding park and streets afoot anyway.

My gut instinct? Flank over into that park behind the S.O. but my eye caught a disturbance on the way down the major intersection just east of the jail. A cluster of people and stopped cars. Four lanes of rush hour, east/west traffic stopped cold. The rest of us saw it too, and I veered back with them.

I ran past the county building and spotted jailer Barry Bale, sitting on the ground, all multiple hundreds of pounds of him, his back propped against a tree, hair messed up, shirt tail out, gasping for breath. He must have chased Rice as he escaped, yeah, all of about 15 feet and collapsed. Acting like he was near a heart attack another jailer attended to him and pointed us east.

"They went that-away," he *actually* said to me. (well, it was Texas.)

"Thataway"…was up ahead on the northwest corner of a major intersection, in a small patch of short bushes and foliage of the Civic Center parking lot, were multiple official types and a downed man. When I closed in, I saw that the face-downed guy was Reilly Rice. Ranger Weldon Lucas was standing over him, with his hands on his hips, huffing and puffing. A city patrolman showed up.

Then our CID Captain Bill Cummings drove up and bailed out of his sedan.

In so many words, Weldon told us he shot Rice. Okay. You must be thinking can police shoot fleeing, unarmed suspects? First off, this was Texas many decades ago. Back then there was a running joke that if you ran 7 feet from us. We would start shooting at ya'. That also included driving away from us too. Rice was a child-raper and killer, otherwise known as a dangerous felon, we could not allow to escape. Just couldn't. Shooting at fleeing felons. I have, trying to scare them into stopping.

"Stop or I'll shoot!" "Stop or I'll kill ya!"

These warning shots or "scare" shots have been deemed illegal almost everywhere by now, but they sure have worked for me more often than not. Hate to see it go. Great peace-keeping tool, but they are gone.

Anyway - back at the scene, I examined Reilly Rice. Prone, he was panting from his mad dash, but otherwise he seemed just fine. None too messy. An EMT was patching up the side of his head. A head shot?

"Where's he shot?" I asked the EMT, kneeling beside him.

"Earlobe."

"Ear...lobe?"

"Earlobe," he repeated.

I looked at Weldon, and Weldon shrugged.

The TV news crew was setting up for an impromptu shoot. A patrol sergeant was organizing traffic control to allow the far lines to pass. The EMTs were standing Reilly Rice up and preparing to transport him…back to the jail, not even the hospital. After all, he was only shot in the ear lobe. Our crime scene guy, Russell Lewis showed up and began photographing the "scene.: Not much of one really. More county officials jogged up.

"Hock, you got this case," Captain Cummings told me. Though this involved the Sheriff's Office and the state police via the Texas Rangers, the shooting did occur within our city limits, and it was also our city's official problem. I knew that people from the Rangers and Austin would eventually be involved in this, but there was work to do right then. First, documenting the crime scene-event, which ran from the S.O. courtroom to the intersection.

Weldon and I stepped off a bit, and he told me what had happened. I paraphrase here a bit, but he basically said,

"I heard the shouting that Reilly Rice had escaped out the front door. I ran out and saw him running this way."

Weldon had worked on the Rice arrest and case and was well aware who and what Rice had done.

"He ran into the middle of traffic and turned east," Weldon told me. I took off after him and got in the middle of moving traffic, (four lane) chasing him. He had a big lead. It was getting bigger. I felt like he could get away. I couldn't shoot at him because it was rush hour. Cars and people everywhere. But, Rice started angling north and in front of him was that brick building."

Weldon pointed to the two-story brick building behind us, and to the northeast corner of the intersection… The building looked pretty big, as close as we were then.

"I could see he was going to pass in front of that building, and it was my only safe shot. I drew my pistol and fired one shot when he crossed in front of the building. Rice went down."

"How far away were you?" I asked, thinking about the ejected, spent shell from Weldon's .45 handgun.

"Up there," he pointed west, up the avenue. We both grimaced at the sight of the cars being filtered into the right lane, albeit slowly, and allowed to pass the intersection by our erstwhile patrol officers. Oh well, life and cars move on. At least they were moving slow. A crushed shell would be better than a no shell.

My unmarked detective car was back at the station. I approached an officer and asked for one of their distance measuring wheels and some chalk. This is like a walking stick, with a wheel at the bottom and distance counter. Back then, the numbers rolled on the handle like a slot machine. The officer pulled it from his trunk. Weldon and I started from where Reilly Rice took his dive and we walked west on the avenue, marking off the feet.

I hit about 30 feet and I asked Weldon, "Anywhere around here?"

"Nope." My eyebrows raised.

We kept moving in between the cars and impatient drivers. Our eyes were scanning the roadway for that single spent shell. We hit about 60 feet!

"Anywhere here?"

"Nope."

Nope? How far was this shot? We continued.

"Right about here, I think," Finally, Weldon stopped me. He looked around.

I looked at the scrolling meter. It read "ninety-seven feet." Good God, could that be right? And sure enough, to our right, untouched, unbent and pristine, lay the spent shell in the middle of the street.

"Ninety-seven…98 feet, Weldon. Thereabouts" I told him. "Maybe damn near 100."

I looked over at Weldon, and he was staring back at the intersection. "Yup. This is about right," he said, nodding his head.

I shouted for Russel Lewis. He saw me and with his camera, instinctively knowing why I was there, jogged our way. He took some photos of the shell and of the brick building from there – which looked way smaller. I put the shell in my pocket.

"Shit, Weldon, this is like a circus shot, like a wild-west show, shot."

"I reckon," he said.

"Was it a moving shot? How exactly did you do it?" I asked him.

"I was running. I saw my chance. He was running in front of that building. I pulled my gun. Two-handed grip. I think maybe I stopped to shoot just for a second. I think. Kinda. I shot. Cars out here were whizzing by me."

"Well, go on back, and I'll start taking some other measurements."

I recorded the distances, "triangulated" them from the surroundings, the shell scene with other related landmarks. Nowadays I guess they use GPS and satellite photos.

Weldon went to our PD and started his own statement on one of our new, electric typewriters. There was much for me to tighten up, and I wanted as complete a report as possible before the state bigwig, Ranger shooting team started showing up. The only loose end was the bullet, it obviously did not stop at the ear lobe, and hit that brick wall. It might take a major deal to find and recover that slug, as we couldn't see it with a quick walk-by that afternoon.

Two high-ranking Rangers were there at my desk the very next morning, and I had a good, solid report for them to kick off with. As we went over the details, I got a call from the Sheriff's Office CID Captain Ron "Tracker" Douglas. He told me the latest news.

"Hock, Reilly Rice hung himself last night. He's dead."

"Hung himself! How? Where?"

"He was first booked in wearing his own socks. We let them keep their socks. You know, like those long, white tube socks? Well, late last night, he got one end around his neck, tied off the other end on a bunk bed and hung himself."

"Dead?"

"Deader than hell. Dead right there in the cell," Tracker said.

"Damn."

Shocking for sure, but I really didn't care. Yeah, yeah, yeah, he wasn't officially convicted on the case, but the case was airtight with a confession that led to other evidence. I mean, the son of a bitch was a child rapist and killer. And "death by sock" was too damn good for him in my book. Too damn good.

"You gonna' call Weldon?" I asked Tracker.

"Already have. Just did."

And we hung up.

"Well, gentlemen," I told the Rangers at my desk, "looks like our ear-pierced, shooting 'victim,' hung himself in the jail last night."

They exchanged glances. They collected my reports and their very next visit was to see Ron Douglas at the S.O.

I next made it a point to try and find the bullet itself. It wasn't that important, but I knew many would be asking. I would have loved to dig the bullet out of that brick wall and tie Weldon's perfect shot package into a bow. I made two trips out there, one with a goodly height of ladders and a metal detector trying to find the slug. It was tedious work, and I just couldn't find it. I would need a third trip with a fire truck ladder or utility cherry-picker to do it, even though the shot could not have been that high off the ground. How high up could the slug be? Around the time I started making calls for a city lift, nobody really cared about the bullet anymore.

There was no further case to pursue as the county and the state declared it a closed investigation and justified shooting. The local DA, the state, no one found any fault with the actions of Ranger Weldon Lucas taking that single shot and winging, or "lobing" the dangerous, fleeing Reilly Rice. That bullet remained in the wall until the building was torn down years later, I reckon. Who knows? Did it miss the wall? No matter where it went? It went, effectively, nowhere anyway.

The shooting of - at, escaping felons laws in the US have been evolving since about 1978. The general, modern letter of the law requires that to shoot someone, it must be in defense of yourself or to interrupt the imminent serious injury of others. Seeing the back of a head, ass and pumping elbows of a fleeing felon does not constitute these imminent categories. But many state laws include shoot/don't-shoot and the fleeing felon problem. Many states and police agencies say that permitting the felon to escape would pose a grave and continuing danger to public safety. Shooting them is an option. Not misdemeanors, mind you. Felons. A criminal justice bulletin,

"1978. UNDER TRADITIONAL RULE, FATAL SHOOTINGS BY POLICE OFFICERS OF SUSPECTED FELONS WHO ARE FLEEING FROM ARREST GENERALLY HAVE BEEN HELD PRIVILEGED AND THUS NOT SUBJECT TO LEGAL SANCTION. THIS PRACTICE, HOWEVER, HAS BEEN COMING UNDER INCREASING ATTACK."

That was 1978, Today? "As of 2026, based on established U.S. Supreme Court precedent (specifically 1985's *Tennessee v. Garner* and *Graham v. Connor*), a police officer is generally not allowed to shoot at a fleeing suspect solely to prevent escape. However, an officer may use deadly force if they have probable cause to believe that the fleeing violent felon poses an imminent, significant threat of death or serious physical injury to the officer or others."

If you are a citizen? I wouldn't do this, by the way. As for police officers, different states have differing laws about this. Even police departmental policies may be stricter than state law. And local county, state, and federal prosecutors and grand juries can have some say on the subject. If driven by politics, they may weave some charges in and around the laws. Then, there are the civil lawsuits! Shooting your gun can always be messy.

When I think back about it today, it was the greatest shot I've ever seen, given the circumstances. I'm sure there are many record-breaking, amazing, military sniping shots on the books, quick-kills and all, but think about it. Think about this one and why it is so unique.

- The shooter was a Texas Ranger (already cool).
- The shot was taken in the middle of moving, rush-hour traffic.
- It was about a 100 foot, high-stress shot with a pistol.
- Weldon waited until Rice had a safe background.

- Rice was a confessed, dangerous, escaping felon/murderer.
- Rice was a moving target.
- Rice was shot-clipped only in the earlobe, and it knocked him down.
- Rice didn't even require a hospital visit. The escaping Rice was returned to jail with an ear lobe bandage. What could he sue Weldon and the State about? What Texas jury would award escapee Rice for damages, for an ear piercing?
- The state police had no defined policy at the time for shooting dangerous escapee felons.
- The passing bullet did no further damage.
- Any possible, crazy, residual legal problems were over when Rice hung himself in the jail.

We know it would be impossible for Weldon to actually aim at an earlobe, at a dead run, in a split second at near 100 feet. Sure, and all the events played out so very well and with minimal, post-shoot problems, it makes for the best shot I have ever investigated.

And I must add, for a while there was a running joke in the county. Wishes were that all prisoners would be issued extra-long, tube socks upon their jail book-in. Who knows what they would do with them?

As Ranger legends go, many retired and became Texas county sheriffs. Weldon slipped right into that mold. Weldon served as Denton County Sheriff for 12 years, from 1993 through 2004. He passed away on January 15, 2011, at the age of 68 following a stroke. He and I worked numerous big cases together. All that knew him, will say he was a totally unique person.

Police Detective Notebook...

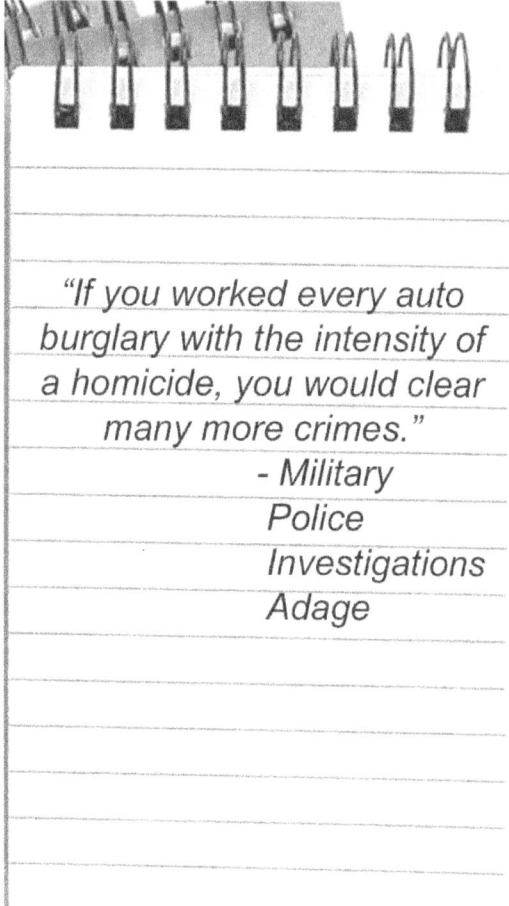

"If you worked every auto burglary with the intensity of a homicide, you would clear many more crimes."
- Military Police Investigations Adage

Chapter 4: "And Hock, You Take the Back!"

When I walked onto the Criminal Investigation Division floor to start my evening shift, I could tell something was "up." The day shift guys were scrambling to get their tactical vests and assorted personal and standard-issue, shotguns.

"Hock!" said one of them, "Hurry up here!"

They directed me up to the third-floor meeting room, which was a large room constructed like a small theater.

"We will hit this house...."

...and the briefing went on, conducted by a SWAT team sergeant who also was a rather new detective sergeant. I'll just call him here, "Sgt Barry."

Down in our city's projects, in an old, two-story wooden, house bound for demolition, a local crack/cocaine dealer, ex-con named Willy Vics was running a dope house. It was a magnet for bad guys and hookers from the region. Our narc guys had a freshly signed warrant in their hands.

"David, Benny, Jeff...you three will enter here and will move upstairs...Tony...you..." and Sgt Barry laid out the plans while waiting for the warrant to be written and signed.

There was a somewhat discreet effort to rest the SWAT team a bit in those days, on various raids. Recently, a certain team had set a house on fire with a flash-bang, shot through a window that had ignited a curtain, and the house burned down! That and, well a few other "events," there was a movement, you might call it, to tone down militant appearances a bit.

At some point Sgt Barry decided some of his detectives should do this one, not our SWAT team. So, his chalkboard was filling up with tactical brilliance. White arrows were laid down aggressively, but there was a bit of a problem manifesting. The back of the house. It emptied out to a big yard connected to a neighborhood of other yards. The arrows ran out of people to cover these escape routes! I would say there were at least eight detectives assigned arrows on the board. Most going into the house.

Sgt Barry looked up at the newly arrived me. I was gearless at this point, just in a suit and tie, and he said,
"...and Hock...you take the back."

Ok. The back. Take it. Pretty big back though. And I didn't even rate an arrow! A few of us had run dozens of these deals through the years and we all had... "taken the back," at one point or another. Still, this was a pretty big. Nothing new here, though. Most of the time, the suspect, and-or suspects, upon hearing officers at the front door, would peek outside a rear window, see an officer standing guard back there, and surrender.

Usually. Some hide in the house. We have had to chase a few. (I would often put something across the back door causing a fleeing felon to trip.) I witnessed one investigator throw a brick and hit a back door, fleeing suspect in the head. Took him right down. He couldn't shoot him! So...he bricked him.

Within a few minutes, everyone hit the streets in their unmarked cars. I threw on my body armor and raid jacket and left the shotgun in my car (too cumbersome in close quarters for me on deals of this nature). The plan was to give me a minute to park down the street just a bit and trot up to the yard. This was a corner house. Then, several cars would skid up to the house front, men bail out, destroy the door, and rush in. The usual, subsequent yelling and threats would follow.

I barely had time to surmount the tall backyard fence, when I heard the sound of skidding tires and men yelling. It wasn't difficult to exactly coordinate such timing. You know, me say on the portable, "89 in position." But no.

There were about six back windows and a back door. The first floor extended beyond the second story. There was a sloping, large ledge-like roof over the first floor and under the upstairs windows. I tell you this now because in an instant, every hole in the back of this building had people pouring out of it, as people leapt, hung and dropped from the ledge to escape.

"Halt! Police! Stop!" I say! I yelled from the middle of the yard, my .45 drawn.

HA! I recall at least 10 people running by me as though I was not there. Fat hookers, skinny dopers, you name it. Stumbling, loping. Looked like a zombie wave. If I had started shooting at any of them? Well hell, I'd be writing this from the penitentiary right now.

BUT! One of the escapees was Willy Vic himself! The whole subject of this little endeavor. He ignored me, too, so I figured since he was the subject, I would at least chase him. The sprint was on. Willy had to vault that fence, and I was counting on that slowing him down.

I holstered my weapon. I couldn't shoot anyone here anyway. He jumped onto the fence and started climbing, and I reached up and grabbed him. He clung like bat on the chain link. I reached around, cussed and slapped his face a few times from behind. Hammer fisted his hands, loosening his grip. Distracted, he…we dropped.

Thereupon came the scuffle. Willy landed on his back and my mission was to get him cuffed, which he didn't want. He still had "rabbit in him" (which was Texican lawman talk for he was a runner). He was a big guy, but in his mid-50s and while these guys are still dangerous when excited, plus I was still surrounded by his escaping doper customers and his gang who could double and even triple the odds in Willy's favor. Ever try to fight a mean, angry, fat hooker?

Meanwhile, the "team" was SWAT-tiptoeing through the house as though terrorists with sub-guns were around every corner. I could hear them yelling, "Clear! Clear!" as they secured every empty room and closet.

One thing was very "clear" to me, I was all alone in the yard, fighting a guy right beside all his buddies, who I hoped were all content trying to escape. I had to toss a few snappy body punches into Willy, all the while yelling for him to give up. He quickly ran out of gas, and I cuffed him. There was no loyalty among these thieves, and all the confederates got over the tall back fence, or the shorter side fence fences, or the side gate to the street. I stood alone with the drug dealer, and I was, all at once, a failure and a success.

I pulled the portable radio out of my back pocket and called Sgt Barry. I reported that I had caught Willy Vics in the back yard. I hooked his arm and walked him to the front porch of the house where those few, shocked folks who had remained in the house that were cuffed and sitting on the steps. It made for great front page, local, newspaper photo of about six arrested guys, Willy now among them, cuffed and sitting dejected on the front porch steps, sternly observed by our guys in raid jackets with shotguns towering over them.

I stood off from the photo-shoot and was a bit disappointed in myself because I had let about, oh, 11 people get away. I was about 38 years old then and had very high expectations for myself. Hell man! "One riot? One Ranger!" Audie Murphy and Sgt York took hundreds of prisoners. I couldn't stop about eight dopers and four fat hookers?

But it all became quickly apparent that, in the end, I had caught the big fish they were after, and there was a tactical mishap in planning.

This mishap became an "inside joke" with the troops for a while. For the next year or two there was running joke with CID that anytime we would plan anything, (even a party), it would finish with, "...and Hock, you take the back!"

Sgt Barry, if he heard the rib, took with good nature. Barry was a unformed patrol officer at heart and a temporary detective sergeant, in a foolish game police admins did and do, moving people all over departments blindly. One should keep good people where they are good at. Barry eventually returned to patrol.

There was an old comedy bit done by the now disgraced Bill Cosby about the Lone Ranger and Tonto TV show. The Lone Ranger would say, "We've got to go to town and find out what the gang is doing," meaning that *Tonto* himself, alone, would have to go to town. Whereupon Tonto would routinely be beaten up. Cosby said he and his pals would scream at the TV, "Don't do it, Tonto! They'll beat the snot out of you!"

Bill Cosby suggested Tonto say instead, "Who's 'we,' Kemosabe?" Which kind of became a cultural remark for the times.

But that one day? I was the Tonto "out back" for sure. And Lone Rangers were nowhere to be found.

"Tonto. You take the back."

Chapter 5: Shadows and Reflections: Multiply Your

Lines of Sight

It is not uncommon these days for police and military entry-and-search training to have a few paragraphs in their PowerPoint presentations on the use of reflect-able surfaces, shadows and light.

In summary, while searching for the enemy or suspects, one should take advantage of any car or business glass windows, clock faces, picture frames, and certainly mirrors, etc., to see beyond normally where they see. This might reveal the position of your opponent-suspect-enemy. In fact, in the trunk of my patrol and detective cars, amongst other items, I always had:

1: a hand axe. (To bust through most walls between beams, and so forth.)
2: a length or rope.(for many reasons, one being pulling open doors when expecting gunfire from the inside.
3: a mirror with an extendable, telescopic handle. (For another line of sight or seeing around corners without exposing my head and one eyeball, or other chores.)

May all your enemies be untrained and ignorant! In the time-sensitive, half-seconds of a running hand, stick, knife and/or gunfight, reflections and shadows are easily ignored by the bad guys (we hope)...and the good guys too.

In fact, an everyday person, agent, cop, or soldier may need these tip-offs in their everyday lives, not just on SWAT callouts or Baghdad raids.

Before power point lessons, advice was once passed down by the old, savvy hands. Here's an example of one such "sightings."

I was in the middle of working a series of home invasion/robbery/kidnappings. During the crime, one of the kidnappers accidentally called out to his partner by a nickname, which was heard by the victim. (This was 35 years ago, and I cannot exactly remember the nickname so let me say the closest thing I remember is "Shock Knee." It was something like that).

Even with the rudimentary computer systems we had back then, there were records in major cities, and the Texas Department of Corrections maintained a nickname and tattoo file. It was a tedious search to request info, but it was there I decided to start a hunt for the nickname of Shock Knee.

At the time our city sat attached-atop two of the top five major crime capitals in the entire country, Dallas and Ft Worth, and we were constantly going there to find criminals and work our cases. It only made sense to check with the State, then Dallas and Ft Worth nickname files. Sure enough, there was a violent offender nicknamed Shock Knee living in one of the worst in Ft Worth, TX. The state sent me his mugshot. The mugshot was picked out of a photo lineup. This I.D. and nickname were enough for me to write a probable cause warrant.

So, I went on a hunt to arrest Shock Knee. I stopped at first with Fort Worth P.D detective division. A sergeant, lieutenant and a few CIDs were there. They listened to my story. They had no idea who Shock Knee was. I told them that I was going to hit the projects and try to find him. They nodded and said, "good luck."

I am stupidly confident. I have, would and will go anywhere a case took me. So, I went to the gambling houses, bars and street corners, to the card games and domino folding tables under the shade trees that lined the projects. I was met with incredulous faces as I badged them all and dared to interrupt them on their turf with my questions. This was a very racially tense era and times.

One street corner group near an open lot, of 20- and 30-year-olds played dominoes, sat and stood around folding chairs. To their amazement I parked and walked right up to them and with a causal James Garner-*Rockford Files* manner started asking questions. They were so surprised some were jaw-dropped smiling. To them, I was either so stupid or such a badass to be there talking to them like this. I was neither. I just go where I got to go and do what I got do.

They did a verbal dodge and dance with me, and as I turned to leave, I put on my sunglasses causing me to look down just a bit as I walked to my car. The setting sun on the street under me cast long shadows, and I spotted a rushing shadow dashing up behind me! It flew across the ground like a shark in the water!

I instinctively spun. My hand went up as I saw one of these guys suddenly stop cold just a few feet from me, his face in an expression of surprise that I turned on him. His on-looking friends had faces of thwarted anticipation. In fact, my shadow-man was caught.

I turned my extended arm and the fingers of my hand into a fist with a pointed finger,

"ONE more question!" I declared with an emphasis on the word "one." The guy remained frozen like a silly, still picture of someone who was caught mid-jog. I then walked right past him and addressed the group again. It was like a "Oh, oh, one more thing," a Peter Falk, "Colombo" style moment from the TV show.

I left again. As I got to my car, looking at the reflection back at the group from my car windows. I wondered what would have happened had I not been alerted by the shadow of this shark on the ground? My gut instinct was that this idiot was going to run and just slap me on the back of the head or maybe kick me in the rear and dash back. Of course, he could have hit me and knocked me down, took my pistola and killed me?

Looking back, my "Colombo" routine actually defused this little strange situation. I had outsmarted the dasher. And I de-escalated the whole thing with a quick Colombo question act.

I was alone in deep, enemy territory – what we use to "politically incorrect" call back then, "Indian Country" (this was Texas) and in this case Colombo was better than Rambo.

A super street tactician would never let me go there alone in the first place. But all my fellow detectives were juggling the same backbreaking caseload as I was. Nothing would or could get done if we constantly paired up and spent time like this.

By the third day canvassing and prowling the projects, I stopped a lone man walking with bags of groceries. I asked him casually, "Hey man! Where's Shock Knee? You seen him? I need to talk with him," out the window of my car.

He smiled at me. He told me right out where Shock Knees could be found. With his mother.

When I got back to HQ, my CID Captain Bill Cummings and I were at the coffee table.

"How's the Fort Worth search going?" He casually asked.

"I told him.

He was immediately pissed, "What? YOU mean no Forth Worth detectives went with you?"

"Nope."

"You are NOT going back there alone."

Hours later he called me into his office.

"I found out…do you know that Fort Worth patrol and detectives are not allowed to enter those projects alone. They go in with minimum two or even more officers."

"Didn't know that."

"And CID did not offer to help you!"

"No sir."

"You have a warrant on Shock Knee now?"

"I do."

He dialed a number and asked for Texas Ranger Weldon Lucas. As you know by now we worked with him a lot. Weldon answered and Cummings told him what happened. They hung up.

"Weldon said he will go back there with you and find that guy. As long as it takes. Fuck Fort Worth P.D. I can't believe it!"

Which was handy anyway because all Rangers have full-state authority. Two days later, I and Weldon found, caught and arrested Shock Knee at his mother's address.

He eventually did 12 years for armed robbery.

Reflections and shadow applications work in many more ways than orderly retreats like this one and in hot searches. I have been on numerous surveillances where I have used reflections to observe hotspots, track and follow suspects. When you set up on a location, try to calculate these reflection factors into your positioning. Turn your "line of sight" from two eyes into four or six eyes!

When contacting, passing by, or interacting with questionable folks, you must check out your surroundings, watching yourself and them in bits, in the reflections of nearby windows, car windows or by the shadows cast on the ground from lights or the sun. Even many darker painted cars, or their chrome accessories, can offer you a reflection to work with. This must come to you as an instinctive process through time. You may even spy more of a 3D version of the person you are talking with, or other views of opponents and their sides and backs, plus watch the movements of multiple people.

Remind yourself of this in the reflection in your mirror each day. Reflect in the reflection. Or when you walk up to your car door window and see yourself at the beginning of each day. Remind yourself. Remind your colleagues. Surprise your enemy. Play the glass and play the shadows. They are all around you.

The winner of the hand, stick, knife or gun fight is the savvy cat that outsmarts and out-thinks his enemy.

Patrol. Detectives. Military. Sometimes even citizens, you don't just go to work. You prowl.

Chapter 7: A Murdering Cop I Knew. His Fall from the Ledge

If you're from around "these parts, "the North Texas region or if you watch international crime documentaries on network or cable TV or read the dog-eared true-crime paperbacks stacked in airport kiosks, then the story of Police Detective Bobby Lozano murdering his wife in their North Texas home in the summer of 2002 was more than news. It was salacious. It was seismic. Even Dateline NBC devoted an hour to it.

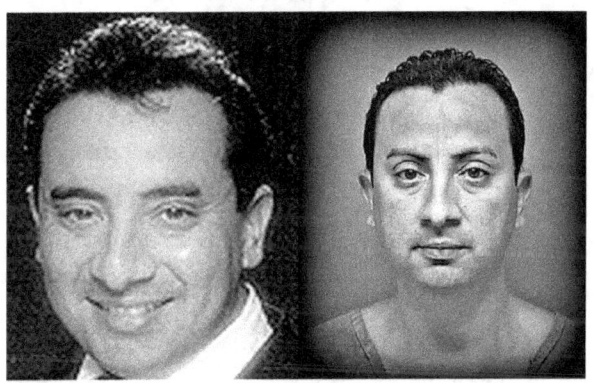

Lozano the dashing detective.   Lozano the inmate.

In a way, part of me is glad I had been retired five years when this case tore through the guts of North Texas law enforcement, doubling it over in pain. You see, I knew Viki Lozano. We all did. And Bobby? He was a friend of mine, ours, and many others.

Bobby and I, along with the rest of our detective squad, worked side by side for years on all manner of cases. It started with this one.

My story with Lozano goes back to the 1980s. Rumors drifted in to us that a small child had been murdered, some kind of confrontation, threat, revenge over a drug deal on the south side of our city. The information rippled hard enough that our CID administration assigned Juvenile Investigator Mike Baker to the case and paired me with him since it involved a possible homicide.

The alleged crime occurred in a poor Hispanic neighborhood. When Baker and I began canvassing, we quickly realized many potential witnesses didn't speak English.

About that time, patrol had a new, sharp rookie named Bobby Lozano who spoke fluent Spanish. Baker and I went to our captain, Bill Cummings, and requested a temporary transfer from Patrol to help us work the neighborhood. Cummings agreed. Soon, Bobby was ours.

We reworked the area with him. I also put him in plain clothes on a bicycle for several days and evenings, letting him hang around, talk, ask questions. It wasn't exactly undercover. He was overt in his questioning, just minus the usual police trappings. That often helps.
He checked in daily. I quickly saw he was smart, personable, and possessed that detective's instinct, the ability to cut angles and get to the quick. We eventually sent him back to Patrol, but we never forgot him.

The child's case took us all over the county and into West Texas, chasing leads, rousting dopers, even digging in rock quarries for a small body. We never found one. There was no official missing child report. The two men originally named passed polygraphs. The case evaporated. We found nothing. But we did find Bobby Lozano.

Becoming a Detective. Years later, a CID investigator slot opened. Lozano applied. Part of any detective's job is keeping a thumb on the pulse of crime in your jurisdiction. I'd read his reports. They were solid. Others had too. I spoke up for him. He was a first-round draft pick. Back then, detective wasn't a paid promotion.

It was more like joining the everything team. We were SWAT before SWAT was formalized. Hostage calls, major felonies, oddball disasters, it all fell to CID. We fixed it, mopped it up, straightened it out, and passed it to the district attorney.

One night patrol had an armed hostage situation physically surrounded. When I arrived, the patrol sergeant and lieutenant essentially handed me the scene.

"CID's here. All yours."

Gulp. That was the culture of the old times.

The Ledge. Bobby's first or second week in CID, I had developed an arrest-and-search warrant for a burglar and his apartment. I told him we'd hit the place at 7:00 a.m., catch the suspect asleep. We'd meet at 6:30 at the PD and roll.

One glitch: I was on call and got pulled into a major crime that night. Worked straight through. At 6:30 a.m., I was at my desk labeling evidence, dog-bone tired. I'd completely forgotten about the warrant—until Bobby walked into the bay, bright-eyed and smiling.

Oh no. Okay. Let's go. We climbed to the second-floor apartment, listened at the door, knocked. Muffled voices inside. Two people.

"Police! Open up!"

No answer.

The apartment office wouldn't open until 10:00 a.m. All the windows faced the street. I stepped to the outdoor stairwell opening and looked.

I saw a ledge. Solid-looking. Wide. So, being half an idiot, I stepped out of the open stairwell and slid my feet six feet over to the first window. I saw inside, our burglar and a woman sitting frozen on a couch, staring at the door. The apartment was basically one open room.

The window was cracked open a few inches. I lifted it.

I climbed in halfway through "Police!" when the suspect sprang up. I had to draw my weapon, straddling that second-story window, and order him to freeze.

He froze. I squeezed fully inside and went to open the door for Bobby.

He wasn't there. He was climbing through the same window behind me. Two half idiots?

We arrested the suspect and searched the place. Not much evidence, but just enough to salvage the warrant. Back at the station, after processing everything, I told Bobby.

"You know that guy could've run out the front door."

He grinned. "You didn't expect me to let you climb through that window alone, did you?"

That was Bobby-charm and recklessness in equal measure.

I knew I'd acted impulsively. I also knew he was half-crazy like the rest of us. Willing to climb out on the ledge.

And that's how it went for years. Case after case. He liked catching bad guys. He liked working angles. He liked specialized units. He liked SWAT. And married Bobby… also liked the ladies. I mean *really* liked the ladies.

A Lesson in Womanizing. That patented Lozano chuckle won witnesses, confessions, juries, and women.

"Womanizing." It's an odd word when you break it down. Woman. Izing. The "izing" of women. There are womanizers in every profession. Policing has its share, maybe more than its share, given the testosterone environment.

When I was hired in the 1970s, Lieutenant Gene Ray Green walked me through the department. In a hallway he stopped us and said:

"That badge will get you a lot of women. But it only takes one woman to get that badge."

Scary math. I've seen badges come and go over that equation. Womanizing didn't just cost Lozano his badge. It put him in prison for life.

The murder case was summarized by media. On July 6, 2002, Virginia "Viki" Lozano, 36, a schoolteacher, mother of an eleven-month-old, and wife of a Denton, Texas police detective, was found shot to death in the bedroom of their home in Denton County, one day after their 16th wedding anniversary.

Bobby claimed she had been cleaning his gun, and it went off. In bed.

In his initial account, he said he had planned to clean his firearm, but left to go to a tanning salon, and later returned to find her dead on the bed. A self-inflected accident while cleaning Bobby's gun?

Authorities (my friends) struggled with a brutal question: Could one of their own, Detective Bobby Lozano, really have committed this crime?

Paramedics believed Viki had been dead significantly longer than Bobby claimed, possibly ninety minutes or more before he reported finding her. The condition of the body and scene didn't align with an accidental discharge or suicide. There was no gun-cleaning oil on her clothing, despite the weapon being oily. Signs pointed to staging.

Investigators uncovered multiple extramarital affairs, complex personal entanglements that shredded his credibility and suggested motive.

BUT! The Denton County District Attorney at the time was Bruce Isaacks when Lozano was first indicted in December 2002. The case seemed to stall. Then in 2004, Isaacks dismissed the murder charge, citing insufficient evidence and concerns raised about the medical examiner's findings. He stated when he dismissed the 2002 indictment, he relied in a large part on input from the medical examiner suggesting the death could be suicide or accidental, and that this medical opinion really weakened the homicide case against Bobby Lozano.

Isaacks said he sought an outside expert opinion from "out of state." He said the expert raised concerns about the strength of the forensic evidence. This explanation was given publicly. later reiterated in interviews (and later a very controversial part of the trial).

Case dismissed? Then came Donna Fielder. A reporter with the Denton Record-Chronicle, she refused to let the case die. When Isaacks closed the case in 2004 as unwinnable, Fielder dug deeper. No record of *any* out-of-state expert was found. The original autopsy ruled the death a homicide. A new D.A.'s office - subsequent prosecutors - could not locate documentation supporting a suicide finding. Questions mounted about what Isaacks had relied upon.

Fielder's investigative series ignited public outrage. When that new district attorney, Paul Johnson, took office, the case was reopened in 2008.

The 2009 trial followed. Spurned lovers testified—one after another. I have never seen womanizing laid out in open court so clinically, affair by affair.

I cannot do the totality of the case justice here in a short review. Donna already has. I suggest you read ***Ladykiller***. Yeah, I know Donna, and she's my favorite newswoman, but this book stands alone as a terrific, painfully truthful, murder mystery and story.

The case was ultimately built by people who had once worked closely beside him, city detectives, county investigators, Texas Rangers, prosecutors. Friends. He had spent years working successfully with us…out on the ledge. Then the years rolled by…and Bobby Lozano fell off the ledge.

Police Detective Notebook...

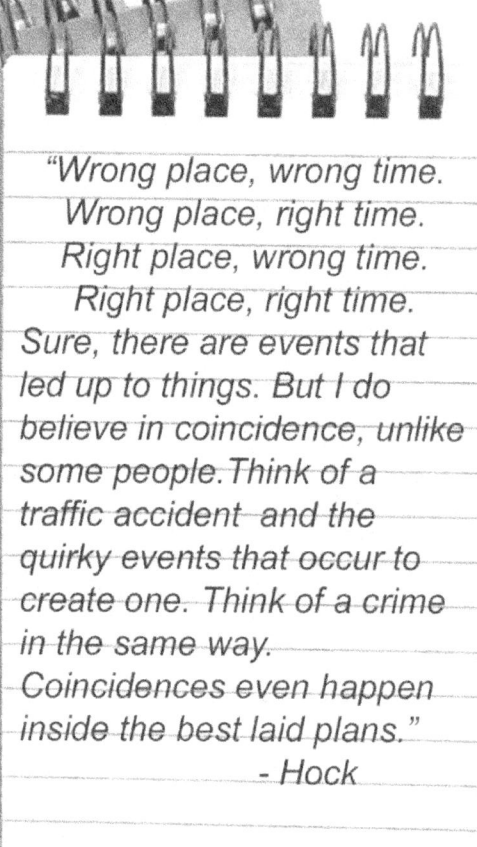

"Wrong place, wrong time.
Wrong place, right time.
Right place, wrong time.
Right place, right time.
Sure, there are events that led up to things. But I do believe in coincidence, unlike some people. Think of a traffic accident and the quirky events that occur to create one. Think of a crime in the same way. Coincidences even happen inside the best laid plans."
— Hock

Chapter 8: Libby, Bozo and Sidney

As a city police detective, I've probably been a case agent on about 50 or so rape cases and worked on more while helping out with other detectives' rape cases. On one of these serial rape cases, I developed a suspect that we'll call here, Sidney Green. In the '70s and early '80s, you didn't hear the term, "serial rapist," but Sidney was one.

This suspect was a black male in his 20s, about 5'8", and a good-looking, friendly-faced kid. His MO, modus operandi or method of operation, was to roam the many apartment complexes and two major college campuses in our city, pretending to be a college student. He would ingratiate himself with groups and had unusual success at apartment complex pool parties. He would linger until almost every person had gone home and singled out the last girl at the party. With charm, he'd find his way into her apartment, and there, once inside, he went about his insidious work.

One other method Sidney used was just to knock on an apartment door and see if a woman answered. We don't know if he stalked these women or roamed these complexes. He would ask for any stupid thing, use the phone, get a drink, whatever, and once inside he would attack the woman. And that is how I became involved.

My involvement began late one hot, summer, evening shift. I was dispatched to a rape scene to discover a woman, and I mean a woman not a "college girl," shivering at her kitchen table, being questioned by a patrol officer and Russell Lewis, once again our "CSI-guy" you might call him now in modern terms. The victim let the suspect in to use the phone.

The rest is ugly, violent history. The woman, I'll call her Libby here, was in her late 20s, early 30s and a graduate student working on her masters or doctorate. She also possessed something else, a real "hippy's" attitude you might say, against guns and against the police. She was a '60s generation type. Hell, so was I!

She acted like she distrusted and resented us from the start. Especially me. If only she felt that way toward strangers at her door? But I was very annoyed at the boldness of the suspect and maybe it showed. Russell was disarming and charming as usual and got a lot of information. Her night would be long. A trip to the hospital and the medical rape kit, the exam to collect bodily evidence. Rape Crisis help. Long night. Libby was married, and her husband worked nights.

We worked the scene and a prowl car took her to a nearby hospital emergency room for the rape kit. When I arrived at the ER, her husband was there. Nice enough fellow, in his 30s, red-curly, haired-afro, (Bozo-hair, I'd call it) and well, I could tell his hero was an Abby Hoffman, not John Wayne. We'll call him Abby, not Bozo, although he screwed up like a Bozo a few nights later. He too was a peace-nik, non-violent type. Perfect for Libby. Love at first yawn.

We ended up back at their apartment. They expressed natural concern about the suspect returning, and how she'd been singled out? Did he know the working hours of her husband? I didn't know.

I suggested they get a gun in case he returned. Suddenly, my Gestapo status skyrocketed. They both bolted upright on the couch and each gave me the "I abhor guns" speech. Bad guns. The waste of hunting. The waste of war. Cops shooting minorities. Okay then. I politely said goodnight. I told her not to answer the door alone and only if Abby was home. The suspect was a door-knocker. Otherwise, they should answer the door together. No more of this random door answering.

The waste of hunting? I thought to myself as I left. I don't care what people hunt as long as they follow the rules of hunting. Through time, I learned that shooting birds and small or big animals is nothing like hunting people. Hunting people? People I like to hunt criminals. Being successful at it just takes an extra commitment, a deeper study of personality, and staying out on the trail longer than your average detective will stay. We called it having "teeth." In detective candidates, I used to look to see if they had the teeth for the job.

It always amazed me that a detective would gladly sit in a deer blind at 4 a.m. waiting for a passing deer but bitched about waiting in a drainage ditch for a felon to come home. Confusing isn't it? I would take the felon hunt any day over a deer hunt.

So anyway, I left Libby's apartment with few new clues for the hunt. I wonder what they expected their hippy version of a brutal detective would do? And if the suspect resisted arrest, what would "a Libby and Abby" certified hippy detective do? Plead for peace? Ask for no bond?

The next day, Libby came into the station, and I constructed a composite drawing of the suspect. Our conversation was cold and her trip to the police (Nazi headquarters) station a total strain on her sensibilities. I found her a strain on mine, too.

But I did learn that the once happy, hippy Libby was now afraid of life. Afraid of every corner, every alley, every hallway. We always encouraged getting help for this, and the Rape Crisis people were our ace in the hole to steer them to get that help. I cobbled together a decent drawing as those kits go. You've seen them. Generic features.

The next few days, I used the local media as well as two universities to spread the word, now with this new composite drawing of this suspect. I even used the new police department copy machine (remember, I started in the world of carbon-copy paper) to make copies and visited the office of EVERY apartment complex in town. Area officers and I tried to stop by any college pool parties we spotted. (Tough, tough job, ain't it?)

I continued to collect suspect sightings and from canvassing of parties and publicity and found new attempted-rape victims who managed to foil Sidney's charming ploys. I filtered a collection of conversations he had at these parties down to some conclusions. It seemed logical that he was from Missouri and his first name was indeed Sidney. I got this info from extraneous people he did not need to conceal his identity from. He lied to the girls, but not to guys here and there. I found the guys. Basically, if a student was from Missouri, Sydney could converse about its geography.

The heat was on for our Sidney and, as I feared, one result of such a tightening net, he might have decided he needed to flee. That "closing net" thing. But he decided to make one last re-visit before splitting.

Yes! He actually knocked on Libby's apartment door, again! Only this time her husband was home. Libby and Abby answered the door together, and there stood her rapist from a week earlier. She screamed. A smiling Sidney turned and slowly walked away. Bozo Abby stood there and let him slowly escape. He turned for the phone and called the police. We had no 911 system back then. Of course it took a while for us to arrive. We all searched the area first and then I went to the apartment. An officer and their new friend from the Rape Crisis Clinic, were interviewing Libby and Abbey when I walked in.

This skunk's return was Libby's worst nightmare. I scratched my head and asked why Abby hadn't jumped his wife's rapist. He was a full foot taller and bigger than the criminal. He remained pale and speechless, and I gathered, feeling all confused and pretty bad about it.

Libby was in a state of shock and part of it was the realization she was married to real hippy-dippy....non-violent Bozo. I mean, every time they answered the door, they were expecting the rapist to return. Sounds like paranoia, but this time it wasn't, was it? Why be so unprepared?

The rapes and even the Sidney sightings dried up. I extended this search information from Texas to Missouri and contacted state investigators up there and all places in between. About a month later, I got a phone call from a Fulton, Missouri detective saying that officers had arrested an armed robber I might be "interested" in.

"Do tell," I said.

He told me that a man with a shotgun held up a store, kidnapped the female clerk and shoved her in the trunk of her car.

With her keys, he escaped in her car. Luck! A witness saw this. A police chase ensued, and he shot at the officers. He crashed into a tree or something I can't remember today, and was arrested on the scene. The clerk was rescued from the trunk. Unfortunately, they did not kill the somabitch. The Fulton investigator told me he had some papers in his effects and within his wallet were some items from my city in Texas. He was a black guy. And, his name was, you guessed it...Sidney.

I got some mug shots mailed to me. I put together a photo line-up. Libby was the first victim to come back to the station, and she identified him as her rape suspect. I used this ID and got a search warrant for Sidney's hair and blood. I packed a bag and drove up to Fulton to collect this evidence. I tried to interrogate Sidney. By now, a week had passed since the robbery, and he was well lawyered-up and wouldn't talk.

He apologized to me that we couldn't talk, the charming bastard. They had great cases on him up there, least of which was attempted murder of a police officer. I returned with the evidence and some great facial photos.

I also carted this new photo line-up around to all the other Sidney victims and sightings. Positive IDs. Blood/sperm tests matched our victims. He was convicted in all Texas and Missouri cases. Texas was scheduled to take over when his Missouri terms expired. Possession is 9/10s of the law so to speak, and the folks of the "Show Me" state possessed Sidney at the time.

But this story is not about Sidney. Instead, it's about Libby. About a year later, Libby called me to check on the court case, and she was apparently in great spirits. Her life had undergone a sea of change, it seemed. She'd taken up shooting, carried a pistol now and, by the way, divorced Bozo. She told me she couldn't tolerate his inability to jump Sidney that night as he slowly walked away from their front door. Reality strikes. Many realities and issues were brought to a head about life and death, violence and non-violence.

Libby, it seems, is a survivor. I hadn't been treated well by the old passive-aggressive Libby, none of us had, and this phone call was actually kind of an apology for all that, too.

Many theories and idealisms exist in an un-popped, delicate, social bubble. But in our diverse and radical world, sometimes, something rolls along and pops that bubble. Sometimes that's real communism, or terrorism, or even just a guy named Sidney...

There is an old adage, "I've never met a liberal that's been mugged." And honestly, that's been my usual experience. Though I know there are some deep-dish hippies out there. I have also learned another piece of advice: never marry a hippy, Bozo.

Never marry a hippy, Bozo.

Police Detective Notebook...

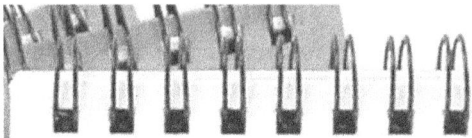

"Crazy, unpredictable bullet paths once inside a body are caused by loss of 'gyroscopic stability' which leads to tumbling (called yawing), fragmentation, and deflection off of bones.

Take care in examining these paths and don't jump to early conclusions.

Let trusted experts explain the sometimes fickle paths of bullets."

- Hock

Chapter 9 A Barbershop in Waco

Another story you won't find in the Federal government archives or Texas Ranger Museum in Waco is a small and revealing moment during the David Koresh, Branch Dividian, Waco raid/standoff that captivated the world for months. Still to this day for many "Waco" represents a transitional time in law enforcement history where police officers...peace keepers... donned militant uniforms and performed a compound-size military assault operation. Or, they tried too...

The initial mission was based on a search warrant for illegal weapons and an arrest warrant for Koresh. The primary reasons included:
1. Illegal Weapons Stockpiling: Authorities received tips that the group was illegally converting semi-automatic rifles into fully automatic machine guns and manufacturing explosive devices, such as grenades.
2. Arsenal Details: Investigation showed the group had acquired over 200,000 rounds of

ammunition, 136 fircarms, and grenade-launcher attachments.
3. Child Abuse Allegations: While not the legal basis for the ATF's federal jurisdiction, allegations of severe child physical and sexual abuse (including Koresh's "marriages" to minors) heavily influenced the government's decision to act.

Results…

- Total Deaths: Including the initial February 28 raid, a total of 82 Branch Davidians and 4 ATF agents were killed during the siege.
- Children: Among the deceased were between 20 and 28 children.
- Survivors: Only 9 people managed to escape the burning compound on the final day.
- Complete Destruction: The sprawling Mount Carmel Center complex, which included a gymnasium, cafeteria, and chapel, was burned to the ground.

In the '80s and '90s as a Texas detective I've worked with Alcohol, Tobacco and Firearms (ATF) investigators quite a bit, especially in the '90s when they were "tasked," and-or under DOD pressure to attack gun crime. They would hit the streets along with us looking for gun felons and gun cases with Federal "hook-ins."

When the Davis Koreash standoff occurred from February to April 1993, I was in the Philippines training for some of that time. Some of these Dallas agents I knew were ordered to Waco, attached to the Koresh case and told to suit up in black and participate in that fateful opening day when the compound was first invaded/raided. The agents and officers retreated under much Koresh gunfire. Somehow none of my friends were shot or killed. The rest is history from around the world.

David Koresh (born Vernon Wayne Howell) was the leader of the Branch Davidians, an apocalyptic religious sect. He claimed to be the final prophet and a messianic figure who could interpret the "Seven Seals" of the Book of Revelation.

After a long 51-day standoff, the last attempt police raids inadvertantly started fires on the compound. Buildings burned and many died. Many survivors and critics of the raid argue that the fire was either caused accidentally by the armored vehicles knocking over kerosene lamps used by the members, or deliberately by the FBI's tactical assault.

Through time, knowing many of the agents and many Texas Rangers, I wound up attending various events, barbecues and dinners etc. (at one time there was annnual Texas-country-style gathering were ATF and favored PDs...we shot all the various guns the local ATF agents recovered for the year. After which – brisket and whiskey. Pit fires. Bring your own camping chair. (What could be more fun!)

These were also informal intelligence meetings, where a growing knowledge of "behind the scenes," first-hand information spilled out from the insiders. One such story gossiped over by federal agents, then later even newsman and magazines like Texas Monthly, goes like this:

"In the inception planning of the Davidian compound raid, many agencies were present. The raid was ramrodded by the Feds of course, but as routine, all related agencies with jurisdiction were present, city, county, state, etc. This meant Rangers from the local Ranger company were also present. Paraphrasing the words and memories of these Rangers, the Feds treated the whole operation like a D-Day invasion, and they were all dressed accordingly. Many of the ATF agents had no SWAT training and were just case-agent-trained. Yet, they dressed like SWAT, and assulted like the Army."

The big fear in these initial plans was – and it did come to pass – it would be a big military shoot out. A replica of the compound was built. At one point in this initial planning, a Texas Ranger (while chawing a pinch of tobacco – I know him) interrupted the invasion strategies and the the Fderal group and he said,

"You know...(chaw) ol' David gets himself a haircut bout every third Wednesday downtown. Why don't we..(chaw) just set up there and we'll walk in, catch 'em in the chair and arrest 'em. Put 'em in jail that way. Then we'll drive out to the compound in a couple cars, and have a sit-down talk with the folks at the compound. Without David there, they won't put up no fuss. We here know mnay these people."

Story goes that all the decked-out, militant commanders exchanged glances. Oh, no cowboy. This was *their* war, by God. The idea was immediately nixed. I'll bet this vocal Ranger was thought by more than a few buzz-cut, Spec Ops types to be a hick-simpleton, a foolish and out-of-touch, bumpkin.

There is no doubt in my mind, and now a many others that this barbershop idea was a better plan. First off, isn't the visage of the barbershop solution a very cowboy and western setting? That ironic note aside, I do see here the "old school" way to solve some problems, not all problems mind you, just some.

The Waco event represented a key moment for the national scene I think, a transition movement to militarize the police in clothing, jargon, tactics and approach.

In the 90s and early 2000s we could hardly find ANY gun or police magazine on the marketplace that doesn't didn't depict police officers as SWAT warriors. The same for many of the period police recruiting posters. "Join the police and got straight to SWAT.

Here's a popular USA police history chart…

Look at the far right end. The most modern cop has transformed into a soldier.

This all has a lasting subliminal effect on our young officers and agents. These magazines and catalogs worshiped the Middle East "contractor" look too. In both worlds, everybody's got a machine gun and just the right clothing!

And these vests! I believe the Brits introduced the police vest look, once trimmed down, the vest look has gone ballistic with USA law enforcement (and security guards). The over-packed uniform vest has the look of someone dropping into Afghanistan for a week of mortal combat. The Batman utility belt on steriods. (is there Bat-shark repellent too?"

I believe we the police are supposed to officially be "quasi-military," and we can't forget the quasi-part, a mix somewhere between Andy Griffith and Rambo, but not either one all the time. Many adults today have never seen a single "Andy Griffith" episode, but I hope we never forget to consider the old-school, "barbershop" options as viable plans sometimes? Not very police arrest or raid needs to be D-Day.

Chapter 10: Fear and Loathing of the Killer, Henry Lee Lucas

Ranger Phil Ryan walking with Henry Lee Lucas early on the murder cases.

It was a head. I mean a skull. Just a skull. Laying there on the ground before me. And I realized why I was there.

"Must be a murder," I said aloud but to myself.

I was there because of the radio message:

"CID 89, Meet Texas Ranger Phil Ryan at the southwest intersection of 35 and 380."

That message came over the air and not from the regular police dispatcher, but rather from my CID Captain. It was unusual for him to be on the radio sending anyone, anywhere.

"Ten-four," I said, wondering what was going on. Ranger Ryan worked the next county over and not ours. I had worked with him many times and he was a quintessential Ranger in looks and life. I knew he was a dedicated hard-worker and would investigate a trailer theft as hard as a triple murder. He sure had a doozy this time...

I drove across the city to the west side and under Interstate 35 overpass. Just west of the highway, south of 380 was nothing but scrub brush fields. North of 380 was busy hotels and stores and a major interstate truck stop. Why was I going to this southwest corner?

Clearing the overpass, I looked over the fields and saw several men walking around in the distance. I could see that two of them were county deputies from neighboring county, along with a small, thin man. It was easy to spot Phil Ryan, who dressed like the classic Ranger, white shirt, white hat and big, tooled, brown gun belt.

I turned onto the field and parked my unmarked sedan on some low grass, got out of the car and made my way to these wanderers. It was then and there I saw it. The human skull. Laying in the open. Not 40 feet from the road and right across the street from a busy truck stop, cars buzzing by every which way. The loud hum of interstate traffic loomed.

I walked across the field and up to Ranger Ryan.

"Hi, Hock," he said quite normally.

"Hi, Phil," I said.

"We're out here looking for a body," he said.

I saw the strange, thin man with a bad eye, unhandcuffed, standing around, and he smiled at me.

"Hock this here is Henry. Henry Lee Lucas," Phil said, "he killed a girl and cut her up out here. Buried her parts. He's killed some other folks too."

"Well, I about stepped on a skull back up there by my car," I pointed my thumb over my shoulder back toward 380.

Phil looked at the deputies and Henry.

"I didn't put no head up 'thare,'" Henry said with a quizzical face.

Phil started out for my car and we all followed. We knew that animals would spread body parts all over, and these fields often contained bobcats and coyotes to name a few critters.

I keyed up my handset and asked the dispatcher for our crime scene man, if Russell hadn't already been notified by Captain Cumings.

Phil walked over by me to explain.

"Henry killed a woman in county. He confessed, and when I got him to talking, he wouldn't stop," Phil said. "He said he killed his girlfriend Becky here in this field. He killed her, had sex with her body, then cut her up and buried her in different spots."

The longer story, the one I found out later was that an 80-year-old, Kate Poor of Ringsilver, TX was a small landowner and she'd vanished. She frequently let some travelers stay on her property in exchange for labor around her farm. She suddenly disappeared, and her friends contacted the police about it. As the case grew more suspicious, the local P.D., a small department, asked for help from their friendly neighborhood Ranger Phil Ryan.

Phil began questioning everyone, and Henry's actions and words didn't add up. Then, Phil found and collected a "deadly weapon" on Henry, and Phil put Henry in jail.

The next day Henry called out to a county jailer, "I've done some bad things! I need to talk to that Ranger again"

And so it began...

Back at the scene...we walked up on the skull, and we all solemnly looked it over. Henry kept sizing up the field and the distances.

"I kilt her over 'thar," he said. "How'd her head get here?"

"Probably animals, Henry," Phil said calmly. I knew that he'd stay calm and friendly with him for as long as possible to keep him talking. I would also, in the coming days, and he would confess even more.

CID Sgt Howard Kelly pulled up and so did our crime scene guy Russell Lewis. We filled them in. Russell started on the skull and its area, and we all walked back to the center of the field.

"I buried parts of her here," Henry said. "You'll find her leg bones over there and her arms bones over there."

Sounds like a lot of digging. I looked at Howard Kelly.

"Hock," he said, "bring Henry in. Get a statement from him, if you can."

This meant booking him in and arresting him. Then talk to him.

"I'll get some of the boys out and start digging," Kelly said.

I have done some digging for bodies before, and I thought this arrangement might get me out of that ugly, shovel chore. I will go ahead and ruin the suspense for you right now. It didn't. I dig quite a bit over the next few days.

"Hey, Henry," I said, "we need to take a little trip downtown. And, I have to handcuff you."

He was expressionless. I cuffed his hands around back and walked him all the way back to my car.

Phil told me, "He's been strip searched down to his toenails."

I let him sit up front in the passenger seat. This was a detective car with no screen or cage. But it was my method sometimes to remain at least partially friendly with suspects.

"Where ya' from, Henry?"

And it went like that. Light conversation. Very light. I took him into our jail and drew up a quick arrest report. Printed him and I took the classic mugshot below, a photo used in dozens and dozens of news reports, about 30 or so books, and on true crime TV shows.

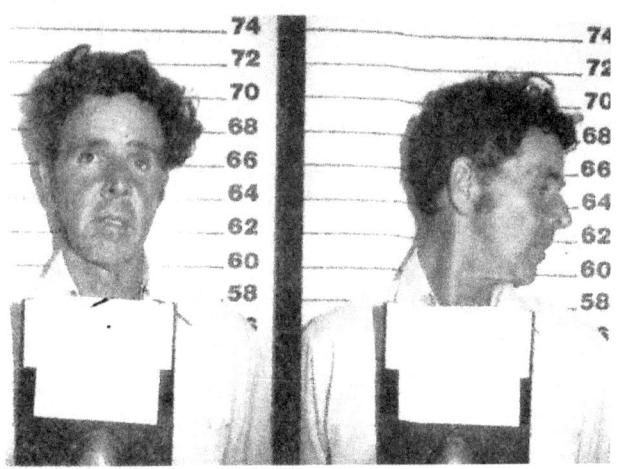

and I took this classic mugshot…

"Come on with me," I walked him down to my office in the CID section of the building.

I sat at my desk and put my feet up. He sat in a chair, now handcuffed around front, and we relaxed.

"What in the world is going on?" I asked.

"Well, like I told Ranger Phil, I killed that ol' lady out in the field, and…"

"Before we talk about this," I interrupted, "let me go ahead and read you your rights, otherwise you know we can't talk. And I want to talk to you for sure."

"Okay."

And talk we did. But first I got us some coffee. Then covered the classic Miranda warnings. He told me that he and his girlfriend, Becky Rowlett, this girl in the field, hitchhiked away from their county and were dropped off at the Interstate by the field. They bought some food from the stores at that intersection, with stolen money from Kate Poor, walked to the center of the field, started a fire and camped.

They had some kind of an argument. She slapped him, and he pulled his knife from a sheath on his belt and stabbed her right in the chest. He watched her die. Then he had sex with her body. (As you get to know Henry, you learn this happens a lot).

With that same knife, he cut up her body, head off, arms off, legs off. He put some parts in pillowcases that he traveled with. He decided to gather up his belongings and cross the street to stay in a motel.

He hitchhiked around the and walked around the state for about two weeks and returned to that campsite. He told me he wanted to bury her.

"Why," I asked.

"Because I loved her."

"Okay," I said.

Henry said that when he walked out onto the field that dark night and saw her decomposing body parts, he buried most of the parts he could find. He told me that his and 14-year-old Becky's relationship was like a father-daughter "thing." He had pictures of her in his wallet, and he carried those photos from jail to jail, state to state, thereafter. How did this Texas killer go state to state later? A Texas Ranger Task Force, that's how. Stand by on all that.

We were about three cups of coffee into this by now.

I need to get this down in writing, Henry. We need a statement about all this from you. Can we do that?"

"Yeah. I already fessed up to Phil. So, yeah."

And I got a statement on the murder, which was my job. Other crimes in other jurisdictions would be secondary to me tightening up this one. We finished off that typed statement. I typed line by line as he told me line by line.

He read. He signed. We relaxed.

"I've got a problem," he said.

As if I needed to confirm my suspicions.

"Ever since I was a little kid, I've been killing things. Dogs, Sheep. Cattle…and having sex with them. Something just snaps in my head, a sex thing. He told me about a man named Bernie who "taught" him how.

"When I kilt my mother…"

"You killed your mother?"

"Yeah."

Keep in mind this was the early 1980s. There wasn't much literature and psychology officially collected and disseminated on serial killers. The FBI VICAP (Violent Criminal Apprehension Program) was fairly new and largely unheard of at the time, and frankly, were not very helpful when we needed them through the years. It was organized in 1985, established by the Department of Justice to act as a national repository for tracking and linking unsolved violent crimes, particularly those involving serial offenders, across different jurisdictions In short, they match up violent crimes around the US and develop profiles of suspects.

So, what has become this textbook case of someone killing small animals and the sex was news. Serial killer movies like "Silence of the Lambs" were not popular. (But Hitchcock's "Psycho" was! Norman Bates killed his mother and dressed up in her clothes. Weird was weird.)

Lucas killed his mother when he was 24 years old. He told me (and other psychiatrists) that he had sex with his dead mother, but years later he denied that. He killed her in the kitchen with a knife and then fled the state in a stolen car. He ditched the car and was arrested while hitchhiking in Ohio. He said that was his first murder.

So, I am sitting in this office with a lunatic who killed his mother about 20 years ago. What was he doing out and roaming the streets? Obviously, somehow released, like...parole or something?

"How did you get out of jail," I asked him.

"I was in mental prison. The doctors said I was alright one day. I wasn't, you know. But they said I was. One morning they just let me out the front door."

He started to tell me about all kinds of murders, all over the country that I just found hard to believe. It started to look like he wanted to shock me, like a braggart. I still have these details in my notes. And I knew we would be talking about all that again and all too soon.

I walked him back into the jail and locked him up.

Then I jumped back in my car and drove to the site by the highway. A lot was underway there. Four detectives and Howard Kelly were combing the area and digging up body parts. Newspaper and TV crews were showing up.

"You get a confession?" Howard Kelly asked me.

"I did. He's a real nut-job. He killed his mother, that woman in the county and this girl. And he started telling me he's killed a bunch of women all over while hitchhiking."

Howard's eyes widened and head tilted down. He had a certain way of looking at you over his glasses.

"We are going to have to spend a lot of time with him," I said.

We had about four unsolved murders in recent years that we would simply have to run by him as a matter of routine. Then, there's the county, the state and what now? All 50 states? Boy howdy, how far could this go?

"Well, Phil will hep' us on all that," Kelly said.

I got my "crime scene shovel" out of my trunk.

(This wasn't my first dead-body-rodeo.) and got with the guys and started digging.

The Justice of the Peace was finally called. I say "finally" because I remember he was really mad at us. He'd heard the news at about 11 a.m. He needed to be called out to the death scene as soon as possible. And he knew that we knew that. Frankly contacting the J.P. was not my job with so many supervisors present. We had body parts he needed to officially preside over. No one called him all day until it was his dinner time. He got out to the field at about 6 p.m., and he really pitched a high-holy, embarrassing fit.

"You know I could have you all arrested!" he yelled at us. "By law you are supposed to notify a magistrate as soon as reasonably possible! I could have all of you arrested right now."

Whew! The judge looked like he was about to have a heart attack, but he finally calmed down. Dinner is really important to some folks! But apparently not so much to us as we worked well into the night. We called a funeral home to transport the remains of the body to the forensic morgue in Dallas.

Nowadays, police agencies have special forensic, "archaeological" teams that sift through the turf like they are looking for T. Rex bones. Not back then. We just had five shovels, a Polaroid camera and some trash bags. (More or less. We also had a tape measure and a 35mm camera.)

Since this was my case now, I drew up diagrams of the parts in relation to fixed objects in the field, triangulating the dig sites. Ranger Phil Ryan and the county deputies went home. Lucas was in our jail, and we felt we could leave the field until the next day. End of day one. The field was city property. No need for a search warrant by the way.

I drove home a filthy mess and stripped naked in the back yard. Bad news. The itching started. It was getting worse and worse. I was covered in chigger bites that were growing and expanding into a leper's landscape on my skin from my sock line up to my chest. I ran into the bathroom and got into the bathtub while my wife tried to look up in a medical encyclopedia what to do. It started to drive me insane. Finally, I took pain-killers we had left over from my various police and martial arts injuries. That took an edge off. That and a little whiskey.

I know some folks reading this won't know what a chigger is. I hope you never do. A chigger is a bug I've only run across in Texas. Virtually invisible, they get on you and scamper up as far as they can. They bite and burrow into your flesh. Lives. Parties, and legend has it, then procreate in there until for some reason the original clan dies off. (Experts say they die quick and don't reproduce, but once bit, it sure feels like chigger generations stay and have an orgy.)

I arrived at work the next morning and all of us that had toiled in the field, even the poor angry, judge I heard, were suffering from chigger orgies. And we had to go out there again! Not without a visit to the pharmacy for nuclear, bug protection, though. But Detective Preston had another plan.

"You see this raw potato?" Jack said, holding one up.

"Yeah."

"If you keep a raw potato in your pocket, chiggers won't bite you."

"That so," I said.

"I got some potatoes out in the car for us."

"I think I will stick with the nuclear, bug spray, thank ya' kindly."

"OKAY then!" Preston said, as though I were a city-boy fool.

We returned to the field and worked all morning. By lunchtime, we were through. I hadn't accumulated any more bites, that I could tell anyway over the red rubble of my lower chest and legs. But Preston? His chigger bites had chigger bites. I can't really say I remember for sure, but I think he went to the emergency room at the hospital that night. I think the chiggers even ate the potato.

In the afternoon, Kelly and I sat back down with Henry at the police department. We ran some unsolved murders past him, showing him photographs. This is routine in a situation like this. A kidnapped and killed young teen, found in a Dallas gravel pit. Strangled woman found out in the woods by some railroad tracks. At first, he said no to them, then fudged on his "no," and said maybe. I watched him look at photos of the victims and had a feeling that they were strangers to him.

Howard and I talked in the hallway. We didn't believe him, but we were obligated to test him through and through.

"Me and Preston will run him around these crime scenes. You catch up here," Howard said.

There was plenty for me to catch-upward-with. Reports. Warrants. Body parts in the morgue. Confirm that Henry was at that hotel. Etc.

Howard and I spoke about the two full days with Lucas and in summary, we discounted all the other Lucas verbal confessions as lies. Becky's murder, however, was bone solid, as was Ranger Ryan's murder case on Kate.

I filed the only case we had in our jurisdiction. Henry was then quickly out of our hair, and Ranger Phil Ryan's hair too.

Henry was convicted and sentenced to many decades in prison. Phil Ryan had his county case. But Henry would not shut up about killing a lot of people. I mean a LOT of people. So many, Austin responded and Henry was next embedded with a special Texas Ranger Task Force to examine his stories. Ranger Ryan would be involved with the team only in the beginning, to shift Henry over to them. (Phil didn't believe all the murder confessions either.)

The Dallas Observer newspaper reported, "A special task force, manned by the Williamson County Sheriff Jim Boutwell and members of the Texas Rangers, was formed to help other agencies sort out the stream of horrors that Lucas couldn't confess to fast enough. Soon, he was being jetted all over the country to lead investigators to crime scenes and recount the terrifying manner in which his victims had met their fates.

Henry said to the task force and visiting detectives, 'I done it every way imaginable,' he liked to say. 'Shootings, stabbings, strangulations, drownings. Killing somebody, to me, was just like walking outdoors.' For good measure, he occasionally added details of post-Mortem sex or experiments in cannibalism."

None of us locals thought Henry had killed all the people he'd suddenly claimed at the time. We read in the newspapers that the toll was running up to 300 people. What?

Phil told me early on, that he'd accompanied one of these early crime scene visits with other detectives from another Texas city. The body was found under an overpass. With two detectives, and with Phil and Henry in the back seat. Sitting in a office later, Phil once recalled for me what happened on that trip.

"Henry had been shown and had studied all the crime scene photos before we left the station. He collected enough of the crime story and evidence in the course of the first "did you do this one," interview. As we drove up the highway, they kept asking him. 'Look familiar? Look familiar?'

Finally, at the next overpass, Henry said, 'Stop here.' We all got out and looked around. Henry pointed to this or that. Back at the station he gave them a bare-bones confession to the killing. I said to Henry later,

'Why did you take that killing, Henry. You didn't do that?'

Henry smiled at me.

I asked, 'How did you know which overpass to stop at?'

Henry said, 'Well, the driver kept slowing down and slowing down, and I just guessed.'

Henry didn't kill all those people, Hock. He's working the cops."

Working the cops. Then one morning, about two years after I snapped that popular mugshot of Lucas in our jail, I bought a weekday copy of the Dallas Times Herald and a headline declared that the Henry Lee Lucas murder spree was all false. A local reporter Hugh Aynesworth, had

constructed a map and a time line of Henry's confessions and found it physically impossible for him to travel all across the United States and commit most of them. Hugh inserted into the time-line, proven facts of Henry's whereabouts. For example:

Henry collected a paycheck on one date, than claimed he killed a girl six states away later that same day. Aynesworth concluded, "Lucas would have had to drive 11,000 miles in the space of a month to have murdered all of the victims on his confession list."

Now, I ask you, why didn't this Texas Ranger Task Force run a simple chart like this on their headquarters wall? We all asked this. Phil Ryan did too, and we couldn't believe the mess. Why did it take a local newsman to do this?

In the middle of this is an odd tale of the Waco, TX. Prosecutor Vic Frizzell, which is another complicated story. But in summary:

When Lucas was brought to Waco and linked to several local murders, Feazell grew skeptical, particularly because his office already had other good suspects or conflicting evidence in those cases. He openly criticized state and federal law enforcement, particularly the Texas Rangers, for:
- Relying too heavily on Lucas's confessions.
- Possibly *feeding him information.*
- Closing cases without proper evidence.

This was, at the time, extremely controversial and seen as a public rebuke of powerful agencies. Then came retaliation and legal battles. Feazell claimed that, after he began openly questioning the Lucas confessions and initiating investigations into the task force's methods, state and federal agencies turned their attention to him. He was investigated and later indicted on racketeering-related charges, which he defended in a federal trial and was acquitted. Stinks.

The New York Times concluded, "After his arrest in 1983, Lucas claimed to have killed as many as 600 people around the country, and detectives from 40 states talked to him about an estimated 3,000 homicides. Mr. Lucas later recanted, and many of the murder cases attributed to him were never reopened. He attributed the false confessions to a steady diet of task force tranquilizers, steaks, hamburgers and milkshakes fed to him by investigators, along with crime scene clues that he said he had parroted back to detectives."

Henry also got to travel, play cards and watch television and enjoyed numerous other benefits at the "Lucas Headquarters."

Lucas' lawyer Don Higginbotham, said that, "Henry lies to everybody. That's how he maintains control over his situation. Anybody in authority. He's playing with the system."

Now get this mess. While I was hanging out with Henry before he went hog-wild with tall tales of killing, he told me about his traveling, murdering buddy Ottis Toole, and how they killed people. He also told me that Ottis had kidnapped and killed young Adam Walsh, the son of John Walsh. John had gone on to become the famous host of "America's Most Wanted" TV show. Was this yet another lie? Not up to me to decide, so when the dust settled a bit, I called the detective division of the Hollywood, Florida Police

Department and reported all these details to them. A CID Sargent listened to me. Never heard back from them.

Years later, Toole became infamous thanks to Henry's popularity. But, apparently my early '80s phone call to Hollywood, Florida CID fell upon deaf ears! And unchecked? Then months later I learned the Texas Ranger, Lucas Task Force called them also with the same news I gave about Toole. Read what Time Magazine wrote about this:

"The FBI would credit 'America's Most Wanted for helping nab at least 17 of the agency's '10 Most Wanted' fugitives, John Walsh had to wait 27 years for the Hollywood Police Department to both admit that drifter and serial killer Ottis E. Toole abducted and murdered his son and apologize for investigative mistakes that transpired during the early years of this investigation, as police chief Chad Wagner said in a news conference."

Years later I was hired to help Fox security protect John on a book tour. We discussed my first call about Toole.

Toole first confessed to the Walsh killing in October of 1983, but, as the department's police chief told TIME in the mid-'90s, Toole and his accomplice Henry Lee Lucas were notorious for 'confessing to crimes they didn't commit.' Toole would end up dying in prison in 1996 while serving five life sentences for other crimes."

But, there was also supporting evidence against Toole. Walsh would later write a book about this. In the late '90s, Walsh was on this book tour, and I was hired to assist FOX security with protecting John on his trip through Texas. I had a chance to get to know John and we discussed this overall situation. Ironic, isn't it?

And now for even more madness and weirdness, in the mid-1990s, then sheriff Weldon Lucas (no relation to Henry) called me at home. Weldon, as described in the previous chapter, was a former Texas Ranger and was indirectly involved in Henry's local case with us. He told me there was some new ado about a woman claiming to be the *real* Becky Rowlett in the media and coming to our city, perhaps to appear in court for a hearing. Becky alive and well? Whose skull was that I'd almost tripped over that fateful day? He warned me that there might be a quick, new court date/hearing over the issue.

But, this was quickly dismissed as a fraud. Some bizarre married woman named Phyllis had befriended the imprisoned Henry. You know, first pen pals. Jail visits. Then, "prison love." For sick people. She thought she could somehow throw a monkey wrench into the works of Henry's death sentence by suggesting Becky was still alive. She was quickly arrested for this fraud. Like the entire Henry Lee Lucas penumbra, this too was very, very strange. Years later, even Geraldo Rivera did a TV show on the Henry and Phyllis connection.

Of course, Henry's story morphed into books, documentaries and even a movie. All of these are available on the internet for further investigation, with the proper names and locations. I was interviewed once in a while by them, but Lucas disgusted me so I didn't add much more to their stories. I have only decided to tell my small involvement in this book, from a personal historical perspective.

I feel as reporter Lucas expert Carlton Stowers felt when he wrote in the Dallas Observer when he said:

"The furor over the latest Lucas scam attempt had already died when, one evening, I answered the phone to hear a long-distance operator say that I had a collect call from Lucas (in prison). "Will you accept charges?" she asked. 'No,' I replied for the first time. Then, realizing that he was likely listening to my response, I added emphasis. 'Not only no,' I said, "but hell no.' Finally, I had too belatedly realize, the time had come to put the life and lies of Henry Lee Lucas behind me."

I guess I should sum up by saying that Lucas died in prison from a heart attack. All the stories about Henry's killing spree, lies, and manipulations still fascinate people, but all agree that he did kill "some" people, and the murders they mention as real include our Becky case and Phil Ryan's case.

Of course, others and I are also convinced he killed Becky in our city. I still remember that afternoon, all of us standing in the field west of the interstate, and Henry pointing to the ground and telling me, after I almost tripped over a human skull,

"If you dig here, you'll find a pillowcase with arm bones in it. Right 'chere is where I buried them."

And we did.

Police Detective Notebook...

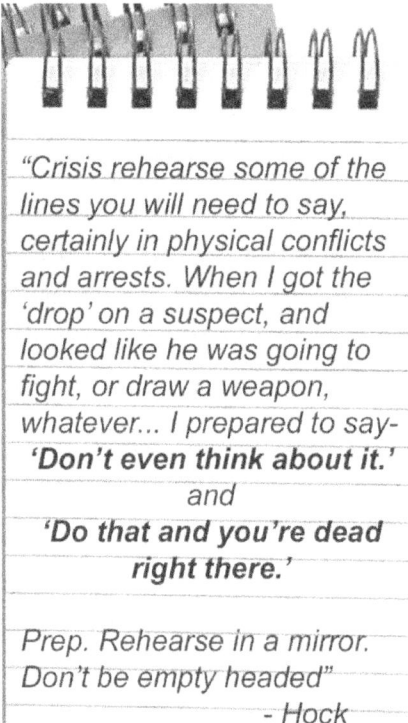

"Crisis rehearse some of the lines you will need to say, certainly in physical conflicts and arrests. When I got the 'drop' on a suspect, and looked like he was going to fight, or draw a weapon, whatever... I prepared to say-
'Don't even think about it.'
and
'Do that and you're dead right there.'

Prep. Rehearse in a mirror. Don't be empty headed"
— *Hock*

Chapter 11: Jailbreak! And the Psycho Martin Crebbs

It was afternoon in August in the early 1980s. Egg-frying, Texas hot. That is to say that if you plopped a raw egg down on the street, it would sizzle in less than a minute.

CID Sgt. Howard Kelly and I were cruising back into our city from a long day of looking around the countryside on the north side of our county. Looking over open, condemned land. Howard had caught a tip that a ring of car and truck thieves were stealing vehicles, stripping them down and discarding the remnants out on the vast fields and farmland very soon to be flooded-covered over by a major lake project.

If we didn't find any striped vehicles soon, they'd all be under about a hundred feet of water. Howard had an idea about this location, and we hoped we might catch the ring at work. Who in the world would be working out in this laser heat, though? Still, we had to try.

We were in my assigned Chevy, but Howard was driving because he knew where he wanted to go. I had my hands up on dashboard to collect the air conditioning shooting it up the short sleeves of my damp dress shirt. No matter the heat, we usually had to wear a tie and a sport coat or a classic suit. Had to cover the gun back then. Kelly almost never wore a tie, or a jacket for that matter, and "they" (admin) were kind of afraid to tell him otherwise. He was the *NCIS, Jethro Gibbs* of the detective division, if you get my drift with this modern analogy.

We hit town, turned down Chester Ave and into the busy downtown area, talking about who knows what all, when a screaming man yelled over the police radio,

"Jailbreak! Jailbreak! A whole floor is loose!" It was the county dispatcher. He was desperate.

"All available units report to the SO, ASAP."

This news quickly went out over the city radio airwaves too. This did not sound like the usual "suspect bounding out of the first-floor, book-in room" and off to the city park north of the Sheriff's Office.

Howard and I looked at each other. We were about 100 feet from the County Sheriff's Office! He pulled onto the lot. We bailed, pulled our guns and ran into the building. We could see some city police cars zipping in, and some officers running across the field from the neighboring city PD.

We got inside and three county investigators were standing by the doors, guns up and at the ready, as the one main elevator descended from the cell floors above. What was this? Were escapees coming down? Howard Kelly and I pointed our guns at the doors too.

The elevator descended. Descended. The doors opened. On the elevator floor lay a jailer. Johnny Yale. He was howling and quaking. There was blood all over his torn shirt.

"He stabbed me!" he yelled. "They stabbed me. The whole third floor is loose!"

S.O. investigator Jim Wilson hit the kill switch on the elevator wall and knelt beside Yale. Lt Jim Neel also knelt.

"Who stabbed you?" Lt. Neel asked over and over, "Who?"

"Crebbs! Crebbs did this. It's a jailbreak up there. He turned everybody loose on the 3rd floor," Yale yelped, almost crying.

"Everybody" on the 3rd floor of the county jail was about 75 inmates.

"Block off the stairwells!" Jim Wilson ordered. Some deputies near there with shotguns and pistols took positions.

Crebbs. I looked up at the ceiling, my .357 Magnum revolver in my hand. Crebbs. I'd put that raping, stabbing, psycho Martin Crebbs in this jail last month. I caught him. I put 'em in here. And now?

I thought, "Now I'm gonna' go upstairs…if he has a knife or shiv in his hand. I'm gonna' kill him.

Who is this Crebbs you ask? How did I catch him? Why did I think he suddenly needed killing?

He was Martin J. Crebbs. Years ago, back in the 1970s as a patrolman in Texas, I'd heard of a rape case from crime updates. A woman had been awakened in her bed by an intruder. The intruder controlled her with one of her own kitchen knives he'd collected from her counter on the way to her bedroom. She was raped at knife point in her bed. Then she was abducted to another house and tied up and raped again. Held for hours, she escaped. Our detective squad caught this teenager, also a known burglar. He was convicted and sent to the Texas Pen. Somehow, don't ask me why, perhaps his age? Perhaps the trying times of overcrowded penitentiaries? He was released on parole. The man's name was Martin J. Crebbs.

Then, years later, there was another home intrusion rape in the neighborhood, and a series of aggravated robberies and burglaries throughout our city and in North Texas, and by this time, I was a detective.

May 19	Paroled
June 12	Aggravated robbery
June 12	House burglary
June 20	Aggravated robbery
June 20	House burglary
June 20	House burglary
June 20	Attempted rape
June 23	Attempted rape/home invasion
June 24	House burglary
June 26	Aggravated robbery
June 26	Aggravated robbery
June 30	House burglary
June 30	House burglary
July 1	House burglary
July 4	House burglary
July 5	House burglary
July 5	Aggravated rape
July 8	Aggravated robbery
July 12	House burglary
July 12	House burglary
July 14	Aggravated rape

Other crimes too…

Also, I might mention that not all of these local crimes listed were within our city limits. Some occurred outside the city, in the county and in the counties north of us on up Oklahoma. Who knows about Crebbs and Oklahoma?

In the 1980s we were not in "lightening" touch with each other as we are today. It would take days, even weeks, maybe even a month or two before regional crime patterns over multiple jurisdictions could be recognized and organized.

Where and when did I come in? July 14. The a.m. hours of. There was a pool of detectives in our squad, all taking general assignments and some of these crimes were routinely spread out among us.

I happened to be the "detective on call" so I was summoned to an old house on the northeast side of the city in zero-dark-thirty hours of the 14th of July. A home invasion, rape case. Crime scene specialist, Russell Lewis was also dispatched. In route to the house, I was informed that the victim was rushed to the hospital and with the crime scene in Russell's expert hands, I turned off my path to speak with the victim and oversee the rape kit process.

At the hospital, I learned what I could from this poor exhausted, bruised woman, I'll just call her "Judy" here, before she was rolled into an examination room. I left Judy with a patrolman to gather her info for the basic, crime report. Judy had a good friend who quickly met her at the hospital, as well as the ever-handy "Friends of the Family," a group of female counselors we used to help rape victims. Judy, the friend and the counselor promised they would all be at the police station by about 11 a.m. for a detailed statement.

By 6 a m, I was at the house. Russell and I had to swap stories to really know how to scour the residence, yard and area again. The open kitchen window of the older, wood framed house, and the big kitchen knife (from the victim's kitchen drawer) and the bed left in total disarray, and the strips of cloth used to tie her spread hands and feet to the bed frame...well...they all told much of the overall story. The three-hour ordeal.

We stepped through the yard and with the help of the rising, welcome, dawn light and with our giant flash lights, we saw four, dry, Marlboro cigarette butts by the doghouse (there was no dog) in the yard. We collected them. I found another cigarette butt by a big tree in the yard. Another place to hide and watch from? Russell photographed and printed.

We carefully folded up the sheets and pillows hoping for fluid stains and head and pubic hair and so forth. Was anything stolen or missing? I wouldn't know until the victim could return to her house and take stock. You never know how fast you might need this info, and the first few days are a thirsty rush for intelligence.

Up all night, and by mid-afternoon, I knew a few things. The suspect was young, white male, 20s maybe, long blond hair. He surprised Judy when she was in bed. He had one of her big kitchen knives. He treated her "like a candy store," as she described it. He brandished the knife until she was tied up and even after, at times, while she was tied. The tip was at her neck.

He told her as he left, "Don't bother calling the police. They'll never find me."

Forty-plus something years later as I type his last "never find" words to her, those words still burn my stomach and piss me off, not unlike when I heard them the first time.

Judy, nor anyone she knew, smoked cigarettes, least of all Marlboro cigarettes. The presence of such butts in the yard was mysterious to her. Perhaps we could run some successful saliva tests on them? She said she'd looked over her house and thought she'd lost one piece of jewelry. It was a customized piece. I learned she was an art student, and I asked her to draw the suspect and draw that customized piece of jewelry. She did, and man! Did that come in handy later.

(Left) The rape victim was an artist and sketched her own profile of the suspect. The resemblence to Crebbs aided the investigation.

I started a neighborhood canvass around dinnertime on the 14th, looking for any and all information about people, cars and suspicious things.

That began an amassment of suspects. One of Judy's next-door neighbors was a parolee, who had killed his wife back in the 1960s, and was a known "window-peeper." Another "weird" guy lived a block away, the neighbors told me. Plus, we had an occasional "butcher-knife" rapist working that side of the city for years, but he was a little older and always brought his own butcher knife. Neighbors reported their usual, suspicious "hippies" and one of these "weird hippies" was wanted for assault. I wasted a day running him down and arrested him inside a college night club. I quickly cleared him of this crime.

Russell Lewis checked in with me to report the fingerprints were smudges and not comparable. He sent other evidence off for testing.

Meanwhile, I'd also caught "talk" of this Martin Crebb's parole, once again from general "cop gossip." I cannot tell you how important just gossip and talk was and is with fellow, area investigators, especially back in those non-tech, days.

When on day shift, after the morning crime briefings, a bunch of us would go eat breakfast at a series of restaurants. We, the county and the state investigators would congregate, talk smack, hunting, sports and oh yes...crime! Some of us on evening shift would still eat breakfast for this. Ignorant police supervisors and bean counters who'd never served as investigators, would oft times complain about this "laziness." But, they were just plain ignorant and frankly, pains-in-the ass.

At one breakfast, someone from the state, warned us to watch out for,

"Hey, a crazy somabitch, Martin Crebbs was paroled and he is a little psycho, crime machine. A robber and a rapist. He's got relatives in this county and up north in Cook."

So, I looked into Crebbs and contacted his state parole officer in Cook County. After this phone conversation, I could see it deserved a drive north to look at his file, which the officer said was thick, and always a pain to fax back then. Faxes were a bit foggy to read, especially if you received copies of copies. Better and quicker to make the 90-minute drive.

Once in the state building in Cook County, I sat down with the Crebb's file. The parole officer said that in just the few short weeks Crebbs had been on parole, he was already a growing problem. He lived with his parents in a rural area in Cook County. His picture matched the suspect description and Judy's drawing. Some of his prior rape conviction details did match those of Judy's crime, but still, many rapists share common denominators. Had robberies increased since his release? Yeah. Burglaries? Well, yeah. But they come and go. Maybe up here in Cook too? I took one Polaroid photo of Crebbs' face, like a mugshot from the file, and collected some copies of ID data.

My next stop was the Cook County Sheriff's Office where I met CID Captain David Bone. Bone and I had worked together a bit in the past. Bone was about 6'5", a power-lifter, former Texas Tech lineman, ex-rough-necker-oil field worker and smart as a whip on fire. What little we had and knew about computers back then, was already Bone's new interest and his specialty. If I ever build a Dirty Dozen, police force, Bone will take up two slots.

Cook County CID Captain Bone and me.

He had a very simple business card that had two things on it – the word "BONE" in the center in capital letters, and his phone number in the lower right. Not Captain, not Sheriff's Office, just "Bone." If you got one of those stuck in your front door, knowing that Bone had been there looking for you? And you're a shady character? You'd better just pack up and head on out to Mexico, bubba. You do not want Bone after you.

"Martin Crebbs!" Bone said to me. "I am right this instant, looking at him for an armed robbery of a convenience store." South part of the county. I need to talk to the clerk. Let's go."

Go we did. I climbed into his sedan and took the front seat, passenger side. I felt like a small child there. Bone was such a giant that he'd removed the front seat and welded a new foundation for it, moving it back a few more inches than factory spec, so that he could fit his giant self behind the wheel and work all the pedals. So, though my own 6'3" self, felt like a kid in there. I drove his car once on another case we worked and could barely reach the steering wheel, and I needed a Dallas phone book to sit on. But I digress. Back to the case....

The robbed county store was not that far from the Crebb's family house. The owner himself was robbed, and he thought the getaway car he spied parked up the road from the store was familiar looking "Seen it around," he said.

The masked man with a gun reminded him over-all of someone in the area, but he couldn't say for sure whom. The man said that the .45 pistol aimed at him was very old and even "rusty-looking."

Right then I recalled that we too, in my city, had two armed robberies where a masked suspect, about Cribb's height, held an old .45 pistol.

Back at the Sheriff's Office, Bone and I made a plan. We would take turns surveilling the Crebb's family house and if that dried up in a day or two, we'd march up to the house and question everyone. As Howard Kelly would say,

"When you hit a brick wall, go shake the tree."

That might not make sense, a "wall" and then a "tree." But it meant that when all leads fail, go shake up, and mess with the suspects. Sometimes they react in a beneficial way. What have you got to lose? You never know what will fall out of the wall...er, I mean...the tree.

The next day I asked Judy to make a return visit to the P.D. I showed her a photo line-up with Crebbs and with similar males with blond hair. Since the rape occurred in darkness, she just couldn't be sure enough to pick Crebbs out. She gave me a maybe on Crebbs. I can't work with a maybe.

I did a "shift" on the Cooke County house. Bone did a shift and he had a deputy do one too. We never saw Crebbs, and only observed the comings and goings of a large rural, family. Nothing interesting happened. Not even a sighting of Crebbs.

We decided to do that "march" and "tree-shaking" after three days. We drove up the dirt road to the two-story house and knocked on the door. What we found was a mad mom, a mad dad and a mad uncle. Not mad at us. Mad at Crebbs! We all sat down in their large living room.

"I just know that little shit is robbin' places! I know it!" the dad exclaimed. "The day after he got out of jail, his little sister took him to Boydston, to a pawn shop, and he bought a gun."

"What kind of gun?" I asked.

"It's an old Army pistol," he said. "I've seen him with it."

"By old you mean…"

"Like World War II? An automatic."

It was very common to call semi-automatic pistols, "automatics" in those days.

"He is a hangin' out with that Steve Spitz from Sherman. He's trouble," the mom said.

Bone nodded and said, "Heard of him."

"I'll bet you have. He's a snake in the grass," the dad said.

"They drive around in Spitz's car," the mom said, "some kind of Camaro, dark red. It ain't his, belongs to some poor girlfriend of his."

We collected various bits of other information, like the little sister's name and birthdays. Cars. Etc.

Then Bone and I drove back to his Sheriff's Office and we went straight to their records room. We looked up Spitz. Bone uncovered in the county files that both Spitz and Crebbs were roommates in their county jail years ago under burglary charges. With the Spitz birthday on file, we ran his criminal history and driver's license info. We had mugshots. Spits had dark hair, Crebbs had blond hair.

Back home I collected all our recent armed robbery reports. I was not assigned to any of those robberies. One robbery was at the usual gas station combination convenience store.

According to a customer pumping gas who saw the robbers approach the store, one robber was masked, the other man was still donning his mask while running across the lot. This almost masked man had black hair. And the customer saw the man's face before the mask slipped on. The robbery team got inside, pulled an "old" semi-auto gun and robbed the place.

Who was the witness pumping gas, the customer who saw the face? I scoured the report. The detective assigned to the robbery case had not found out, even after three weeks? I will only tell you that the detective assigned to the robbery...was a slug, and I wasn't surprised.

I drove to the store and working with the manager, looked over the credit card receipts from the crime date and time, hoping the guy didn't pay for his gas with cash, but used a credit card.

He did use a card at the pump. He used a company card. With some long-distance phone calls, we found him, an Oklahoma truck driver. I created a photo line-up of similar white males, and I met this witness at a restaurant on the Texas-Oklahoma border. He actually picked Steve Spitz out very quickly.

The next day, I got an arrest warrant for Spitz and we spread the word all over North Texas.

Meanwhile, I contacted Texas Ranger Phil Ryan who worked the whole region including Boydston. I gave him the info on Crebbs and Crebbs' little sister and asked him to find the pawn shop where the gun was purchased. Ryan, as you already know, was a terrific Ranger. Within two days we learned all the details of the gun purchase. It was an old, .45 caliber, semi-auto pistol.

Days later, my desk phone rang. It was Bone.

"We got Spitz," Bone said. "A state trooper found him driving on Highway 8. Alone in his car. Nothing in the car. I'll wait for you to get up here, and we'll talk to him."

"I am on my way," I said.

Spitz was a real punk, but he knew he was caught and he did talk in the hopes for leniency.

"Crebbs is crazy, man! He thinks he is Joe the Dope Dealer with drugs and Bonnie and Clyde, Clyde the robber. And he thinks he is Jack the Ripper."

In just three weeks these idiots committed a crime wave of felonies with more plans on the Crebbs. Drawing board for supermarket robberies, raping lone convenience store clerks and Crebbs favorite – home invasions, but of families at night. They had even plotted a bank job. Police officers stumbling into these scenes would be taken hostage or shot.

"You know, it was all Crebbs. I...I wouldn't do all that," Spitz said.

Spitz was an emotional mess. Crying. Bulging veins. Pleading. We knew we would have to prove and re-prove everything he said, anyway we could.

I won't bore you here with the skyscraper of paperwork this produced. And all this back in the day when we typed reports on typewriters, maybe electric, sometimes not, with carbon paper, and used expensive copy machines when we could. But filing warrants and cases on 30-plus felony crimes was a paper puzzle. We did, it none the less, filing cases in three counties. Bone was a computer whiz and we used his personal printer.

Welcome to my world. Today, all this would be done by a task force. Back then, it was just me and Bone. (In case I forget to tell you later? Spitz eventually took a 10-year plea bargain.)

We were informed by the angry relatives that Crebbs was still coming and going from the family house occasionally in another friend's borrowed, two-door, light yellow Chevy. Bone drew up a search warrant for Crebb's room in his house, which we searched and turned up nothing. (Crebb's had what we call "a reasonable expectation of privacy," thus the warrant.

Now, all we had left to do was find Crebbs and that gun. The word was out he was a wanted man. We were back to staking out the family house in plain cars. I was driving my personal Ford Thunderbird.

And then one afternoon after a few days, we saw him go by in the two-door Chevy. We pulled a simple traffic stop and an "under-the-gun arrest." He tried nothing. He knew he was surrounded. Cuffed and stuffed, I took a quick look over his car. There in an open compartment in the console was a chain and a piece of jewelry. It looked familiar. It actually looked like the drawing Judy sketched of her stolen necklace! I walked back to my car and returned with my Polaroid camera. I snapped a photo of the console and the jewelry. In a "search of a vehicle, incidental to an arrest," I pulled the jewelry out. It matched Judy's drawing perfectly. Her missing piece! The souvenir of a rapist. I stuck the picture and jewelry into my pocket.

Next, began one of the most unusual relationships I guess I have ever had with a criminal, and I have had many, from Narcs, to Cowboy Mafia-men to dopers and killers. Back at the Cisco jail, Bone and I sat down with Crebbs in an interview room. We read him his Miranda rights. He waived them. I think he was dying to talk and see what we had on him. At first, Crebbs denied everything and was only concerned with the evidence we had, trying to play all the angles he could. He yelled and swelled up with pitch-fits of innocence. He called us crazy.

I pulled the chain and pendant from my pocket and held it up. The pendant swung like a hypnosis watch.

"You took this from a woman," I said calmly.

His head shook slightly, just back and forth, not side-to-side, not yes, or no, and he almost smiled. Then I proceeded to tell him a list of what we had on him, step-by-step, to include a complete confession from Steve Spitz. Then I told him about the evidence the lab was working on. He listened intently.

"You're good," he said.

"No," I said. "You're just that bad."

He was impressed with me and Bone. His whole demeanor changed, and he sat there and told us everything, almost as only an actor could, playing the part of psycho, talking about someone else, not him. He spoke in a passive, monotone voice. He did slightly giggle over some of the rape details. He bragged about the houses he "shafted." He criticized his accomplice's inadequate performances.

"Did Spitz lie about anything?" I asked.

"No, I don't think so," he said.

It was pretty clear we were dealing with a psychopath, who viewed the rest of us as mannequins to his passing fancy. Bone and I took long, separate typed confessions from Crebbs. He was quite proud of himself and his...achievements.

Over the next few days, Bone and Cooke County kept Crebbs as they worked on paperwork and court appearances for the crimes in their county. Meanwhile with Judy's jewelry and the confessions, I obtained a few more arrest warrants on Crebbs and pushed the local paperwork monkey further up the tree.

By this time, Texas Ranger Weldon Lucas caught wind of all this and wanted to help out. In about a week, Weldon and I drove up to Cooke, served the warrants and transferred Crebbs to our county jail in cuffs and a hobble.

Once ensconced, I visited him frequently and I took him out to cruise the city and further document the locations of his rape, robberies and burglaries. I never once talked down to him and always treated him "normally." And we talked about a lot of things other than crime. This is an important strategy for every detective to try. You either have this knack, or not. Now, this method of "questioning/interrogation" has been quite formalized by the FBI and now even for fighting terrorism.

Crebbs sat in the passenger seat of my car, cuffed around front to drink coffee and eat from drive thru, fast-food places. This was a treat for a bored inmate. I knew he would kill me in an instant, but I had a detective in the back seat right behind him that I could really trust and who would…seriously intervene. It was another detective in our squad, Danny McCormick.

I knew this was tricky and dangerous, but it was the confession game I was playing. A risk I knew I was taking. Danny and I go way back in rough times, and I knew without question, Danny would just shoot the son of a bitch, if Crebbs tried to kill me in the front seat.

In the process of his first local court appearances, he was appointed an attorney, who immediately shut all this interaction down. This attorney, first-name Gary, was a sharp guy, and we were friendly adversaries, as I was with almost all local defense attorneys. Gary could not conceive the unusual mountain of evidence and confessions I'd obtained from Crebbs. Within a few weeks, I would have a sperm match with the rape kit and a saliva match on the cigarette butts from the yard. Solid, solid case. This surely looked like a major, plea bargain to all of us. When Crebbs was eventually transferred from our city jail to the county jail, he told our city jailer to tell me goodbye.

This had all the earmarks of a plea bargain indeed, but we had a new, go-getter, assistant district attorney I'll call here "Hal Sleeve." Hal craved the Crebbs prosecution. He asked me over for a meeting at the DA's Office, and I expected a puzzle-piece, plan to bunch the crimes together into one big, plea bargain with a hefty jail term.

"I am going to start with the rape," Hal said.

"Start?" I repeated.

"This guy is an animal, and we are going to try him one felony at a time."

Okay. Hal's the boss, and that is what we did. That was a whole lot of cases! Sleeve really was one helleva an attorney too, and he did quite a job.

So, within a few months, with Crebbs in our county jail with a "no-bond" the entire time, a trial eventually began. When I walked into the courtroom, Crebbs waved at me, and I nodded at him. Do you see what I mean by strange? When I was called to the stand to testify and Gary could not shake off any of the evidence we presented, especially the confessions I took from Crebbs, that I had to read aloud before the jury. I was dismissed. I had to walk past the defense table and Crebbs nodded at me again. Strange. I just fried him alive, and still he acknowledged me.

Crebbs got about 30 years in the Texas Pen for aggravated rape. But, the next trial date was set a month off, and Crebbs remained in his cell on the third floor of the county jail. And during that wait? Crebbs called a friend on a pay phone for a pick-up, escape vehicle for a planned date and time. He took small pipes off of a jail exercise bike, sharpened one end of each, wrapped the other ends of the pipes with a small, hand towel, tied the towel with some string, and tried to kill a jailer named Yale with seven stabs.

Yale fell screaming. Crebbs took the jail keys off of Yale's belt. With the jailer's keys in hand, he turned the whole 3rd floor of the jail loose, and they gained access to the office off the elevator. There were various staff weapons up in that office.

And now you know why on that hot, August afternoon, with wounded jailer Yale screaming bloody murder on the floor of the elevator, 70 or so inamtes loose on the 3rd floor, and the S.O. in chaos, I stared at the ceiling, gun in hand, and wanted to kill Crebbs.

With the elevator sealed, with just a few moments ticking off, we made our move. There was one stairway to the 3rd floor. Me, Howard Kelly, a city patrol officer named Jim Tom Bush (who was a decorated Vietnam War sniper and now brandishing a shotgun) and LT. Jim Wilson gathered at that doorway. Wilson opened the steel door, and we heard the raucous yells and crazed chants from above. With all our guns pointed upward, just me, Kelly, Bush and Wilson ran up the stairs. For some reason? <u>No one else followed us up</u>. I can't imagine why. The city guys and one county guy?

Oh, you might think, "Now wait a minute, isn't this a job for SWAT?" But back in those thrilling days of yesteryear, only places like Tokyo and Los Angeles had SWAT teams. Back then, we were the SWAT team. In my department the detective division was the SWAT team. Same with the County Sheriff's Office.

We got to the big, vault-like office door on the 3rd floor, which led to the cells. There was a window in the door, and we saw the inmates walking around, yelling, throwing stuff. Unlike modern jails with open pods, this jail was mostly a series of hallways and cells on either side, and some open, sitting and eating areas. Wilson unlocked the big door, shoved it open, and we marched in, guns up.

"Back in your cells or die!" we shouted, pointing our guns at everyone we could see. This was Texas in the 80s and they knew that we were not bluffing. Mostly, they did return. Some were shoved.

"You cannot get out of this building. Get back in your cells!" We said.

I also was on the visual hunt for Crebbs. I couldn't find him. I couldn't see him. I ran down an empty hall to one of the day areas. I heard a voice. Angry, pleading. His voice. I turned the corner to see Crebbs on one of the pay phones. He was yelling at someone about his car ride escape. He held the shank in his hand. Jail keys hooked on his pants.

"HEY!" I yelled.

He turned. He dropped the phone. And pissed-off, stared at me. We were completely alone in this end of the wing. The ruckus in the halls seemed far away.

It was another one of those moments in my life. I could have shot him. Shiv in hand. Dead right there. No one would have doubted or questioned the action under these circumstances. Somehow, I had this odd feeling that shooting him was just not good enough.

There is an old expression in Texas, "If you shoot em', you can't beat em'."It was a gut feeling. I holstered my gun and walked toward him, pointing my finger,

"Drop it! Drop it. Drop it."

He didn't. He didn't. He didn't.

He raised it as I got close, and we had a fight. I can't specifically remember each step of this, but (as a "karate" guy) I beat him down pretty bad. He'd had a lit cigarette in his mouth, and I hit him there first, which was hard enough to make him drop the shank in his hand. After that? Confusing mess. When it was done, I Cuffed himand picked him up off the floor.

A deputy ran down the hall and shouted, "You okay?"

"Yeah, can you get that?" I motioned to the shank.

I marched Crebbs back down the hall as Kelly, Bush and Wilson and another deputy or two locked up the last of the loose inmates. I took Crebbs through the office, down the stairs and was sort of surprised how no one else had really joined us. No one else was in the stairwell, until I got to the bottom, where some officers stood an anxious guard.

Why didn't they help us upstairs? Maybe they thought we would just take back the floor's office? Shut the office's solid metal, jail door, and only secure the office? I don't know.

I walked Crebbs past the Sheriff, past some of the lingering detectives, officers and civilians congregating on the first-floor hall. The local news was already there, their office building a few blocks away.

All solemn eyes were upon us. Maybe I had a bruise or two on my face. Crebbs did. He was bleeding and limping (but alive). I took him into their CID offices, followed by some of the investigators, and sat him in a chair. Nobody cared about the blood.

"Yale?" I asked of the jailer when CID Captain Ron "Tracker" Douglas walked in.

"He'll live."

"He's all yours. Let me get my handcuffs," I said.

And some of the S.O. detectives stood Crebbs up, and we exchanged cuffs.

"I caught him on the pay phone. I'll write you up a statement right away and get it back to you," I told Tracker.

I needed out of there. Needed air. I walked outside. My car was still outside, and Howard Kelly could simply walk across the parking lot to the City PD. This was a county crime, and a county arrest. I didn't need to do that usual ton of city paperwork. The county did. I just needed to type a statement. This whole thing took about 20 minutes. From the second we heard the radio call of, "Jailbreak!"

I saw my car in the crowded parking lot. I could squeeze it out between all the emergency and news vehicles.

I was going to make my own clean, little escape from the mayhem! I could of killed him. But I didn't. I was certainly prepared too, and, holstering my pistol, confronted by such an armed inmate – who'd just stabbed a guard! Well, it might be considered real dumb on anybody's paper. But as a karate and jujitsu practitioner, maybe not so dumb. And we have a suspect alive not dead. Anyway, it's a hard to describe feeling. I just wanted to get to my office and type up a short, concise, statement and ship it to Tracker Douglas.

As I backed out of the parking spot, I saw in my mirror, Tracker Douglas outside, running toward me and waving.

"Oh no, what now?" I said to myself. I rolled down the car window.

"Hock. Crebbs said he wants to talk to you."

"Talk to...me?"

"Yeah. We need a statement from him, and he said he would talk only to you."

They really didn't need a statement. Yale was alive to testify about his attack. But to be thorough, a statement is always...you know...nice to have. I pulled back into the parking spot and got out. Tracker and I made our way back to the CID offices.

We found the interview room with a desk, and there sat Crebbs in a chair, with a cuffed wrist to the arm of a chair. A deputy with a shotgun sat outside the door.

I walked in, closed the door and sat half on the desk. I said in an astonished tone, like two old friends talking,

"What in the fuck happened up there?"

And he began and wouldn't shut up. He told me everything and I mean everything. I got off the desk and sat in the other chair. He told me that with the rape conviction and more trials coming, he realized his life was over and he had to escape.

"Well, the only chance you have for any kind of leniency is to explain...explain your...your desperation. All this in a statement. If you don't get your voice heard, you'll just be like a cool-blooded killer. An attempted murderer," I said. "You know your attorney Gary won't let you speak up in court. The prosecution will really tear you apart if you take the stand."

"Yeah, I know," he said. "Yeah, I'll make a statement."

Now, technically, Crebbs was still under the auspices of Gary the attorney. In some locales, this might shed a darkness over any statement Crebbs might give. But, on the other hand, this is a separate incident, and any criminal could waive his or her rights at any time and offer a statement. So, I went with that angle. Worse came to worse? They would just outlaw-dismiss the statement. And Hale would be the victim, witness on the stand.

And so, I began the statement process with Crebbs yet again. I got a standard confession form with the Miranda warnings on the top, and I began collecting a confession from Crebbs. We went line by line. When it was done, I told him, "Good luck," and handed Tracker the confession. It had various details like who the getaway driver was supposed to be. And so, to my memory that was like the 18th or so confession I had collected from Martin Crebbs. The last one, I had hoped. But oh, no. No.

The next morning, prosecutor Hal Sleeve called me. He wanted to know the details of the escape from my perspective. I told him. In those days, video tapes were a growing interest in the legal system and Sleeve had massaged the DA's office budget into buying some expensive camera equipment. He was a real advocate for maximizing the use of video in court from crime scenes to confessions.

"So, he confessed," Sleeve said.

"Yeah," I said.

"Would he confess again? I mean on tape? Could you get him to confess again?"

"I don't know. Maybe. I don't know. What would Gary (his attorney) say?"

"Gary's on vacation for two weeks. Crebbs waived his rights. What can he say if Crebbs agrees? Would he confess again," Sleeve asked, "up on the scene. Would he walk you around the 3rd floor and explain what he did? Could you get him to do that?"

"Can you get an S.O. detective to do that?" I asked.

"You know he won't do it for anyone but you. Go try, Hock."

I didn't work for the DA's Office, but I kind of did, you know? We all do in this business, and the police chief and sheriff are really just anal retentive, hotel managers. And, as the old Al Pacino movie line goes,

"Just when I thought I was out, they pull me back in."

Sleeve set it all up with Tracker Douglas. 1 p.m., the next day. Two days after the escape attempt. I went to the S.O. Sleeve was waiting there for me. Their crime scene people and operators of the video equipment were at the ready. Tracker Douglas was also ready to facilitate.

Crebbs was brought down to the same interview room and there we were again. Just me and him. He was surprised to see me. This was the kind of guy that, if you fight him? And you beat him? He respected you even more. And, after some conversation, like a damn salesman on cue, I reluctantly began my requested pitch.

"Listen, Martin, it would be a great service to this agency and all the other agencies to hear you describe how you did all this yesterday. You know it's a new world with these video tapes. And a video like this would be helpful, also make it look like you were trying to help us, and fully cooperate. Show full cooperation. It might show the jury that you have some...you know, hope? Compassion? Whatever."

I guess he had nothing better to do! Why not. His face was expressionless.

"Yeah, sure," he said.

And we did. Uncuffed, he stood beside me, on the third floor, with all the hooting and hollering of a hot, un-airconditioned day in the county jail. I read his Miranda rights yet again this first time on film, but maybe the 20th time overall? He waived them again. I asked him to start explaining what happened. He walked us to the exercise area, showed us the particulars on the exercise bike where he got the two pipes for his shanks...showed us everything, right up to the point where he and we had our little, physical confrontation in that day room by the phones. I was wondering how he would handle that, describe that part of the tour? Just at this point, I asked him a question and broke his chain of thought.

Video done. I left again.

I got back to our station and sat down in Howard Kelly's office, stretching out.

"Is it over?" Howard asked.

"I think that part is over. Now comes the rest of the trials."

I didn't see Crebbs for about 3 months until the next case came to trial. The jailbreak case was put atop the list in his crime wave. He was charged with Attempted Capital Murder with a Deadly Weapon. In the hall Gary the attorney looked at me, half-smiled and shook his head.

"I don't know how you do it," he said.

I think I knew what he was talking about. Should I have waited for Gary to return two weeks before I questioned Crebbs? That whole protocol thing?

"He said he wanted to talk to me, Gary. They pulled me off the street to see him. Then he kept waiving his rights to counsel."

"And yet? I am still his counsel," Gary said.

"And yet you are." What else could I say? Crebbs agreed to it all making it all very legal.

I don't think Gary was so keen on defending this crime wave, career criminal. He was just doing his job too. In court, there were arguments for and against both the written and taped confessions. The judge ruled in the state's favor and both confessions were admissible. I did a lot of testifying that week. The jailer testified. Sleeve's great, closing argument was another patriotic, crowd pleaser. In the judge's chamber, awaiting the jury verdict, Hal Sleeve was ecstatic. At one point he even put his head on my shoulder and said, "Thank you."

Prosecutors don't always get such cases.

Somewhere in the annuals of the county court evidence records, in a locker somewhere is that very strange video tape of Crebb's confession, taking us on a violent tour of a jail stabbing and mass escape.

Crebbs was convicted, received nearly a life sentence and following that, the prosecutors from various counties joined together for a big plea bargain. There were aggravated robberies, rapes, burglaries, drug charges…what a bundle. He wound up with over a hundred years to do.

Somewhere in all this, and I don't remember how, nor is it in my notes, I somehow recovered that "rusty old Army" gun. Crebbs must have told me where it was. But I got my hands on it, and I do recall, and do have notes, that I traveled around and showed it to the robbery victims in our city to further close up our robbery case files. One woman I showed it to jerked back at its sight, like it sent an electric shock her way.

And that is the Crebbs story and his jailbreak scheme. I sometimes think about the victims of his crimes. And that line,

"Don't bother calling the police. They'll never find me," Martin J. Crebbs told Judy the rape victim as he left.

Well, guess again, dipshit.

Updates: Just a few months after his confinement in the Texas Pen, Crebbs was almost beaten to death by fellow inmates. I received no further information about this.

Just a few months after this beating, Crebbs was stabbed four times by another inmate. He survived. I received no further information about this.

After a few years, Crebbs was killed in prison by another inmate. Once again, I received no further information about this, nor did I care. This is a typical end for a psychopath.

Police Detective Notebook...

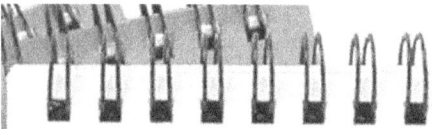

"If I were officially involved in hiring new officers, or selecting detectives, (which I never was), I would be investigating just how clever and CHARMING they were, or could be.

Clever and charm have a lot to do with making connections and getting information. Things not on any hiring or promotional, paper tests." - Hock

Chapter 12: You Can't Hide Your Lying Eyes

Truth. Dare. Or consequence. Ever played that game? Heard of it? Many citizens think that the lie detector is used to clear innocent people. But I used a lie detector test as a tool to ferret out facts, manipulate suspects, classify witnesses, and move investigations along much more than to expect the pure truth. Sure, I was often looking for the truth, the dare of taking one, and-or the consequences.

The mystery remains for all - CAN YOU BEAT THEM?

As of around the late 2010s, (yes, that is the latest research) estimates suggest about 2.5 million polygraph tests were being given per year in the U.S., mainly for things like employment screening in public safety fields (e.g., paramedics, police, firefighters) and internal investigations. The exact number today (2026) is not centrally reported by a government agency, so estimates are based on industry figures and academic reporting.

Other studies estimate several hundred thousand to over a million tests annually in the U.S., though exact numbers aren't centrally tracked and figures vary depending on the source.

Government agencies (including intelligence and law enforcement) also use polygraphs for background and security screenings, and agencies use them for internal leak, theft and corruption problems.

Worldwide usage? There's no comprehensive global tally of polygraph tests given each year. Many countries either don't track tests centrally or don't make data public. According to some professional estimates, polygraph testing is used in law enforcement, national security, and private sectors in more than 100 countries worldwide, with millions of evaluations annually across those sectors. That's a whole lot of work for a machine whose results are questionable. Still used, but controversial. They are widely regarded by scientists and many courts as unreliable indicators of truth, and results are often *not admissible in criminal court* without agreement of both parties.

Many psychologists point out that decades of research haven't significantly improved polygraph machinations and that they remain prone to false positives/negatives. In other words, truth that are lies. Lies that are truth.

When you are on the very cusp of taking a lie detector test for a new job or a routine "checkup" some jobs have or even a crime, you will often be talking up the wonders of polygraphs.

"How good are they?"

"Can I beat them?"

"Will they call me a liar when I'm not?'

"I am innocent, and will one make me look guilty?"

"Well, if it's not admissible in court, then I shouldn't have to..."

Before the internet, there were some books in the back of stores on the subject. Now the web is wide open for all kinds of science, junk science, the debate on the weird little box, and the quirky funny men who work them.

Who could forget the scene in the remake of ***The Day the Earth Stood Still*** when Keanu Reeves wiped out the weird polygraph examiner? (After that very scene, I think the whole movie went downhill.)

Great movie scene.

The polygraph test compares the physiological responses of breathing, blood pressure, heart, and perspiration rates between clear base questions and ... "questionable" questions. You might ask me,

"If I were charged with a crime I did not commit, would I take a polygraph? Probably not. It would really depend on the circumstances.

These days, suspects who are smart and rich enough pay to take a secret polygraph by a reputable pro. If they fail? It is a secret. If they pass? The government might not like that method, but the defense can wave that pro examiner around to investigators and the media, maybe even show a film of the test, etcetera.

Why would I hesitate to take one? Read on...the polygraph had been inadmissible for as long as I could remember, but the expert veteran investigators and examiners always told me that the polygraph was just a "tool." A tool? I never really understood that concept while I was a patrolman. But when I became an investigator, I began to....

As a patrol officer, military or otherwise, thinking about or using polygraphs was just not a daily priority. When I started working for MPI, (Military Police Investigations), and then later MDDS, (Marijuana and Dangerous Drug Section), despite what should have been the obvious need for polygraphing folks on occasion, the lie detector was some sort of elusive device that required all kinds of okays and approvals up a long chain of military command and had to be conducted off base by "outsiders.

In South Korea? When I was an MP over there? I guess somebody offered them somewhere, but I couldn't imagine getting to use one on a common burglary case. I never heard or saw anyone use it. I'm sure our "FBI" the Army CID was using them. And I was sure that if an MP Colonel had lost his left sock, we'd all have been drawn, quartered, and polygraphed by the hundreds to find a culprit sock-thief.

It was not until I became a rookie detective in Texas that I learned so much about a polygraph test. Very early on in my days in investigation in Texas, I was assigned my first money-theft case at a bank in our city. The main suspect was an employee. The woman denied any knowledge of the theft, yet many elements of the case pointed to her.

One afternoon I sat at my CID Sergeant Howard Kelly's desk, and we were talking about cases and crime. I mentioned my stalemate on this, my first internal bank case.

"Sounds like you need to polygraph her," Kelly said.

"Won't that cost a lot?" my virgin-self asked, still haunted by the stigma of the military process.

"If we hire somebody, it'll cost. And probably the bank would pay. But if the state police does it? It's free."

"Free?"

"Hell, yeah. Call DPS (Department of Public Safety, otherwise known as the Highway Patrol or Texas State Police) in Garland and ask for Charlie in Polygraph. It's free if the State does it. We can hire examiners that we like to use in some special cases, but DPS will do it for free. Just about any case. And, anyway, Charlie is a great examiner and a great interrogator."

Kelly opened up his desk drawer, shuffled through some business cards, and handed me one. Then he stood up to leave, shoving his .45 inside his tooled leather holster and belt line. I looked over this card for Charlie's at the DPS headquarters in Garland.

"Hard to pass. Easy to fail," Kelly said over his shoulder as he left me sitting in his office.

Hard to pass. Easy to fail. I never forgot those simple words, and that about summed up the polygraph's position in the legal system, too. Card in hand, I walked back to my desk and dialed the number.

"DPS Polygraph. Charlie Givens," the man himself answered - and within a minute, I had a polygraph scheduled for four days later. So much for red tape and expense!

Four days later I drove the bank employee down there at the specified time and date and met this

Charlie. But, you see this story wasn't about the bank's money loss, or if that employee got caught lying while strapped into the machine, or really even about polygraphs exactly.

It's really about ol' Charlie and how he was a very influential learning experience for me. Charlie was one of best I'd ever known for showing me how to successfully interrogate people.

Once arriving at the state HQ, each time I went, just Charlie and I sat in a closed-door session and I would explain the entire case, specifically what I needed to find out. He drilled me down on these specifics. If it were an arrested suspect, he'd be a locked room. If my subject was in such custody, I'd try to bring another officer with me to watch over the suspect. Often, I'd ask a patrol officer involved with a case to come down with me so he or she could observe a process that patrol officers NEVER get to see. Or I brought in a new detective. Or a reserve officer. I wished someone had done that with me when I was in my training wheels. A free suspect or witness would be in a small lobby.

After the briefing, then I'd usher the subject in the room. He'd carefully, and emotionally unattached but still in a friendly way explain to the subject what was going to happen. I watched all this in another room, through a classic two-way mirror. He would go over the simple questions, all requiring a yes or no answer.

After the test, Charlie and I met alone again. He had opinions. When he and I were unsure about some answers, Charlie would ask,

"Can I talk to him about it? No re-test, just talk."

"Sure," and I returned to the other mirror room and Charlie would quiz the subject on the questionable parts. His knack was great. The machine was just a steppingstone. Usually, he would re-test and sometimes not. But we wanted to get the subject to try and explain-figure out why his answer sent the needles flying. Usually this was very revealing.

And for me to hear about all those educational interrogations-interviews Charlie conducted first and after the test. Charlie was such a verbal craftsman.

At the HQ, Charlie would book one polygraph in the morning and one in the afternoon so that he would have a good four hours with each suspect if needed. Four maybe five days a week. For many years. Lots of time and grade in interviewing.

Charlie had been a State Trooper and a State Detective and was nearly 60 years old. He'd been a polygraph examiner for almost 16 years at that point, and there was hardly a story he hadn't seen or heard of. Running the case by Charlie, you could see him pigeonhole and filter it all in his mind. He'd flip open and shut his metal cigarette lighter with his thumb while listening, and finally light one up and ask,

"SO ... what you need me to do is see if this kid was a witness or an accomplice?"

He'd usually get to the point like that.

"Yeah, Charlie. That's about it!"

Or whatever the nature of the crime was. He would reduce it to a short sentence question. He would design a few key lines of questioning on a yellow pad and run them by me. I'd add something or not. The questions were brief and concise. Things like...

1. Your name is (the qualifying-truth establishing needle patterns).
2. "Do you know?" "Have you ever been?"
3. "Did you steal, rob, pillage, rape, kill...whatever)

Simple questions like that. Then he asked specific, nuanced questions that mattered in the overall picture. "Pertinent" I believe is the legal term. He would ask the subject these very questions to prep him.

Charlie would methodically explain the machine in his slow, droning kind of way. Seated, he would discuss the case and slowly read the questions he or we had designed. I could see him study their faces as he asked them if they completely understood each question. This alone created a certain stress factor. Each question was made to seem vital, and the person would soon be expecting the pending "Difficult Question Nine" in a crescendo, as he or she answered "Regular Question Three." They knew nine was a' coming. Needles moved.

Then Charlie would rubber tube and wire the person up. He'd turn on the machine and tinker with it like he was setting a difficult radio station connection to Mars or setting a complicated MRI to perhaps peer into a brain and soul. When YOU were in the chair and the juices in your "hidden brain" started squirting?

He'd finish the test questions. That usually didn't take too long. He'd unhook the person and ask him to wait there as he left the room. He'd come in to see me and fire up a Marlboro. He'd look at the guy through the glass and take a draw, then say, "the ol' boy is lying," or not, or if he couldn't decide.

When in doubt, he'd always say, "Let me take a crack at him." Which meant he would sit in there face to face with the subject at the small table, position his cigarettes and lighter on the tabletop, and try out his interview kung fu on him.

You know many of the guys who trained me or who I worked with were vets from the 1950s and 60s. On the mystique of a lie detection machine, there was an interesting story from way, way back. This story went so far back in a time when few people had seen a polygraph. Nor had they seen many ... newfangled ... copy machines!

So, yes, polygraphs can be defeated.
Not because they're useless, but because:
- They measure arousal, not deception.
- Arousal can be manipulated.
- Humans vary widely in stress response.
- Interpretation involves judgment.
- This is why many courts and scientists remain skeptical

In the 1960s, two old detectives in our agency who shall remain nameless here, knew that a certain "Mr. Charles" had knowledge about a series of business burglaries and the burglars. They picked up the old gentleman and took him to the police station for questioning. Both told me that they liked Mr. Charles and did not want to interrogate him harshly.

"Nozzah! Nozzah," Mr. Charles insisted, "I don't knows nothin' about no kinda' burglars."

"Now, Mr. Charles, we know you know. And we have that new polygraph machine, a LIE DETECTOR!

I am sure you've heard of it. We will test you on it to prove you know."

"You what?"

The detectives rolled into the room with the first ever copy machine our agency ever had. They plugged the copy machine in and hit the start button. Mr. Charles' eyes widened.

"Now step up here, Mr. Charles." They lifted the lid on the copy machine. "Put your palm right there on the glass."

"Will this hurt?"

"No, sir."

They closed the lid over his hand.

"Do you know about the burglaries and where the stolen property is?"

"Noozah!"

They hit the copy button. Mr. Charles' eyes widened as the machine scanned-bathed his hand in an almost religious, bright, white light.

"Here's the report now," a detective said snatching out the photocopy from the machine's tray. He casually let Mr. Charles peek at the copy of the handprint.

"Hmmm. HMM!" the detectives said while shaking their heads and looking over the paper.

"You are lying, Mr. Charles."

"Oh, Lordy!"

Long story short for Mr. Charles he thought he was scientifically caught in a lie. He then took the detectives to a suspect's house that contained the stolen property. So even a copy machine in the right situation, the mysterious "box," can be a tool in the investigation!

So goes the polygraph. Do you think things have changed much with" the box?"

Police Detective Notebook

> *"Does your detective candidate have the "long teeth" for the job. To dig in, to bite in and work a case for the long haul it might take. The commitment. The 'obsession' if you will?"*
>
> *- Hock*

Police Detective Notebook

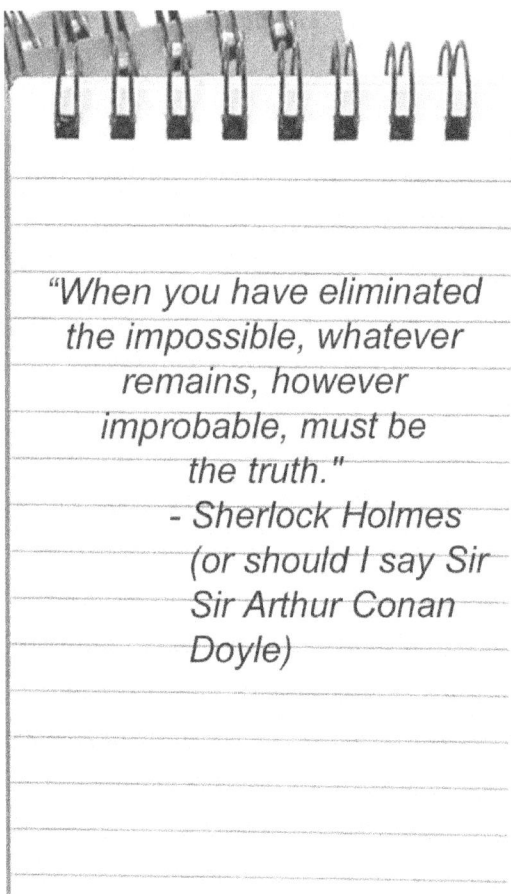

"When you have eliminated the impossible, whatever remains, however improbable, must be the truth."
- Sherlock Holmes (or should I say Sir Sir Arthur Conan Doyle)

Chapter 13: The Face Mask Murders
Part 1: Dead Head on the Beach

It was such a lovely day. The sunset temperature was perfect as one might expect of San Diego, California, a place where it was said that God kept a summer home. Any couple on the planet would have loved to stroll on the beaches of San Diego at such golden times. But when William and Maria Cass took their shoe-less walk there on the soft sands late one afternoon, rolling up in the froth on the beach beside them was not a tanned surfer dude, an ornate shell, or some tossed seaweed.

"What is THAT?" Maria gasped.

"I ... I don't know," William answered.

In a crouch, they timidly stepped over to it, then...

"It looks ... like a head. Is it a head?"

"It's a head! A skull!"

They both looked around as one is likely to do under such times, and then William grabbed Maria's hand and pulled her off the beach. They ran and ran until they found an open snack shop.

"We need to call the police! Call the police!"

William breathlessly insisted to Cameron Delone, the proprietor, "there is a dead head on the beach."

The fact was that it was a head, a fresh head more or less, but more precisely one whose flesh and internal inner skull parts were half gone. Not a stripped-clean skull per say. The skull must have been used like an underwater ice cream bowl for various sea life to come scooting in and slinking around and to take delicious nibbles of this brain part or that eyeball.

Within an hour, one of the rotating San Diego homicide detective squads showed up on the beach and conferred with the patrolmen standing guard. Other men took some pictures and measurements; but the crime scene "CSI" action we see today on TV and the movies was not quite the norm for 1982, progressive California or otherwise. In other words, no one was collecting things like DNA samples back then. And an open public beach is just not the greatest of crime scenes to work. Shifting sands of time and all.

Still, veteran Homicide Detective Dale Borlan had some hunches. He knelt in the sand by the head and commented, "Looks like the fish ate his face off first." Great guess. Great instinct from a generally messy-looking, lopped-off head. But not correct. Their job would be to identify that head, eliminate the slim chance of a decapitation accident somewhere (stranger things had happened), and presumably find a killer who took time to cut said cranium from somebody's torso. But they would have to hurry because their rotating team caught or was assigned several murder cases a month.

Dead head on a beach. Might make a great song title for a Jimmy Buffet-Grateful Dead collaboration, but that was not music to the homicide team's ears.

Me? A few thousand miles away. I was busy minding my own cases, working on a variety of criminal investigations in the heart of north Texas-land. It was a beach-less place; and if you wanted my honest opinion, God kept no summer home there and just kinda' passed through sprinkling blue bonnets over his favorite places along the way.

A "Lawman's Life." They say that in dog years, dogs age faster than people. In detective years, there was a similar time warp. When you figured that each month I was assigned about 20-25 cases on average of any and all types. That meant 25 complainants, 25 times multiple witnesses, and 25 or more suspects to deduce and catch. Compressed people, problems, pressures, puzzles, and cases. Each month built a taller pile of previously unfinished faces and cases. It was a rat race that never ended, and you were always supposed to do a perfect and brilliant job.

Part 2: Technicality Was a Dirty Word
"What the...?"

On the hallway wall outside of our detective offices hung a large cork bulletin board full of wanted posters and regional intelligence bulletins. One rather unique, new intelligence poster, not a wanted poster, caught my eye one morning and stopped me cold in my tracks.

A "warning poster"? The block letters "WARNING!" appeared across the top. That sheet of paper contained a large disturbing photograph of a man shown from knee-high and above. He seemed very tall with a long dark jacket and a large collar turned up. Wild, long, combed-back, dark hair. Forty years old? Thereabouts. Gaunt face. He was tall and thin. And ... posed. Posed slightly sideways as if coached by a portrait taker. Behind him was an open field, and I swear it looked like a sunset. Just a creepy, odd photo. That was certainly not your average police photograph or any kind of mug shot. I tell you it looked like a horror movie poster. It did! This photo must have been swiped from the guy's house or from a friend. I took a closer look at the face, which was small on the page.

"Alice Cooper in make-up? Ichabod Crane," I whispered.

Captain Bill Cummings walked down the hall and spotted me talking to myself.

"That's a real-deal killer right there," Cummings said, "that guy killed three airmen in West Texas four or five years ago. Torture deal."

"Queer deal?" I asked. (Hey, come on. Look! That's just what we called those kinds of murder cases back then! Politically incorrect but historical correct.)

"Yeah. I remember when it happened," he said. "The investigators screwed up the case, and the courts released him about three months ago over a technicality. That county sheriff's office mailed this flier all over the state. And triple murder was not all he'd done."

I stared at the face. Cummings thumped the poster several times with his index finger. "That's the most dangerous son of a bitch in north Texas right there," and he walked off.

If the west Texas detectives wanted to scare you with a poster, they picked the best picture. There were some paragraphs of text above and below the photo. They told a synopsis of the three Air Force Base air servicemen murdered. It mentioned some of the other felony attacks he committed throughout his lifetime. From then on, I nicknamed that guy "Ichabod Crane."

Now Crane was free on a technicality. Texas and the whole country at the time were in a correctional and penal crisis. The penitentiaries were seriously overcrowded. In Texas, circa the 60s and 70s, a feller could get life for possessing or selling marijuana. Those plentiful Mary Jane smokers took up a whole lot of cell space. Plus, the country was in an uproar over the early parole releases of violent criminals AND the continual release of felons over small mistakes made by the police and prosecutors. Crane here was a giant mistake of serial-killer proportions. I could only imagine that the west Texas detectives had tried every trick in the book and every stretch to get this killer behind bars. If I did find out those details way back then, I didn't recall them now to tell you; but "technicality" was sure a dirty word we hated to hear.

"That's the most dangerous son of a bitch in Texas right there." I thought again about what Cummings said as I left headquarters to work on my cases. Little did I know, (a phrase literary experts hate) within eight months I would meet this lunatic face to face and track him all over the country.

The bulletin board in the hallway went through its own warp of change. It was a changing place of news, photos, and announcements. The foreboding photo of Mr. Ichabod Crane was soon buried under layers of alerts, tragedies, and be-on-the-look-outs for missing people, cars, and who knew what all had gone stolen and/or missing. Eight months to a busy detective could mean one, two, or even three normal people's years. I didn't know about a police dog's?

In the ninth month, in one morning detective squad briefing, CID Lt. Gene Green handed out the morning assignments among the investigators. He had a daily few for me:

"Here's a duet special just for you, Hock." He looked at the report through his bifocals with a big Gene Green grin. "William Mars is at the Westwind Hospital. He said that he was shot by an unknown person who drove by him, a drive-by, as he walked down Dallas Drive at 4:30 a.m. in the morning."

Lt. Green held the very tip of the crime report between two fingers as though it stunk and handed it to me. I scanned the report. The victim stumbled into the hospital ER. A detective (Skeens again) was on call, was phoned so late about this, near 6 a.m., that he stayed in bed and let the morning crew handle it. Not procedure, but we couldn't get Skeens to do anything anyway. At the time there was no one to interview because the victim went straight into surgery. There was no known crime scene. The docs would routinely save the bullet for us and call us. Skeens slipped through trouble again.

That was an era, by the way, just BEFORE the wave of rap, before gangland, and common drive-by shootings. (I worked several of them.) So, drive-by shootings were not commonplace. Back then in Texas, killers had the common courtesy to stop their cars, get out, cuss, kick dirt on your shin, and then blow your brains out. Rap music destroyed all those pleasant rituals.

"Then!" Green continued dramatically for all to hear, "then, here is another report of a burglar shot while breaking into a factory. A midnight-shift worker shot him. Coincidentally, about 4:30 a.m." He handed me this second crime report. "I think those two might go together?"

Ya' think? Probably. There were a few chuckles in the room among all of us inhaling bad coffee and dressed in simple, low-end JC Penny suits and polyester Western clothes. I take that back, ol' Clovis George really enjoyed wearing his Johnny Carson-Tonight Show suit line. When the morning meeting was over, I picked up the phone and called both the factory and the hospital floor housing William Mars to set up fast interviews. So allow me to recap the next, fast 40 minutes in some kind of order for you.

Part 3: First Call, Second Call, Third Call
<u>First call to the factory</u>. Dips' Wire and Mesh. Small place on the outskirts of town. We all knew Mr. Dips. While Joe Dips was a worthless, wife-beating skunk, his dad was a hard worker. His dad died and left baby Joe with a lot of money; and with this inheritance, Dips picked up with a local gold-digger, lizard-lounge new wife. And he also bought a small failing metal shop on the east side and managed to stay one step away from the creditors and kept it alive. As a professional, I dealt with all levels of scum.

"Dips' Wire and Mesh." It was Joe Dips himself who answered.

"This is Hock from the police department," I said ... politely. "Heard you had some excitement there last night?"

"Yeah! Our one midnight shift guy was working and shot a burglar breaking in the back.

"Well, he's a hero around here, too," I added.

"He's a hero! He didn't know if he shot him or missed. He just shot at him, and the guy ran off. He called and told the officer he just shot at a burglar."

"We probably have the wounded suspect at Westwind Hospital right now, and I need to get over there to the hospital and get his story locked down before they release him. I need an arrest warrant, but I need a signed statement from your man first. Soon as possible. Can you get him down here right away?"

"He's standing right here," Dips said. "I'll bring him myself."

"Bring the rifle with ya'." Pretty sure we know where the bullet landed."

"It's my rifle. I'll brang' it."

"When you get here, come on down to the detective office lobby. Ask for Millie Miller, and she will get a statement from him about what happened. Just a short one. Something to get me started."

Second call. Second call went to the nurse's station of Westwind. I spoke to the nurse in charge.

"This is Hock from the police department. I am the detective assigned to this William Mars' shooting. He doing okay?"

"Yes, he is. He was shot in the side. But he is okay."

"Is he going anywhere real soon?" I asked.

"Ohhh, no. He's wrapped in bandages and hooked up to an IV. And he'll be here for a while. The doctor will be in to see him this afternoon."

"Is he awake and able to talk?"

"Yes, he is."

"Well. If you will, don't tell him we called. I'd rather leave him in a state of bliss. We'll let him rest a bit. I'll stop in to see him tomorrow sometime," I said. Just in case Mars did get the word the police called, he'd think he'd have a full day to recover and try to crawl out of there before "Johnny Law" would come calling. (We used to hear ourselves called "Johnny Law" often and another winner name I never understood—"Lawsmens." Yes, the word laws combined with, not even just men, but mens. Lawsmens? First one extra "s" and then another one, both unnecessary.)

Third call; this one was to me.

"HOOOCCCK!" Millie, our secretary, shouted from the lobby, "DA's Office, line 2."

"Dang!" I hung up the hospital call and picked up the other. It was a pre-trial interview on another case coming up. I was stuck for at least 20 minutes, maybe more. I snatched up that case file and got cozy for the rambling questions, possible pitfalls, and strategies for another pending trial.

Done with that, I chucked the file in the cabinet, grabbed my coat, and left the office. Who's walking down the hall but Dips and a giant, bald, skinny guy beside him?

"Hey!" I said.

"Hock, this is Roy Tab."

"The hero!" I said, and guided them to the detective's wing and to Millie Miller's desk.

Russell showed up and got the rifle.

"She'll get a statement from you about all this. I have to get over to the hospital."

They sat down in chairs by Millie's desk.

I hustled out of the station and jogged to my car on the back lot and thought, Man! That Roy Tab looked awful familiar. On the drive to Westwind I wondered, where have I seen him before? I have never heard the name Roy Tab before.

When I got to the hospital, the lying started straight away.

"William Mars?" I asked as I stepped into the hospital room.

"Yeah?" the patient said.

"How are ya' doing?"

"They said I'm okay. I ain't feeling no pain."

Mars was a white male, 28 years old. Short brown hair. His torso was wrapped in bandages. Prone in bed. Hooked to IVs, wires, and beeping electronics.

"I'm Detective Hochheim." I flashed my badge.

"I knows' you."

"I know you do. Got a question for ya'. What were you doing walking down Dallas Drive at 4:30 in the morning?"

I got right to it. He didn't like it. The lying started, right there.

"Oh, I was on a lunch break from my job. I work midnights at Leevers."

"Leevers. On Monroe Street?" I asked. I pulled a chair up beside the bed and sat.

"Yeah," he said.

"And you walked on a break over to Dallas Drive?"

"To the 7-11. Only thing open."

"And you walked?" (It was a significant ways a way.)

"Where's your car?" I asked him. The car, a car, was suddenly an important key to this whole deal. Either he had a burglar accomplice, or...? Well, a car was the key.

"My car?" he repeated.

"Your car. The thing you go back and forth to work in, that thing. Even take breaks in."

He also knew that was a key question. I could all but see his little rat-trap mind spin.

"Look, I am the one shot here; why are you...?" he complained already!

"Where is your car?" I asked again.

"It's ... it's back at Leevers."

"How did you get to the hospital?" I asked.

"Ahhh, I flagged somebody down who was driving by, and he drove me here."

"After you were shot by a stranger, another stranger happened by and took you to the hospital?"

Silence.

"William, here's the deal. At 4:40 this morning, a worker at a factory near Dennison shot at a burglar. We got the bullet they carved out of you. We got the rifle he used to shoot that burglar..."

"I ain't no burglar! I was no burglar!" he declared.

"But they pulled that bullet right outta' you. Tell me what you were doing, because all this lying is going to get you in more trouble."

His face scowled. "Shit! Look, this ain't what it sounds like, okay? I was at the 7-11 on my lunch break. This guy came in, and we started talking. Both of us work the midnight shift, and we ... we started talking. He invited me over to his factory. To eat. It's my lunch hour! We drove over there in his car. Mine's still at the 7-11. When we got there, he started acting all weird..."

"Weird?"

"Yeah, sex ... weird. He pulled out this rifle; and he got all kinds of weird, all right? I mean, he ... he made me do some shit! He was holding a rifle on me, and I was in this place all by myself. I didn't know he worked alone in that place. There are 10 guys working mids where I work." I was beginning to get the picture. As we said in the business back then, queer deal.

I will let you pass on hearing some of the sordid details Mars told me.

"How did you get shot?" I continued.

"I had a chance to get away. He put down the gun. I started to run. He shot me in the back. I fell down, and he ran up to me. All of a sudden, he was real apologetic, saying, 'why did you make me do this?' and all. He said he shot me to wound me not kill me. He looked at my wound. He patched it real quick. He said that if I never told anyone what had happened, he would help me. He would take me to the hospital. We made up the story about the shooting on Dallas Drive. He took me to the hospital in his car."

"I need all this in a statement as soon as possible, William." I stood. I had more questions, but I had to quick arrest this 'Roy Tab.' ASAP. "I will be back with a tape recorder, or I will borrow one of the typewriters from the nurse's station and set it up in here."

"You believe me?"

I smiled. "Yes, and no. I just need a statement from you. It will help you."

"Will it ... like ... become public and all?"

"I don't know. I will be back this afternoon."

Roy Tab's whole burglar story was bullshit I thought as I drove back to the station. Maybe I could catch Tab and Dips still at the PD. I raced across town, pulled in the back lot, bailed, and ran into the back door of the station. When I got to the CID lobby, I saw Millie working on some paperwork. Her interview chairs were empty.

"They gone, Millie?"

"They're gone. Just missed them," she answered, never looking up.

"You get a look at his driver's license?" I asked her.

Millie always used it to fill out the top of a statement; and as a notary public, she also liked to validate who she was talking with.

"Nope. He said he left it at home," she said.

"He sure as hell ain't no Roy Tab," I muttered to myself. Who in hell...why was he so familiar looking anyway... tall, gaunt, ugly... hey, could h... could he? I marched down the hall and started peeling bulletins and reports off the hallway bulletin board. I found it.

Ichabod Crane. He was now 10 years older. His head was shaved. But Roy Tab was Ichabod Crane-Alice Cooper. I plucked the sheet from the wall.

"What do you think, Millie?" I asked her.

Her eyes widened. She sneered, and nodded.

"Yeah!" I said.

Just 15 feet away was Captain Cummings' office. I stuck my head in the doorway and held up the paper.

"Remember this guy? That is the guy in the factory last night who shot a so-called burglar. Only the burglar wasn't a burglar." I quickly told him the new version of the William Mars' story I had just learned.

"I'll be damned. Go get him. And take somebody with ya!" he insisted.

"On it." And I was. That great rush and mix of excited, focused, and pissed all in one. Dips and Crane probably went straight back to the factory. Or maybe eat breakfast somewhere? But! But if Crane knew I was off to see William Mars? He knew I may well find out the truth from Mars. Trouble. I made a pass through the CID offices. In one, Clovis George was hard at work. Clovis was a good hand, and we had been in some tight spots together through the years, even back in patrol.

"Clovis!" I held up the Crane warning sheet, and his eyebrows rose. I said, "Let's go get this som-bitch! Bring your shotgun!"

The two-story metal factory, shabby and decades old, stood gray and rusty upon what looked like flat, dried-up farmland. Mad Max paradise before the movie was made. The grounds were trashed out with junk vehicles and, well ... tons of junk. Scraps and piles of metal works and car and truck frames. Just an eyesore mess.

"I'll go in the front," I said while pulling into the dirt driveway.

"I'll take the back; and if he runs out the back, I'll shoot him down! HA!" Clovis declared. You would have to know Clovis to appreciate his sense of humor. And, yes, he probably would have.

"Sounds like a plan to me."

I stopped our sedan beside some pickup trucks parked out front. I had no idea what Dips or Crane was driving. Clovis jumped out with his shotgun and jogged to the rear of the plant. I passed on my scatter gun and decided to try this with just my .45.

The morning air was chilly. The world out there on the outskirts of town was still and peaceful, oblivious to all the drama. I opened the metal, front door of the factory and stepped inside. It was way darker in there, and I hung by near the door for a few seconds letting my eyes adjust. As the interior materialized in focus before me, I could see the place was really just a metal barn. Filthy inside. Smelled of burned oil and old grease. Not a sound. Flat creepy. I pulled my gun, held it low beside my thigh, and walked in. I halfway expected to be shot at by a hidden Crane and then halfway not.

Anything could happen. In one corner I saw a sleeping bag, a pile of wrinkled clothes, and some grocery bags. The deeper I went, the louder I heard a conversation. Two men. They were out back. Outside. I could hear Clovis talking. Ahead behind a wall in a corner, I spotted a back door. I hustled to the door and stepped outside.

Clovis, his shotgun low and casual, was busy talking to Dips.

"He's gone," Clovis told me.

"Gone? Gone where?"

Dips sucked on a cigarette and shrugged his bony shoulders. I took that as a "I don't know."

"Where's he live?" I asked, holstering my pistol.

"I don't know. Here?"

"Here?" I thought of the sleeping bag. "Maybe because he lives here? I saw that sleeping bag inside."

"He wasn't just working a night shift, was he?"

Dips shuffled his feet. "Nahhh, he did a little work at night, too. but he stays here a lot."

"Where'd he go? How did he leave?"

"In his car. As soon as we got back, the moment we got here, he left my truck and walked straight in the shop. He grabbed a knapsack and left. He got right in his car and drove off."

"You tell him what really happened?" I asked Clovis.

"Yup," he said.

"You too are lucky to be alive I think."

"Did the patrol officer search for an ejected round?"

He shook his head. I would have to come back on that point.

"What kind of paperwork you got on him? Next of kin? Anything?"

Dips dropped the cigarette to the dirt and twisted it dead with his boot. I couldn't really tell if he was being uncooperative or just dull-headed. Probably both.

"I got something. Let's go inside."

Clovis followed him into the office; and I stopped in the hallway, turned, and walked the whole place scanning for a spent .22 shell. Nearly impossible without an idea where to look. I searched the sleeping bag and gear. I used a metal pole to prod and sift through the debris of Crane's life. I went through the pockets barehanded. Nothing personal. Nothing helpful. Just fowl, stained, and stinking clothing and a crusty sleeping bag. Junk food in bags. He probably had a hiding hole of more important stuff in there somewhere, but I'd be damned if I could find it that morning, though. I had to find him first while the finding was good!

I heard Clovis laugh from the office. The way it sounded, Clovis was getting along really well with Dips, as was his way, and I was too pissed at him to do any real good anyway. I wandered the plant again looking for blood stains or anything else we might need for a case. Clovis and Dips emerged from the office. Clovis carried some papers and winked at me.

"After I get a statement from Mars, I will have to come back and take some pictures," I told Dips. "After I find out from Mars what happened and exactly where inside here. I may have to bring him out here and have him point things out to me."

We left. As soon as we climbed into the car, Clovis told me what he had learned. "I got a copy of Crane's employment sheet. It's all bullshit. Phony name, phony everything. Roy Tab this, Roy Tab that. He worked there for about four months. Good worker. Dips said that Crane owned a black 70's, banged up Cougar."

"Any chance of..."

"No license plate," Clovis finished the thought for me.

I was pondering the next "right-away" steps as we drove back to the station –

1. APB on Crane and a black 70's Cougar. Unknown plate.
2. Call that old S.O. for ANY and all background info on Crane to start the hunt.
3. Get a very detailed statement from Mars.

4. Get a crime scene search done of this plant. Russell Lewis would come back with me.

I feared that before I could get any substantial leads, this son of a bitch would have a great head start. If only I had recognized Crane from that intelligence poster, albeit he was 10 years older and bald. No one else felt that way about what happened in the unfolding span of those 2 hours. Quite a number of officers from the first responding patrolman and detectives in the station saw Crane as the hero at the front desk and did not recognize him. Anyway, this hunt was on big time.

Part 4: To Mother's House I Go....

Dusk. That same day. I crept up on the small country house through the trees. Interior lights were popping on. There was movement inside. Detectives from west Texas said that our man was probably at his mother's house in Gainesville. And any good nut he was over-obsessed with his mother. The serial killer's black Cougar car was in the dirt driveway behind the house...

His mother Lily "Crane," still lived up there according to Creeks County utility records. Back then, getting that kind of information was an easy phone call. Now it would take three search warrants and the CIA to find that out. I called the Westwind hospital. A nurse fetched Clovis from the Mars' hospital room where he was taking a statement.

"Clovis George," Clovis said.

"Clovis, I got to go up to Creeks County and see if Crane is at his grandmother's. Can you get a warrant on this guy? Take the signed statement to Jerry Cobb or

Freddie Marsh before 5 p.m. and get an arrest warrant on Crane."

"Yup," he said, Russell's at the factory. Working it."

As far as I was concerned, Crane was now what we called "a flight risk." He fled Dips' for obvious reasons! He knew given his past he was in big trouble. If I did find him, I would arrest him as a flight risk and let the arrest warrant catch up with us later. I figured I could argue "flight risk" and with good intent. I showed legal due-diligence by organizing Clovis in this manner.

I'd grabbed a portable radio from the charger. Then I drove home. I changed clothes. Dark clothes and shoes. I strapped a good gun belt on under a large, untucked shirt. I pulled a "John Deere Tractors" ball cap on my head. On the outside, I looked like I'd just jumped off a dump truck. On the inside, I was the freakin' Lone Ranger on steroids. (Bulletproof vests were too expensive back then for us.) I tossed all my gear, shotgun, ammo, flashlights, binoculars, etcetera, into my 1970's Ford Thunderbird. That was a giant boat of a car, but a "civilian" car; and I needed something low-profile to snoop around in.

It wasn't exactly department protocol to leave like this and in your own car, but we all did it. We had to time-to-time. Even our captain used his Ranchero on many a stakeout with us. If we banged up our own POVs (personal owned vehicles), we were shit out of luck. (One insurance company canceled me once because of my penchant to do police work in my own cars.) But a driven fanatic had to do what a driven fanatic had to do. I was sure my wife (second at the time) grimaced as I drove off loaded for bear in our family car on another crazy mission.

I filled the T-Bird up (about 50 cents a gallon back then) and raced up to the country hills, ranches, and farms of Creeks County. I hoped that my portable radio would work that far out, but I really knew it wouldn't. I could maybe at least switch over to our county channel and might reach our county dispatcher from up there. Probably couldn't. We did not have a Cooke County Sheriff's Office frequency channel. There was a lot of talk back then about bouncing radio messages around, but I counted on the radio not working. Hell, we couldn't get the radios to work inside our city limits sometimes! They just didn't ... bounce. Anyway, I did plan on just a dry-run snoop up there anyway. I would get to a pay phone if possible and call Cooke County for help if I really needed any.

By late afternoon, I was in the rural area of Momma Crane's. It took a few passes on the route to pinpoint the right house. It sat isolated and back and down in a grove of trees in some lowlands. Mom had herself a few acres. I found a couple of dirt roads near a pond where some ol' boys were drinking beer and fishing. I parked my car near them. Perfect and not at all suspicious. Only fishing was not on my mind. Hunting was.

With a flashlight in one back pocket, a radio in the other, binocs looped over my neck, and a gun belt to beat all (all hidden under a long shirt), this here imposter wandered off into the woods ... to mother's house I go.

On these kinds of deals, you start off walking tall at first and as you get closer you start crouching over and tiptoeing in. I was near the crawling stage when I got a good look at the side of the Crane's house. Now at times like these? You had to worry about dogs. Loose dogs. So far, no dogs here. No water bowls outside even.

It was dusk, and lights were popping on inside the house. There it was! There was the black Cougar on a dirt road behind the house! And another older sedan. I pulled the binoculars up and started a study of the house windows. Momma Crane was all I could see in the kitchen.

I had to hit the house because of the car. I backed off a ways and pulled the radio from my pocket. I switched it on.

"CID 89 to Sheriff's Office," I said several times into the hand-held. No response. I may as well be throwing rocks at the moon. No help! But I had to hit that house!

There was no way I could approach that house by myself. If I so much as knocked on the front door, he'd go out the back door. I had to retreat away, get to my car, and drive to a pay phone. Get some more bodies out there. I'd passed several gas stations and convenience stores earlier on the way up. They all had pay phones.

BUT I would lose sight of that house! I couldn't leave without at the very least getting the license plates number on the cars. I slogged my way slowly around the east and then south of the house. I shimmied through some thick brush and found a few open breaks to traverse. I turned toward the back of the house and stalked into the yard.

Closer, quieter. Closer, lower. It was getting darker; and just about that time I got to all fours and could see the blurry white triangle of a license plate, it was dark. But the darkness was also becoming my friend. I got a bit gutsier and continued closer inward with an eye peeled on the back of the house and the one lit window and door I could see.

I got completely behind the Cougar. I pulled my notebook out and jotted down the license plates and with some neck stretching got the plate on the other sedan in the yard. God, I'd love a peek in the Cougar. There had to be blood in there. What if the doors were unlocked? But I knew that anything I seized from this car at the moment would be illegal. We would need a search warrant from a Creeks County judge to seize and use anything in court. But I sure would at least like to unload that gun and put it right back! If things got hairy later?

The back doorway held a screen door and a wooden door with windowpanes at the top. Curtains. If someone came to it, maybe I would see a shadow first? Maybe I would have a few seconds to duck? I pulled my small flashlight from my back pocket. (Small flashlights back then still were of the two D-cell-size honkers.) I made some quick glances at the door and lit up the interior of the car. Junk inside. Clothes. Fast-food bags. Torn seats. The doors were locked. I dropped back behind the car.

If I knocked on the front door, he could go out the back. If I knocked and she let me in, then I could be inside with not one but maybe two crazies. I had been attacked by mothers before. I could walk right in and be like that stupid cop in all the movies you watched, and you screamed out, "Don't go in there, stupid! He's got a _____." (You fill in the blank.)

I had to back out of there, circle the house, get back to my car, and drive to a phone. Wait for county backup. Who knew how long that would take? In doing so, I would have to abandon the house, the car, and the suspect. Me no like. Not at all. On my gun belt was a 5-inch, fixed-blade knife in a sheath. I pulled it and stabbed the right rear tire. If we got into a car chase with that guy later tonight? At least I would be chasing a Cougar with three tires!

This trek back wasn't easy in the darkened dark. But I worked my way back to the pond and my Thunderbird. The fishermen were all gone. I cranked it up, backed it up, and hit the rural route to where my memory recalled the nearest Stop-n-Rob was. It was farther than I thought and liked. There was a pay phone on the brick wall in front of the store.

I dropped in my quarter, got an information operator, and in a moment a dispatcher from the local Sheriff's Office. I explained my dilemma, and they dispatched the District Deputy and a supervisor.

I walked inside the store and sniffed the coffee pot. The sludge had been made that century, so I bought a cup for a thin dime and cooled my heels in the parking lot for what seemed like hours but was probably only 20 minutes.

These days, a wanted, armed, known killer in a house would spur a SWAT raid. But none of us had those newfangled SWAT-things then, and it was just little ol' me and the two strangers in uniform driving my way. I spied the county car coming close; and as it pulled in the lot, I flagged the deputy over with a badge up and out. We talked. He told me his sergeant was also in route. I asked him to take the sergeant to the mother's address, as I wanted to get as close to the house as possible right away and at least watch who might come and go from the driveway. He agreed.

As we talked, I pulled out my raid jacket from my trunk, removed my shirt, and put the jacket on. This had "Police" on the front and "INVESTIGATOR" across the back in large white block letters. We now needed a uniform at the door and a uniform at the back, and this official jacket would have to do for me. I left.

I parked up the road from the house at a point where I could see both directions of two-way traffic. I drummed my steering wheel with impatient fingers until the two squad cars appeared behind me. Then the three of us pulled in the front yard.

The sergeant and I took the front door, and the deputy jogged to the back. I banged on the door. "Yes?" a female called out with a whining voice of inquiry. The more banging, the higher the tone.

"Police, ma'am," the sergeant shouted.

"Oh? Oh!" she said. Within seconds, the door opened.

"Police, Mrs. Crane." I said. "We are looking for your son. Is he here?"

"No!" she said adamantly.

"Then you don't mind if we look," I said brushing right past her; and I felt the need to pull my pistol. Second time today. I did. I didn't make a big show of it, just had it out, down, old school called it "the bootleg." and at the ready. I made a fast pass through the whole small house. First run.

The sergeant stayed in the living room and spoke with mom. I heard him tell her that her grandson's car was there in the yard. Then I made a second, slower pass. Closets. Under the bed. Anywhere I thought a giant Ichabod Crane would hide. In the hallway ceiling, there was an attic door. There was no fresh dirt or any insulation on the floor under it, but I tugged the rope, pulled down the stepladder, and climbed up. Halfway up, I pulled the light cord. No Ichabod Crane. (Few searching police ever check the attic. Many criminals hide up there.)

When I returned to the living room, Mrs. Crane told me and the Sarge that her grandson had stopped by for an hour or so earlier that afternoon; and a friend came and got him.

"What friend?"

"I really don't know. He just beeped his horn, and my son left."

"You say 'he'? Was it a man?"

"It could have been a woman I guess."

"Tell ya' where he was going?"

"Oh, no. He asked me for a suitcase and some things ... you know ... some towels and things. Toothpaste. He was taking a trip with this friend. What has he done? Is he in some trouble?" she asked.

"Well, last night he ... shot a burglar where he works, Mrs. Crane," I told her, "and we have to check out all the possibilities."

"Shot a burglar? He didn't mention a thing to me about it. Dear God."

"Has he been staying here?" I asked with a look around the living room.

"No, but he visits me. We are close."

"My card," I handed her one. "If you see or hear from him, will you call me? We need to buy him a dinner for shooting a burglar."

"By the likes of this, it more looks to me like you want to shoot him."

"Naah. Just call me," I repeated with a smile.

"Yes," she said. But I doubted it.

The sergeant and I wandered the yard and met up with the deputy in the back. I took a few Polaroid pictures of the Cougar. I would let my DA decide if he wanted the car impounded for the case, as soon as I could arrange it. Tomorrow morning. Best…a search warrant-impound would have to be issued in this county, not mine, but our guys (or me) would write it up for a local judge to sign. The victim's blood from his wound would be in there. Back then Polaroids made them happy. I might return with a 35 mm to take pictures in the daylight too.

Personally, part of me would rather leave the car here and "at large." Then maybe someday, even years from now, he might retrieve it; and we would have a method of catching him in it.

"We'll keep an eye on the house and the car," the sergeant told me.

"Crane has a head start. No telling where he's gone," I said. My head was reeling with possibilities. Bus stations. Trains. Airports. Rides from "friends." Lying mom. Possibilities without practical solutions. No manpower. No communication. Just me scratching my head and standing in the dark off a country road.

"Hey, that Cougar's got a flat in a back tire," the deputy called out to us.

"Yeah … how about that," I mumbled.

Part 4: Mail Trapped!

Way back when in the thrilling days of yesteryear, cops often got together for a couple of drinks or beers after evening shift work. You were usually too damn tired after a midnight shift to be hanging out at the crack of dawn. Only sometimes? Those post-evening shift get-togethers weren't inside bars but were outside. If the weather was irresistible after an evening shift, many of us would opt to park outside somewhere and toss a few down and sip a few against the rigors of the day. Maybe we'd meet in an open parking lot, behind a funeral home, any empty business, or even somewhere barely semi-private. Not too private? No problem. You see, because we wuz' the law; and we wuz' wheresoever we wanted to be.

At times, these meetings got a little crazy. One of my favorite times? Several guys had stun gun duels a few of the nights. Man! That was some entertainment! We bet on them. Sometimes the real guns went off, but you know what? All that's still top secret, and I'll never tell. Of course, all those shenanigans would easily be a firing offense in today's world, so all you little worrywarts out there rest easy. Rest assured THAT kind of activity was ... over. Gone. Completely done with. Modern officers today meet for soymilk and diet cookies down at the gospel hall after work.

One night, we evening-shift detectives parked with some state officers and commiserated against the woes of the world. Howard Kelly, my favorite Detective Sergeant, handed me a beer from a cooler when I walked up.

"How's yer' mass murderer case goin'?" he asked, popping the top of a Coors for me.

Before the "Silence of the Lambs" movie, most multiple killers were just called mass murderers.

"Stumped," I said. "He's gone. I've got an aggravated assault warrant on him. Broadcast all over the country."

I ran the whole deal down to him. The crime. The car. The mother. What I did. Howard, with a thumb hooked on a Western jean pocket and the other thumb securing a cold one in a grip, listened intently. Howard Kelly just lived, loved, and breathed a damn good criminal investigation. And he knew I did, too.

"The mother is the only connection I have. But I can't stake out her house every day."

"Get yourself a mail trap," he said.

"A … mail, what…trap?"

"Yup. U.S. Postal Inspectors can place a mail trap on a person. It's like a warrant. You file the paperwork. It gets approved, and the post office will record every letter the mother receives and will send you a copy of the front envelope."

"Christmas. Mother's Day. I got the mother's birthday off her utility records," I said.

"Well, there ya' go," Howard said, then sipped the Coors. "If he ever sends her anything, they'll record it for you. Your felony arrest warrant will be your probable cause for a mail trap because a judge has signed it."

A postal mail trap? I'd never heard of such a thing and I'll bet you haven't either. It was an oddity, but that was the kind of odd, case-solving tricks Howard Kelly knew. I resolved long ago that when I grew up, I would be just like Howard Kelly. Well, except for the Conway Twitty haircut.

It sounds like these parking lot parties were a lot of useless grab-ass. But in the 1970s and 1980s, a lot of intelligence work was conducted over a shot of booze and a six-pack. Everyone from the FBI, DEA, State Police, Texas Rangers, and you name it, were a revolving cast of characters at these. The topic of discussion was often about police work and crimes and the usual business gossip. A lot of good got done that way, back then. Soymilk and diet cookies just don't bring them out, and there're no fireworks allowed at the gospel hall.

The next morning, I called the U.S. Postal Inspector's Office in Dallas, Texas, and got hold of one of their investigators. Two inspectors drove up, met with me, and prepared the paperwork; and we set up the infamous Mail Trap on ma Crane. It had to be renewed every 30 days. I'd renew that trap for years if I had to. I caught the postal investigators up on all the mundane aspects of the case. Crime scenes. Statements. Etcetera.

I even made regular passes by mom's house. The Cougar was towed-seized, tested and in the police pound. Blood on the seats matched our shooting victim.

Otherwise lead-less, I stayed on this mail trap course for over a year while buried deep in a couple hundred other new cases.

Nothing that Christmas.
Nothing that Mother's Day.
Nothing that year.

Then the next June? I opened about the fourteenth monthly trap from the post office and scanned the copies of the front envelopes, the addresses. Around Mother's Day, ma Crane received her first out-of-state letter! The return address was from a guy in San Diego, California. One William Ranch. The handwritten note from my inspector friend said the envelope was "shaped and thick like a Mother's Day card."

This was better than Christmas for a twisted guy like me. I immediately called San Diego Homicide and spoke with a lieutenant. I ran my whole deal down to him.

"Hmm, now wait a minute ... you know ... you need to talk to Dale Borlan. Hold on...."

"Detective Borlan," a voice came next on the phone.

"Your lieutenant thought I needed to speak with you about this," and I related, yet again, this sordid business.

"William Ranch!" Borlan said. He grunted and rustled some papers. "William Ranch lives at that address! Weird bastard. Weird looking. We know that guy. We have questioned him."

"About what?" I was excited and about to come out of my chair. I love it when a case comes together. In my mind, I was buying my own plane ticket to southern California tonight. The city wouldn't pay. But I would. He continued,

"A bartender disappeared here a few months ago. His severed head rolled up on a beach a day later. We questioned people who frequented the bar where he worked. A...William Ranch was one of the regular customers there."

"Ichabod-Alice-Cooper-Crane-looking motherfucker?" I asked.

"A scary-looking son of a bitch. About nine feet tall," Borlan said.

"He's your man. He's wanted in Texas. Active warrant. I will fax you everything right now. The moment you need me, I will be on a plane," I told Borlan, gripping the phone with not-able-to-be-right-there anxiety.

"We will go back and stake out his house and arrest him there. See what's inside. We will use your Texas arrest warrant and all your PC (probable cause) for a search warrant. The DA's office may need to interview you. Give me all your phone numbers."

I gave him the office phones, the dispatcher's non-emergency number so they could call me over the radio if I was out, and my home phone. He needed them all.

The dispatcher radioed me later that afternoon. She told me to call a prosecutor in the San Diego County District Attorney's office ASAP. I did. I spent about an hour on the phone answering questions for a prosecutor, with Borlan on another phone extension. That way he could testify and sign a search warrant right there based upon what I told them. Apparently, I was somehow a credible…source.

Later that night while hanging out with my kids at my house, the home phone rang. It was Borlan.

"Hey, Hock!" he said. I could tell he was excited beyond a simple arrest. "We caught Crane at his rented house. Searched the place. Guess what we found? Guess what we found in his refrigerator?"

"What?"

"You won't believe it."

"What?"

"Faces."

"Faces?"

"Three faces in formaldehyde jars."

"Faces. Faces like...."

"Faces, like people's faces. Their faces. He's killed some people out here and skinned their faces off. Did a nice job. We assume our bartender's face was looking right at us from one of the jars when we opened the refrigerator."

"Wow!" I said. I listened intently about every aspect of the arrest, search, and weird seizure.

"The arrest was pretty routine. Crane just threw his hands up and surrendered. We are going to sit him down and talk to him next. He is acting very calm. I think he may confess about all of the faces in his fridge."

"Keep me posted!" was all I could do or say.

I knew I wouldn't hear anything new until the morning. I took a deep breath and returned to playing with my kids.

The next day I learned that Crane confessed about all the faces in his fridge. Borlan felt like there were more killings; but Crane, like so many criminals, would only confess to the ones we could prove. Borlan mailed me an envelope of crime scene photos. Inside the collection was a photo of the open refrigerator and the giant glass jars of faces. I'd seen a lot in my time, but I hadn't seen anything quite like that before!

Fast forward about one year. After a postponement, Mr. Ichabod-Alice was due in court for the first murder trial. The DA's office decided that they might need me to testify to the probable cause that cracked the case and arranged my appearance. I flew out on a Sunday afternoon, their expense, and was at the courthouse in San Diego Monday morning at 9 a.m.

As we congregated in the halls of California justice, the courtroom itself was empty and silent. Then the judge stepped in and handled some other quick matters for other cases, shuttling attorneys in and out.

Something about the Crane case was indeed afoot. The routine was that a jury was being picked in another part of the building. That could take all day or more.

Lunch. At 1:30 we returned, and we were all quickly ushered into the courtroom. Two bailiffs escorted Mr. Freak to the defense table. That was the first time in years I had laid eyes on him, not since that brief moment in the hallway of my police station.

His eyes glanced over all of us, over me. They lingered on me. He knew well by now that my work laid the foundation for his demise. I think he just wanted a better look at me, to put a…face…with his nemesis. It was a cold look. No doubt he would like to carve my face off with his favorite knife. Oh, well, I in turn would sure like to shoot him dead with my .45.

The morning delay was over a back-office plea-bargain agreement. Crane took three life sentences to run in succession, not concurrent. The proceedings were over in 25 minutes. Dallas to San Diego, a long way to go for 25 minutes; but I wouldn't have missed it for the world. With those findings, my city and county would close the Texas-Mars aggravated assault case; and I would clear my file "by arrest." And I would call those West Texas detectives and tell them too.

The next morning on the plane flying back to Dallas, I stared out the window at the great southwest canyons below and experienced my usual post-case depression.

My daily life was mired with the muck of common crime, punks, and thugs; and a good challenging case like this came only so often. I missed them so. I hashed over the more ironic moments of this whole nightmare. Irony could be such a harsh mistress. I thought about that dark night, and a wounded William Mars hunched over in Crane's Cougar, another perfect victim for him. Why didn't he turn down a dark country road and make Mars ... disappear into small parts? Keep his face? Why, instead, did he turn west and take his victim to the Westwind Hospital?

Police Detective Notebook...

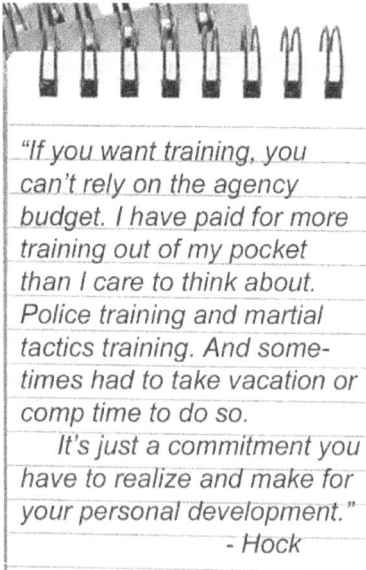

"If you want training, you can't rely on the agency budget. I have paid for more training out of my pocket than I care to think about. Police training and martial tactics training. And sometimes had to take vacation or comp time to do so.

It's just a commitment you have to realize and make for your personal development."
- Hock

Chapter 14: Hacking the Hammer

The world was full of characters; and in the police world, you were forced to meet a great many of them. And then there were bounty helpers...

I had been called many differing things in my life. especially with a last name like Hochheim. Broken up, it is Hock (the "ch" can sound like a "k.") Hoch is the first half of Hoch-heim. The "heim" part rhymes with time. Heim/time. Don't let the two "h" letters in the middle fool you. It was way-back German, but the scores of people one meets, those of varying degrees of education, have various pronunciations and meanings to the name. Citizens have come to the police department lobby asking for me in a variety of versions.

"I need to see the Iranian detective ... that feller Hock-heeem." asked one.

I had to work a case of burglary and vandalism on a Jewish synagogue once. The Jewish Anti-Defamation League was thrilled that they actually had a Jewish detective on the case. But I am not Jewish. No one in my family has ever been Jewish that I know of. I guess the "heim" part fooled them? After all, didn't one of the great racial instigators of our time, the Reverend Jessie Jackson, call New York City "Heimy town?"

Or we'd hear, "is Detective Hoke Hokum in?" And some misheard the name and called me Hawk, which I had to correct immediately. I was simply not cool enough to be called Hawk.

"I am here for Detective Hog Head," said another. That name brought many laughs; and to this day if I bump into Steve Camp or Walter Keen, they will yell out to me, "Hog Head!"

Probably the best was Detective Handcuff. Like I was some kind of logo or ... a cartoon character. That was given to me by one Thomas "Redbone" Reed, a tall black feller with a deep voice. He just couldn't seem to wrap his vocal cords around saying Hochheim and always called me Handcuff. His brother Doug called me Detective Hockmans.

Which leads me to a quick Redbone story...Redbone was a guy in the hood and always in some kind of low-running trouble. Years back, he was messing around with a much younger girl in the girl's house; and her daddy came home early. Dad heard the grunts and groans over the Barry White "love music" from her room. He got his shotgun, and surprised the duo. Redbone stood up, grabbed up his pants, and bolted-dove out the window with the dad in hot pursuit. The dad was shooting like hell right after him as he, too, stumbled-dove out of the same window. A foot chase...ensued (police jargon.)

"Redbone, you leave my daughter alone!"

Redbone was shot in the knee, and the blast tore off most of his left baked kneecap. (He was running away in his underwear.) The kneecap actually went skipping across the street like a Tupperware bowl.

Well, we the police were called. Russell Lewis and I were dispatched to the crime scene. Russell picked up the kneecap and put it in a paper bag. We didn't know what else to do with it. A patrolman and I arrested the dad and collected the shotgun, etcetera; and I took the old man to the station. I got a statement or confession from the angry father. Russell put the kneecap in the evidence room refrigerator-freezer after wrapping it in clear plastic.

"89," the dispatcher was calling me.

"89, Go ahead."

"89 it seems we have we have man at the Flow E.R. with a gunshot wound."

"Ten four, dispatch. Does he have one or more kneecaps?"

"Just one, 89."

"Copy that. In route."

"That's Redbone, that son a bitch!" The father said, overhearing my conversation.

Alas, we had a knee-gunshot wounded man at a hospital. Patrol took the dad in. Russell did his crime scene thing. I went to the hospital to see Redbone.

"Detective Handcuff!" Redbone said when he saw me. That man tried to kill me. Looky' here! Look! My knee is gone!"

"Just the cap, sir," a nurse said calmly.

"Well, it's blowed' off, Handcuff!"

I took some notes for a statement. Needless to say, Redbone knew he was in the wrong and declined prosecution if only the daddy would help him with surgery bills. I returned to the station with this deal, and the daddy said he would help pay for a new knee to keep himself out of jail.

The dad made bond the next morning and was released. I put all this down on paper and in place and shipped the shooting case off to the DA's office about two days later.

But guess what? Daddy lied to us and didn't pay for the new kneecap. The good ol' State of Texas eventually did. Your tax dollars at work.

A limping Redbone still did not press charges. All was dropped and with a knee replacement he committed a series of burglaries over the next two years. Danny McCormick and I had to send him to the pen for a spell of some six years. There in Huntsville, Redbone also got new teeth. Redbone got out of jail, got a few jobs, and fell in and out of much trouble. Each time we processed him to the city jail or saw him, we would remind him we still had his kneecap in our fridge. Russell really didn't know what to do with it! Being a human part, the trash didn't seem fitting.

"Oh, I ... I'll come and get it next week, Handcuff," he would tell me when I saw him around town. That was just enough news to keep Russell from disposing of the knee. There it sat in the freezer for years, often right next to Russell's Lean Cuisine frozen lunches.

Then years later, at least maybe nine years after the shooting, Russell wandered up to my desk and took a seat with a big grin.

"Never guess what happened this morning. Redbone came and picked up his kneecap," he said.

"What!"

"Yeah! Said he felt bad about leaving it."

"What's he gonna' do with it?" I asked.

"He said he was going to take it home and put it in HIS refrigerator."

"Fridge to fridge. Another new meaning for the term knee transplant," I added.

Another great translation of my name came from a woman named Helen Shavers. Helen was a tough ol' gal from the projects. It all started when Helen elbowed her way into the middle of my Harold's Garden Center safe burglary case.

There was, once upon a time, a very successful garden and nursery store in my city at a major intersection that bordered the poorer neighborhoods. And one night, it was burglarized. A safe job. Money was taken; but so, too, was a serious amount of negotiable bonds. Those bonds were passable by the bearer, so ANY criminal could cash them. Harold was quite a colorful character and power broker in that poor community. He would even loan money out and give away money out to people in need.

But he wasn't always so good. One of his employees was murdered once, and he paid a man to be a false witness to the crime to pursue a vendetta on someone. But that's another story. With this burglary, Harold spread the word in the area that he would pay a big reward for the recovery of those bonds.

Reward! That news put Helen Shavers and her close friend Louise on the case. Amateur detectives!

But how amateur? I will tell you those women did a lot of "gossipy-justice work" in the area, both good and bad. Those amateur detectives were nothing like an Agatha Christie story. Feisty Helen and Louise hit the streets passing out marijuana for tips and carried toy baseball bats in large purses.

While working the case, we would often pass each other in the projects and on the streets. Helen would yell at me,

"Hacken-Hammer! Who you got yet? Who you got?"

"I got nothing, Helen; who you got?" I yelled back.

And they would bust out laughing. They wanted to solve this mystery. $$$$

"Listen here, you motha-fucka'," she'd yell, "I'm getting that money. Don't chu' get in the way!" Helen would strut off and laugh.

Most safe burglars would be long gone, but elements of this one told me the criminals were local...

And an aside on safe-cracking... back in those days, safe crackers were an interesting lot. They worked in teams and usually traveled a multi-state circuit. There just weren't that many of them, so they had to spread out. They seemed to work in themes, like hitting K-Marts, jewelry stores, certain supermarkets, or whatever. Few opened the safe on the premises like an "Ocean's 11 job" you saw in the movies. Most burglars would take a small safe off the premises and spend days chipping, peeling, welding, burning with acid, drilling away, or exploding them. More common criminals held a gun to an employee's head or took his or her family hostage if the job was big to get the employee to open the safe. But that became armed robbery or kidnapping. Different category and a different kind of cat.

If you were assigned a serious safe job crime, you visited all the hotels and motels over a large radius looking for a lead like a clerk who saw a suspicious group in and out in the a.m. hours. That took a lot of time and work and couldn't be done from the coffee shop.

Anyway, I all tracked and traced those traveling thugs after the fact; and they were usually caught by some Patrol Officer who accidentally interrupted them in some way with a car full of evidence. One such midnight traffic stop or room raid, in somewhere else, say…Florida, and we would clear tens and more of safe burglaries in Texas and all over the country.

Today money is invisible and stolen out of thin air with computer interception. The old safe crackers and check forgers of yesteryear like those of us who fought against them … are kind of dinosaurs now.

The Harold's Garden Center criminals were common local thieves. They stole the whole small safe. I located drag marks on the cement and ground all leading to the direction of our worst city's projects. But anyone with a car and two sets of hands would've had ample chance to load the small safe.

Despite the fact I had no marijuana to hand out and couldn't legally swing a baseball bat at a witness, I worked some contacts and ran down leads; and in about three days, I cracked the case and recovered all the un-cashed bonds. The bad guys spent the cash, but the bonds were hidden in a black plastic trash bag buried by a creek until the thugs could plan on - could figure out how to cash them. They were indeed too dumb to understand the workings of such bonds.

Harold was thrilled with me, of course, we the police couldn't collect any reward; so, he was doubly thrilled he didn't have to pay a reward. Helen was not at all thrilled.

For years after, every time she saw me anywhere, she would pitch a small fit when I drove by her or saw her in public,

"Mutha-fucka Hacken-Hammer. Youuuu mutha-fucka. You tooks' my money. I was on that boy's ass; and in one more day, I'da' had that money. You a mutha-fucka'. You owe me some fuckin' money, you mutha-fucka!!"

For those years, I would get Helen messages from patrolmen and other detectives, "Oh, I saw Helen and she said hi." Benny Parkey or Roger White would tell me, "She told me to tell that mother-fucking Hacken-Hammer hello from Helen, and where's her gottdamn' money?"

Helen was hired to nurse an elderly woman years later. I would often see her push the woman in a wheelchair on walks. She would look harshly at me with wide eyes and whisper with exaggerated lips, "YOU! Mutha-fucka, Hacken-Hammer."

So, in summary, I'll just sign off now....
      W. Hog Hoghead.
      W. Hawk Hawkheim.
      W. Hand Handcuff.
      W. Hack Hacken-Hammer.
      W. Hoke Hokum.
      Sheik Hock-Heem.

Epilogue: Many years later I had my hip replaced. I was warned that within four hours after this major amputation-style operation, I would have to get up and walk around a bit to avoid blood clots. Sure enough, as I lay dazed-drugged in bed, a young guy came to remind me of this nasty requirement. He walked in and said,

"Ahhhh, Mr. Ho Chi Minh? I hate to tell you, but we have to go for that mandatory walk now."

I let that kid call me Ho Chi Minh for 3 days.

Police Detective Notebook...

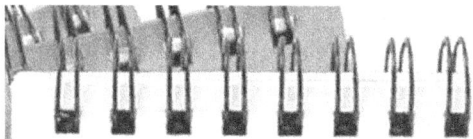

"Every job you want to get in a police agency, like becoming a detective is like winning a lottery to get it. The smaller the agency, the harder it is to get an opening. It can be the same with bigger agencies too. All you can do is get training for that slot. Do a good job where you are.

I had to become an MP in the army, then an army investigator to later get recognized for the Texas job. You have to play the lottery to win the lottery." - Hock

Chapter 15: The Dead Baby

Through the years, I worked on several cases involving dead babies. Dead babies in murders and car wrecks. A rape. Beatings. But one was by far the weirdest and most ironic and not just involving babies.

In Dallas, Texas, in the last few years, the city had started what they called a Baby Moses program. his program was where unwanted babies could be dropped off at fire stations and safe havens with no questions asked rather than be abandoned or killed. As I watched this news feature about the new program on television, my mind flipped off into the various dead baby cases I had worked in the past. Would the Baby Moses plan have helped? All had a snapshot stain in my brain of a telling moment or two. But one sight, one night, sticks in my mind.

That case involved what was probably one of the most ironic moments of my life because it was intertwined with the law, races, friendships, death, abortion, poverty, education, and, ... well, so much it was too hard to categorize it all. I will just have to tell you about it, and I promise you won't know what to do with it either.

I will start by recalling a guy named Sam Till for you. Many of our officers knew Sam Till. Sam lived in one of the projects or "poor" parts of our city; and, yes, it was the black part of town. Sam was a Vietnam vet and a retired, high-ranking Army NCO. He was a hard-working, ambitious person and ran two successful businesses. One was a large, citywide sanitation company; and the other was a well-established funeral home.

On any given day, you might spot Sam supervising a garbage truck or even loading one on a route; or he might be giving a sermon at a funeral or driving the limo to a graveyard. He often came to crime scenes and collected the murder victims or scraped together what was left of accidents and suicides. Sam, like the other funeral home folks, would transport the bodies to the lab for autopsies if needed. Sam pitched in and did it all. Yes, Sam was a black guy.

One day, he and two workers saw a crazed man beating one of our officers and trying to take his pistol. Sam and the men jumped on the criminal and saved the day and the life of the already-unconscious officer. Sam was one of the locals who renovated his house and remained in the projects as many successful people did at that time. It was where he grew up! Where he wanted to be. He was even mildly involved in city politics and became involved with various good causes. He had several good sons who stayed out of trouble despite where they lived.

During my years as a patrolman or a detective, Sam supplied me with a lot of information about people he knew and suspected of crimes. I could go to him anytime for intel and gossip. He in turn would give me a phone call if he thought he'd discovered something. I think he knew I meant well for the community. He also knew that one of the most influential people in my life was a black Army NCO named Gaston; and, therefore, I mustn't have been much of a racist. But racism was an overall problem back then—not as bad as before the 40s, 50s, and 60s, but still bad in the 70s and 80s.

I was a fairly "new" detective (technically new as Texas goes, despite my investigation time in the Army) in 1981 or thereabouts. I was dispatched one chilly, early evening to meet a patrolman about a "family" problem in that part of the city. When I arrived at this sprawling, older home, a patrolman introduced me to a mother and father. The parents had become burdened with a problem, and neither they nor the patrolman knew what to do about it.

I met the officer standing outside on the walkway and alone in the dusk.

"Hey, Hock," the patrolman said. "We've got a problem here. I don't know. I don't know what to do with it." The officer shook his head. He opened the front door and steered me in.

What is there not to know? I asked myself. Then I found out.

"Sandra has not been well, and her friends have told us something," the mother spoke up. "But Sandra was pregnant. And we had no idea."

Pregnant? No idea? I saw the family color portrait on the wall. The parents were big people, and I mean really big people. Sandra, who looked to be about 12 years old in the picture, was a very, very big girl. We all sat in the living room.

"Her friend told us she was pregnant, and she had the baby," the father said. "Sandra has not been to school in a week. She's been throwing up ... we just thought ... we just thought she was sick."

"Where is the baby?" I asked. "Is there a baby ... yet?"

"No one knows," the officer added.

"Sandra's friend says she had the baby last night," the distressed mother said.

"Where?"

"In there," the father said, pointing to a bedroom.

"In there. Have you looked yet?"

"No, Mr. Hock, we were afraid to look."

"Any ... ahh ... crying or...?" I asked with trepidation.

"No. Sandra is in there now. She won't open the door."

"Well, Mrs. Rankin, this is your house; and you can go anywhere in it. Let's go," I said.

We all stood, and the mother announced to Sandra that we were coming in. Sandra wouldn't unlock the door, so I kicked it open. The bedroom was quite large, yet it was stacked and cluttered with ... with just about everything you'd find in a teen's room at the time, times 10. Clean clothes. Dirty clothes. Furniture. Some stuff just stacked and other things grossly shoved and tossed everywhere, all atop a dirty carpet and a few pieces of old wooden furniture.

The mother started to explain to her why we were there. Sandra was now about 15 years old and still quite a large young girl, much larger than the photo I'd seen in the living room. It was possible to live around her and not detect a pregnancy. I guessed. Possible? As they talked, as she denied, I started prowling the room, lifting, and looking. And then I spotted a newborn baby pushed against the wall and buried in towels and clothes. Dead.

The parents knew I'd spotted something. I must have grunted or something. And in an instant, they charged over to look. They moaned and screamed.

"Don't touch," I said quietly. Regretfully. "Let's get out of this room."

I left the house for my sedan radio. I requested our crime scene man, Russell Lewis, to come as well as my supervisor, Detective Sergeant Howard Kelly. Kelly called the crime scene house phone, and I ran it all down to explain the deal to him. He would contact a Juvenile Division Detective to take over any investigation, but that wouldn't be until tomorrow unless something unusual happened. It was my mess until then. I hung up the phone. I knew the girl would eventually be charged for something that would probably be impossible to prove or disprove back then. Stillborn? Starved? Killed? Not too sure what the prosecutors would do. But my involvement would be temporary.

Now I am trying to keep these details brief. Russell came. We snooped around, and he took pictures. Then he left. What came next ... is why I write this. A funeral home was called to handle the dead body after we processed the crime scene. Sam Till's was next on rotation, and he took the call and drove right over as soon as he could.

As soon as he could? Because he was still in his garbage truck! Not the usual Till funeral van, as Sam was out delivering a truck to his office and was already nearby. Sam came in and was greeted by the parents as though they were longtime friends. He sat with them. He listened to them. Sympathized with them, as Sam always did so well. There would be a proper funeral.

The family left the house for the police station, where I would later collect some preliminary statements.

Then it was just me and Sam. The baby would next go to his funeral home and as soon as possible be driven to the Dallas County Southwest Forensics lab for an autopsy.

Sam had a white towel in his hands, and we walked to the bedroom and up to the baby. He was talking about something to me the whole way. The family situation. I don't remember exactly what. He grabbed this baby by the ankles, and with the baby upside down, he and I went back out on the street.

While we discussed whatever it was, he laid the towel down on the passenger floorboard of the garbage truck and laid the baby atop it. He said goodbye.

He roared the garbage truck engine as I walked to my car and unlocked the car door, but I just stood there for a second, you know? What just happened? As he drove away in the garbage truck, I stood rather

dumbfounded on the city street; and I knew I had just witnessed a most ironic, twisted, odd, social statement or situation of some sort. I mean, how can I describe this? The words "dead black baby born in secrecy and removed from the slums ... in a garbage truck at night."

I have a vivid memory of that moment in my head. To this day, I just don't know what to do with it.

Chapter 16: The Dead Professor, True Detective - Murder, Mayhem, and Killer Potboilers

Me, a kneeling Benny Parkey, and Sgt Lonnie Flemming checking the street outside the murder. A newspaper photo.

Murder is the Super Bowl of crime. If you were in the policing business, murder investigation was the most important pinnacle. Sure you would hear all kinds of people slap the backs of the other guys and say otherwise.

"The traffic officer saves lives every day..."

"The police chief sets the standard..."

"The mere daily presence of the enforcement officer is the most important..."

Yeah, sure. But you could have all that stuff. In my small, twisted world, working traffic every day was an upper, not lower, rung of hell to me. I don't care about tickets. There were lower rungs of police hell, believe me. And I never took a promotional test because being a supervisor steered me off my course. I still had to be acting sergeant and acting Lieutenant for periods of time. Was paid for it! But the real action was in the murder case.

I recall one time I had been working two murders at a time. That two-fer caseload was small potatoes, because I had worked with those giant agencies where detective teams were juggling many murders at once. Key word being "teams." In murder investigation, the truth was-is some murders could be obvious, easy, and quick to solve.

Single, double, or more, people were fascinated by the ways and means of murder. You'd hardly find a cop show or movie that wasn't about a murder. It was usually "murder-lite" entertainment. Not the guts, grime, gross drama, and trauma of a real murder. I called it murder-lite such as in the old Angela Lansberry show "Murder She Wrote" or even the popular "NCIS." And all those murder mystery books! They loved the expressions and phrases they read and saw about the perpetrator, the "vic" (victim), the search warrant, and the probable cause.

It took the movie, not the book *Silence of the Lambs*, to really scare the Bejesus out of the world, as they now looked around every corner for the classic serial murderer; or in case they were snared and became someone's brain soup. Look at the TV show Criminal Minds. What writers! How many years has it been on? How many serial murder mysteries have they created for this theatrical task force to solve? Then there's Dexter. I thought that Dexter might possibly end the Hannibal Lector serial-killer run. After all, he's a serial killer who killed serial killers. What could come next?

A few decades back, detective magazines were everywhere. I could walk into a gas station in Arkansas, a 7-11 in Texas, a bookstore in Los Angeles, or a candy store in Boston and find an array of detective magazines on the racks. All the covers were of scantily clad women in various layers of suffering, bondage, or holding weapons. Cleavage, thighs, and guns. The text on the covers indicated the promise of actual mysteries, crimes, and arrests. Just the promise, though, because they were all sensationalized. One title I recall: *"Can a 63-Year-Old Midget Rape Big Country Gals?"*

You can see how politically incorrect those covers became to the women's movement; and soon the magazines themselves disappeared completely from the stands. Gone, too, was the variety of odd police-related ads. The least believable of all was the ubiquitous mail-order correspondence *"How-To Detective Courses,"* which have way gone by the wayside. Yes, by lengthy and expensive correspondence with super sleuths, you, too, could learn to become ... a detective. Live that exciting lifestyle. No doubt, flashing your correspondence course certificate down on the desk of any police chief, even J. Edgar Hoover himself, would have the chief declaring,

"Why, sit right down here, boy. We have a job for an educated man like yourself!"

One of those old mags was named *True Detective*. Then decades later, we had a great HBO series in the 2000s by the same name. Sick of serial-murder stories, even I admired it the first season.

One thing was certain, however; despite the lurid covers, headlines and the sexpot ads, the actual stories in those magazines were fastidiously researched! The reporters usually worked hard, traveled, attended courtroom trials, and interviewed as many policemen and witnesses as they could when possible. So wrapped in all this sexist and culture junk, the case coverage was quite good. The story had to be a little flashy, a little newsy, very violent, or very mysterious ... well, what true crimes do today's TV shows cover? Those kinds of cases.

Two or three of my murder cases caught the detective magazine's attention in the 1980s. Another in our detective squad, David Scott, also had at least one or two stories printed about him. I remember dropping the *Startling Detective* magazine on Scott's desk and David's eyes opening wide.

"You're in this one, bubba," I told him.

"Oh, no," he said, expecting lies and trouble. He read it, looked up, and said. "That's pretty much right on."

Actually, you could write a really good book on David Scott's interesting cases, adventures, and misadventures. Instead, they picked a pretty tame one for the magazine.

In the Army, CID worked all murders. We in MPI just got involved at times. Did various chores for the process. In Texas, I worked on a number of murders either as a case agent or helping my friends with their assignments. There was a period of time when I was assigned all murders and then a three-man Crimes Against Persons unit.

One of my cases selected by the national detective magazines was a real mystery, and the public "loves a mystery," as they say.

One fall in the 1980s, a college professor was murdered in his home over a weekend; and there were no apparent common leads, just a stabbed-dead guy on the dining room floor with his television, some other stuff and his car stolen.

He lived in what we would quickly call a "rich housing addition," one where suddenly, frighteningly, made up of wide-eyed neighbors and shocked colleagues. You get the picture.

I put up a BOLO (Be On the Look Out) for the car. His new Mercedes immediately turned up in the Fort Worth PD auto pound. Towed in from the projects of Ft. Worth, (a different one than the one I wrote about earlier) sans 4 wheels and tires, in a wooded lot. Two Ft. Worth patrol officers found the car in this poor section of the city and impounded it before the body was discovered and before the car was reported missing and/or stolen.

"Was discovered." There was an old sarcastic police expression, "Homicide: Our day begins when your day ends." But sometimes our day actually began the next day, some days later, or many days later. Sometimes years later. The Prof's body "was discovered" by co-workers worried about his missing work fortwo days. The family was called. They collected themselves and traveled to the house. So, the body "was discovered" AFTER" the car was discovered. All those common phrases are tossed out by the mouthpieces of the system and its books, TV shows, and movies. Upon "discovery," there was the gasping, the screaming, the moaning, and the police calling. Patrol got there. I got there next.

The deceased. The prof was on the dining room floor. A bit ripe. Just a bit. Clothes disheveled as from what might have been a struggle. Looked like some stab wounds. The usual blood. Not too much. We had to wait, by law, for the medical examiner to get there to even touch-turn over the body.

No signs of forced entry. We worked the crime scene. I could not find any unlocked, forced-open, or broken windows in the house. The doors seemed fine. Something was missing where a big television set once sat on a stand in the living room. Other than that, I couldn't identify anything else stolen yet. Jewelry maybe?

I opened the kitchen silverware drawer and stared down into it. Such a mix of sets. How could I determine if the prof was stabbed with one of his own knives? The butcher-block knife set on the counter had a knife in every slot.

Canvass the neighborhood. While our crime scene man worked the house, I and some other detectives, Benny Parkey for one, knocked on doors; but few people were home in the afternoon. The college folks, lined up and watching from across the street, told us the prof owned a fairly new Mercedes.

Make and model. I had to find and then scour his household records and taxes. He kept quite fastidious records and had his car serviced a bit more than normal. With those records in hand, I had to drive over to the local Mercedes dealer and get all the "horsepower" on the car. VIN, etcetera. I got the make and model of the car. The tires were surely Mercedes-

Benz 300TDs. I loaded the Mercedes info up on NCIC as stolen; and, of course, an instant hit came in from Ft. Worth. What a fast break! I called Ft. Worth Homicide and told them about the car.

They then had the car moved into a forensic bay away from the common impounded and the outdoor parking lot. I set up a special examination time for the car by their people; one I would attend.

Then I called for and spoke with one of the two impounding officers about the car recovery.

"Yeah, yeah, we find stolen and stripped cars on that empty field. An empty lot. But you would have to know about this lot. Somebody in the neighborhood is involved or did it."

"What's around it?"

"It's a big lot between some old houses. Overgrown grass. Garbage. We found it about 1 a.m. Sunday morning."

"Could it have been there Friday night?"

"I don't think so. We worked Friday. We always checked that spot for stolen, stripped cars. And it wasn't there."

"I guess I will be going door-to-door down there tomorrow, but if you can keep your ears open, that would be great. Any tire dealers and low-running car repair places that would buy Mercedes-grade tires from a thief?"

" In that area? Yeah, well … all of them."

We talked more, and I hung up the phone. Great. Who strips cars down there? Who buys? Now I have to contact the auto theft people, and the State of Texas has an Auto Theft Unit.

The Prof was last seen Friday afternoon at work. So, I had narrowed that down from Friday at 5 p.m. to about Saturday at midnight, with about a one-hour drive to Ft Worth. All that told me my suspect and/or suspects had prior knowledge of this lot and a serious connection with this "poor" section of the city. Yours truly would be canvassing that whole nasty part of town.

There was an old expression in police work. Only one living person really knows the time of death. The killer. It is not an exact science, though it has gotten better and is getting better still. It was not so good, mind you, decades ago.

Next of kin. The Prof's family flew right in, and I asked the sister and her clan to the station for a quiet and concentrated meeting. The sister gave me a working profile of her brother and told me that the prof had engaged in "dangerous, stranger sex," as she put it…with men. Which helped me understand some possibilities. She said he would fly to foreign countries for that activity, which explained some odd vacation booklets photos of happy, happy men that I had seen at his house.

Reward money. I asked if she could raise any reward money. I explained that I would be canvassing various neighborhoods; low-running car repair places that would buy obviously stolen tires and if I could wave some money around, I might stand a better chance of getting information. She said she could. As I recall, it was $3,000.

After about a two-hour session, we all filed downstairs and out into the dark night. I asked them to accompany me to the house and look around and give me their impressions. I walked them to their rental car. I got in my Dodge, and off we went.

At the house, they were much help. It was late; and we all were tired, but we tried.

"Television?" I asked, pointing to the empty spot.

"Yes, there," the sister said. "A big Sony."

"A Sony. Sure?"

"Yes. Sure. I remember when he bought it."

"I will have to get a serial number."

"He kept good records. He bought it three years ago somewhere here in town."

I had a giant cardboard box of his financial records yet to thoroughly sort through. And with that, we left.

It was only about 10 p.m. Having an idea that my car tires and TV were in the projects in Ft. Worth, I still drove over to some local hot spots and snitches and snooped around. Knocked on some apartment doors. Caught some cats I knew walking around.

I knocked on one apartment door. "Chillin" answered. Chillin was known to "buy stuff" sometimes. But he always cooperated with us when we caught up to him. We gave him a few escape hatches from illegal purchases, and he trusted us. We, on the other hand, did not completely trust him.

"Hey, man," he said.

His girlfriend, somebody I didn't know, swooped up and hugged his arm. She was too high to be concerned about my visit. It was about 11:30 p.m. by now, but there was no problem with time.

"Chillin! How are you doing?" I stepped inside. We chatted up some nonsense.

"Listen, I'm working a killing. College professor. Killed in his house. Knife job."

"Okay."

"The killer stole the Professor's Mercedes and his Sony TV."

"Okay. When dis' happen?"

"So far, we think Saturday night."

"Okay. Okay."

"You hear anything? Anybody selling anything?"

"Okay. Okay. Hmmm. You know Willie Richards? Dat boy … dat boy … his momma work forever at Baseheart Cleaners on Earhart and Regal?"

"No, I can't say I do."

"He come all up here Sunday night trying to sell a TV. Yeah. Wasn't no Sony, though. No. It was a big Panasonic."

"Sure? Panasonic?"

"Oh, yeah … no Sony. Hell, I almost bought the thing. But you see my shit." He pointed to a big TV. "I got a hottie already."

The girl laughed with the dual entendre. He laughed. I smiled.

"He wasn't trying to sell you anything else?" I asked as I walked to the door.

"No, he sure wasn't."

"Well, okay. If you hear anything, will you give me a holler?"

"Okay. I will, Hawkman."

Leaving, I pondered the sister's memory of the TV brand. She seemed so sure. Oh well, I knew I had to toss the financial records and see what I could find.

Meanwhile, this brewed into a high-profile crime, a bit of a media event on the TV news and papers. There was some pressure there, but solving the case was enough pressure on me. I would not be distracted.

Making matters worse right at that exact time, my second wife underwent a surgery the day after the crime. I was torn with the case, with her and the aftercare, and keeping up with our two young kids.

Everyone of importance at the PD knew about the operation and that I simply had to take that morning off. When we got home from the operation, I took a badly needed shower; and when I picked up the razor to shave, I spied a hairless spot on my chin. It was about the size of a dime in among my normally cable-like stubbles. What the…? I shaved, putting it out of my mind. We had a close friend across the street who came over at my request to stay with my wife because I just HAD to work on this case. Had to.

Today we have the internet. Back then, we had … phone books. I drove straight to the public library. Yesteryear, most libraries had a collection of annually issued phone books, certainly of the general region. We would often have to mail order phone books from far-away cities for our investigations. We had local phone books at our office but not ones from Dallas or Ft. Worth. We would save these books because people we were looking for might stop "publishing" or "listing" their phone numbers and addresses, but they would still have the same number and home listed in older phone books. A prize book was our cross-reference book. If you just had a phone number, you could look up the number and see the name and address with it. That was some real spy stuff back then. Secret squirrel. If we needed to know the info on an unlisted number? We usually cultivated a snitch, someone who knew someone at the phone company. We would call that person for fast results. Soon that, too, by the mid-1990s became impossible, and search warrants were needed. A real pain. Judges who issued search warrants didn't like "fishing expeditions," but a whole lot of investigations started with "fishing around."

You had the white pages of information on people and the yellow pages for information on businesses. I took the big Fort Worth yellow pages phone book over to a copy machine and made copies of car and parts sales and repair places I determined where in the range of the that older neighborhood. I would cross-reference them.

On TV shows now like NCIC, the funky, perky, quirky, office girl with a taste for fashionable oddity back at the office did that work with computers that rivaled space and time. In real life? We did it. Minus A.I.

As the sun set, I drove to Fort Worth with my copy machine papers and a paper map for my first look around. It was dark when I got to the "hood," and with flashlight in hand, I looked over the vacant lot where the car was found.

It was a classic one like the officer described between two big, old, dilapidated wooden houses. Some junk here and there. Tall and short wild grass. I wondered exactly where the car was on the lot.

I started with those two bordering houses. I was not in a suit because it was after hours, just jeans, shirt, and sneakers. But my unmarked sedan parked on the street was a dead giveaway that the "fuzz" was there. I knocked on the doors, flashed my badge, and as friendly as possible asked them about the stripped car and/or anything else they knew about stripped cars.

Nothing, of course. Zip. They were older folks and smart enough to play dumb. I left my business card and told them there was $3,000 for anyone with any solid info leading to a conviction. That type of news would travel like wildfire.

I worked the whole street. Nothing.

It was about 10 p.m., and I had to relieve my neighbor doing wife-kids duty at my house. So much yet to do!

The next morning, I got the kids off to school and typed up a flier and made phone calls from home. I hung around to care for my wife, but the case was screaming in my brains. She seemed stronger, so I left the house. At the station I made copies with my business card attached and went to the prof's street. I knocked on the doors and spoke to neighbors or left a flier on the doors. About 10 houses in, I got lucky. A woman who had seen something.

"There was a sedan, a four-door sedan that was older, parked in front of his house Saturday night," a woman told me. "It was an odd car for our street. We made some trips to the store; and each time we drove by, it was there. First few trips, it was empty; then the last time, there were people in it. Three black people. One was a girl. Just sitting there."

"Anyone behind the wheel?"

"No."

She gave us as good a description as she could of the people and the car. I told her I REALLY needed a written statement from here. Now. She was certain the car model was exactly like mine she saw me in when leaving. She stopped me on the sidewalk.

"That's it. A Dodge Diplomat!"

My "company car" was gold. This one was not quite gold, but light-colored in the night streetlights. She followed me to the station, and I took a statement from her damn-near trying to hypnotize her to get the most information possible. I now had to type a new flier and add the car info to it. I had to get down to Ft. Worth with this information.

When I could, I would sneak out of my house and work on that case. I absolutely had to be in Fort Worth when the crime scene people dissected the Mercedes in a car bay at their city pound. There wasn't much found.

The Benz was kept immaculate by the professor and still appeared just as clean. Results to follow. That same day, I made a run over to the Fort Worth P.D. substation to present the case in their shift-squad briefing to the patrol shift who worked the area. I also visited Fort Worth Auto Theft.

All the while, there were some nasty fireworks at my house. I wasn't home. I didn't care. The usual. Over that week, I lost most of my beard, one eyebrow, and one set of eye lashes; and small bald spots opened up on my head hair. I called a doctor friend of mine, and he told me the hair loss was probably from stress. Alopecia, he said. I asked him when it might stop, and he said that sometimes it ran all over your body and you become permanently bald and hairless. Great.

But one afternoon, my wife and I had a very rare, reasonable discussion about what I needed to do, why, and how. I guess she was both drugged and feeling better? She said, "You'd better go, then." Huh? And I was gone in a flash.

I spent most of the next week down in those Fort Worth projects waving around the promise of reward money and trying to find a guy selling a Sony TV and those tires to area people, houses, chop shops, or car repair places.

The weather turned gray and cold as a Blue Northern rolled in. I was alone one afternoon working my way down a long dirty street of disarrayed houses that barely stood against the Yankee wind. I knocked on the windowpane of a door, and an old man stuffed in a dated winter jacket waddled to the door.

"Name's Hock, Police Department." I flashed my badge through the glass.

"Get on in heah.' It's freezin' out there," he said.

It was freezing inside his house, too. Everything was about 60 years old. No curtains on the windows. For some reason, the front room was full of old, dead TV sets. Then I saw the sign leaning against the ripped-up couch, "TV Repair." I explained my mission.

"There was a boy here two weeks ago selling tires. Nice tires."

"There was?"

"Saw one tire. Mercedes-Benz 300TD. Said he had four to sell."

I grilled him. It was a black male, late 20s, alone. The tire was in the back seat of a four-door sedan that was a light color.

"He knocked on the door like you did. Told me to look at the tires in his trunk. I did. I rapped on it with my knuckles. Said he had three more he'd run and get if I wanted them."

"Try to sell you a TV?"

"No. Just the tires."

"Hey, have a look at my car out the front windows."

We walked there.

"His car look like my car?"

"It did. Only a kind of blue maybe."

"Tell you what. I am going to type this up at the police station and then come down here with the statement for you to sign."

"I work. I work at Redman's Red Barbecue on Dyson."

"Got a phone?"

He gave me phone number of his home and Redman's. (The days before cellphones.) We made some arrangements. I left.

Out on the cracked sidewalk in the wind chill, my longer hair of the day blowing around like on a Johnny Cash album cover, I looked at all the houses on the street I'd been to, asking about this tire salesman. Yeah. Nobody knew nothing. Nothing.

With the Prof's key in my pocket, I drove back to the professor's house. I simply had to find the serial number on that Sony TV. And I really needed to add EVERYTHING into that box of records I first saw and collected. I turned on all the lights and searched the place inch by inch, one wall and one room at a time. I got to the bedroom he used as a home office. He'd had custom-built shelves and drawers installed and then loaded them with more files. Too many files. Going through them a page at a time, I had the idea that he had been a fastidious guy, a real record keeper, and a loyal customer to local businesses.

I saw some receipts where he'd bought a stereo system from Spinny's Electronics, a locally owned store. It broke down, and he took it there to be fixed. He also bought a washing machine there. I found nothing on a TV purchase. And after the inch-by-inch search, I had no further information I could connect to this crime.

"Raymondo!"

"Hello, Hock," Raymondo said, unlocking the front door of his shop called Spinny's. He was a bit surprised to see me there, anxious at 10 a.m. sharp.

"Ray, I am working the Professor_____ murder."

"Yeah, yeah. Heard about it. What a shame."

"He did business with you, huh?"

"Yeah. A lot."

"You know his TV was stolen after the murder? I really need the serial number for that Sony TV; I was hoping...."

"You mean the Panasonic?"

"The...Panasonic?"

"Yeah, he bought a big Panasonic TV from us. Not a Sony."

"Okay," I said automatically and fully distracted. "Do we have the model and serial number of the TV on file?"

"Yeah, sure, we got that," he said and turned, "Gabriella?"

I was distracted because the words of Chillin flew through my head, "He come all up here Sunday night trying to sell a TV. Yeah. Wasn't no Sony, though. No. It was a big Panasonic."

Willie Randolf. I smiled. The big smile. The grand-slam smile. The Super Bowl touchdown smile. The great sex smile. The lottery-winning smile. That smile.

Raymondo emerged from the back office with a piece of paper.

"Here ya' go," he said.

"There I go," I said back. "Thanks. See ya.'"

Not only did I have the model and serial number, but Raymondo also gave me a pamphlet on the TV. The big TV sets back then were enormous heavy cubes and not the skinny jobs we have today.

I calmly drove back to the station, marched into our records room, and looked up one Willie Randolf. There was a manila folder. William Randolf. A few minor arrests and one for burglary. That meant a mug shot. I got his "number" and revved up the revolving mug shot machine and pressed the go button until his row came up. A few finger flips and there that som-a-bitch was. A front and side mug shot. I carried it upstairs to the CID floor, opened our handy-dandy mug shot books, and constructed the best six-person photo lineup I could. The better the lineup, the better the case.

I drove, yet again, all the way back to my TV repairman in Fort Worth.

"You got that statement?" he asked, letting me in his house.

"No, sir. Every time I thought I was through with it, I had to add another question to it and drive all the way down here again."

He let loose a hiccup kind of laugh.

"Take a look at these guys and see if anyone looks familiar." I handed him the photo lineup, just a thin stack of photos at this point.

"That one. He's the boy."

He picked Randolf.

"Can you sign and date the back of that picture? Can you initial the corner of those others?"

He did.

"Now I will drive back, type up that statement, and get back here for you to sign it."

He laughed. "You'll be needing to buy *YOU* some tires before you're through with all that."

After several attempts at reaching Chillen, I finally found him at home. I showed him the lineup, and he picked his longtime neighborhood acquaintance Willie Randolf as the Willie he knew who came by to sell him the TV. He signed the back of the photo and initialed the others.

It was Friday afternoon at that point, and I simply had to make an appearance at my house. Raging to hunt down Willie and run down that TV set, I managed to act like a normal person for Friday night and Saturday.

Also, the spreading hair loss had quit. My wife was feeling better. By sunset on Saturday night, I had to leave again to work on this case. I wanted to find Willie's car and even question Willie to amass good probable cause for the arrest warrant. I was dressed down in Wrangler jeans, flannel shirt, leather jacket, and a .45.

Armed with the Randolf home address from his file, I took my own car, a big Ford Thunderbird, across town "over the railroad tracks" and into the Randolf neighborhood. I would be less conspicuous in a regular car. I parked up the dark street and watched the house for a while getting a feel for things. No Willie. No Willie car.

In my car was a hardcover-book-sized cassette tape player. I would usually listen to books on tape during such times. It was my understanding that in recent years, a detective doing such an off-duty thing would not only have to inform his or her supervisor about a surveillance, getting approval, etcetera. But approval meant overtime compensation. It had to be decided if it was in the budget? Back in my day? We just worked whenever and wherever we had to. If something serious developed, we'd call it in. Such as this night. We had no such thing as cell phones then. I did have my hand-held police radio.

The house had a bay window in front. The windows were dark, but I saw the flashing lights and shadows of a BIG TV playing in the living room. It finally struck my genius-self after about two hours ...

"Hey! What if THAT is the TV I am looking for?"

I started my car up and slowly approached and passed the house. I could see inside. An old skinny man was sitting about four feet from a big TV set. I pulled over and reported to the dispatcher over my radio,

"Eighty-nine, dispatch."

"Go ahead."

"I'll be out at 914 Alexander."

"Ten-four."

I walked up the walkway and onto the rickety porch and knocked on the door. I saw the old guy get off the couch and come to the door. He turned on the light, an unshaded bulb on a wire.

"Mr. Randolf?"

"Yes?"

"Hock, with the police department." Badge flash. "Is your son Willie here?"

"No."

"Does he live here?"

"No. Not no more."

"Has he ever lived here?"

"Here in this house, here? No. He did live with his momma too, but he stays across town now."

I nodded. I asked that because this big-assed TV playing right next to me in this small front room had to be the professor's TV. And if Willie had never lived there, Willie would have no legal "expectation of privacy" there.

"Where did you get this TV, sir?"

"My boy Willie gave it to me. A present."

"I see. Well, if the serial number on that TV matches the serial number on this piece of paper?" I held up a copy of the Spinny's sales receipt, "we have a situation here."

I took the flashlight out of my back pocket and lit up the back of the set. I found the black and silver plate of numbers on the back. I read the numbers out loud.

"These numbers match, Mr. Randolf. This TV is involved in a major investigation. Can I take this TV with me?" I asked because ... well ... I needed to ask first, but I wasn't going to leave without that TV. No way. Worst case scenario, he'd say no and refuse me and all of my debates.

Then I would have to get a search warrant versus him directly (not Willie directly) to secure the TV. It being a weekend, typing up a good PC (probable cause) warrant and finding a judge all on a Saturday night, etcetera., etcetera… in all that time, the TV could "disappear." I had to take it in.

"Oh, well, go ahead then," he said.

Whew.

"It's stolen, ain't it?" he asked.

I just smiled. I didn't know exactly what to tell him. I unplugged the set, opened the front door, and picked up that heavy bastard and hauled it to the car. I hefted the black box into the back seat somehow.

I walked back into the house and gave him one of my business cards.

"Willie have a car?"

"Not that I know of."

"Where does he live exactly?"

"Over to the college. Some apartments. I don't know. Never been there myself."

"That's such a big TV. Somebody help him carry that?"

"No, he did it."

"Okay."

I left with the TV. Driving back to the station with this booty, I started running the numbers on what I'd just done. My recovery of this TV set from Daddy Randolf's house meant that my suspect, son Willie, would be told, freak out, and go underground. I needed the TV in custody to help get the probable cause arrest warrant. But getting the TV tipped my suspect off that we were after him.

Still, so far, I really only had a car theft or burglary case on Willie. No murder case. A Willie friend could have killed the professor for all I knew. Also, in a perfect world with a perfect case, I would need a signed statement from the dad about all that, too. But my gut reaction, my feeling, was his cooperation would have stopped with the mention of signed statements against his son. I felt it best at the moment to get the TV and attach my statements to the acquisition of it. We could always go back later and bug the old man for a statement. I went over that potential; future sales pitch in my mind. After the case was closed and after a solid case had been made against the son, then we could squeeze the dad for a signed statement. If need be, I could tell him his statement at that later point would not critically hurt his already-indicted and arrested son. But an early statement THAT night would critically hurt his son. Such were the strategies a good detective worried about.

    I humped the TV set into our evidence locker in the basement. I walked upstairs and sat at a typewriter, stared at a blank piece of paper, took a deep breath, and started in on a warrant for Willie Randolf. Burglary or murder? The body of the warrant I would swear to would make a strong burglary and a weak murder. I decided to let one of the DAs decide on the official charge on Monday morning. About 2 a.m. I finished, drove home, crept into my house and slipped into bed.

    Monday morning. We went with murder. A prosecutor punched the warrant up. A district judge signed off. While I had a number of small tasks to do, the hunt was still officially on. I had to write up a flier with a picture, warrant, and all the related horsepower. Then spread the fliers all over. One interesting thing we noticed back then was that when some of our locals discovered they were wanted, they fled, sure, but only as far as Dallas or Fort Worth and then for only a few days. One would think that if you were fleeing the police, you would leave the state! Run to Mexico! Some did. That would make sense. But many of our locals were quite small-minded and considered the neighboring metropolis as major flight.

My gut reaction was that if Willie ran, it wouldn't be far at all. Some of those guys needed a support system to survive; and once away from their environments, they were kind of lost.

My sergeant asked me if I needed any help. I asked for Mike "Batman" Bateman; because, well, for starters, Bateman had arrested Willie in the past and obtained a confession from him. Plus, Mike was solid. Bateman had a history of making good decisions at very key times in several major breaking cases that I was not sure many people knew or thought about and, therefore, appreciated. I did. I sure noticed them. He and I did a lot of hunting around with numerous Tarrant County brisket breaks to keep us going. We began to infiltrate a circle of Willie's friends. Of course, they lied to us at times and tried to manipulate us; but it was becoming obvious that Willie was on the lam and - par for the course - on the lam to Fort Worth not Luxemburg.

He had cousins in Fort Worth. After a while, we found out where they lived. Finally, one night spying on their houses in a circular pattern, I watched them all enter a cheap pizza place. Willie was indeed among them. After they settled in, I also walked in and cornered a worker, flashed my badge, and told her to call the police to serve a warrant.

I sat at a table in clear view of the group and waited a few minutes. I could arrest Willie but not whisk him off into another county and take him straight home. He had to be processed and arraigned in the county's court where the arrest was made. I saw the patrol car pull up outside. I stood, left and walked to the car and walked over to the care, explaining everything. The two young officers in the car were happy to serve a murder warrant. Who wouldn't?

I walked in and they followed behind.

"Willie..."

He looked up at me. His chair scooted back an inch, and his eyes went wild around the room looking for doors.

"Willie, don't even think about it. This place is surrounded as we speak. Get up and put your hands behind your back."

An officer stepped up and cuffed him. This action meant what we needed, a official Tarrant County arrest No gun, just words. I didn't even need to flash my badge. Willie just simply knew. Both were only a second from my hands anyway.

They took him "in" and booked. I picked him up after his arraignment in the late morning of the next day from the Tarrant County Jail; and by late afternoon back at our headquarters, Bateman and I started talking to him. He knew Bateman and trusted him from those prior dealings, so that was cool. In an effort for him to explain what happened, he waived his Miranda warning rights. He told us a fable first; but when we chiseled away at his story with facts, he confessed.

He and the professor met on the street. A homosexual encounter ensued back at the Prof's house.

Willie said he left afterward. Walked away. But then he returned with some friends and their car (the four-door, light-colored sedan) to rob the man. Alone inside the house, Willie stabbed the Professor multiple times and stole the car and the TV. He tossed the knife, his knife by the way, out the Mercedes window on the drive to Fort Worth.

Recovering the knife would be virtually impossible. He named all the parties in the car and numerous other details. There was much work still to be done, but the arrest and confession were the centerpieces. That caused headlines. And about that...

I am told that the major university in our city, the professor's employer, had a monthly deans' meeting of some sort; and the subject of their dead man came up in the conference. All the criminal justice professors started dropping their scholarly opinions. One declared,

"Homicides are usually solved within the first 48 hours..."

"Hemmm-haw, hem-haw," said the faculty choir.

Professor declared, "This case is now a month old. The case will never be solved."

"Hemmm-haw, hem-haw. Here, here," said the academic masters.

"Too bad the 'real' police, like Dallas homicide, aren't working on this."

"Ohhhh, hemmm-haw, hem-haw. Here, here. Yes, yes."

Then the collegiate masterminds all adjourned, left the meeting hall, walked into the lobby and saw the daily newspaper in a stand with the big, glaring headlines,

"Detective Arrests Professor's Killer."

My chuckling spy in place (actually an old friend and the university police chief) said they all snatched up the newspapers and read them aloud in groups. My, my, what happened to their theories? Looks like I got the last "hem-haw" on them.

Addendum: I will never forget the day after the murder trial conviction. Bateman and I drove to the Fort Worth projects, and we distributed some of the $3,000 cash reward to the old TV repairman who first reported the tire "salesman." I felt like a game show host or a lottery board dispenser.

And then Bateman and I had some of the best brisket ever in some ratty, bug-ridden, side-street hovel lunch shack deep down in the hood, an area which, for about three weeks, had become my second home.

Police Detective Notebook...

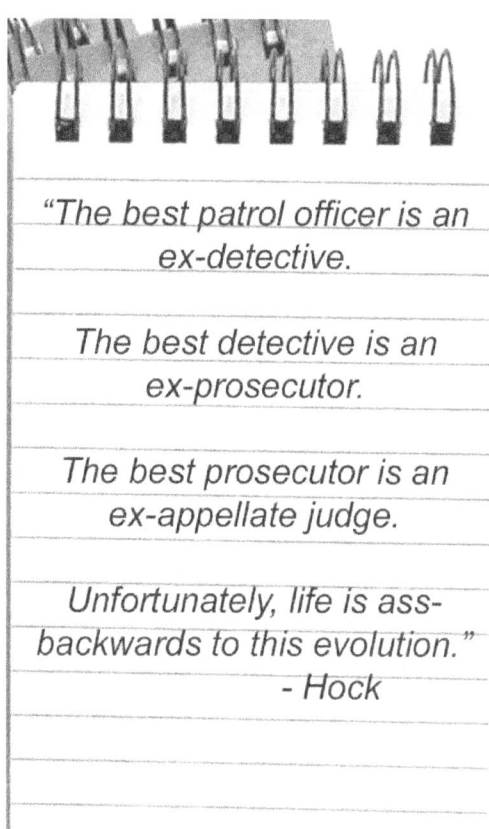

"The best patrol officer is an ex-detective.

The best detective is an ex-prosecutor.

The best prosecutor is an ex-appellate judge.

Unfortunately, life is ass-backwards to this evolution."
- Hock

Chapter 17: Showdown at Jacksberg Lumber Yard

First, before I start this torrid tale of how an armed robber lay dead at the tip of my gun barrel in a north Texas lumberyard, I would like to take a moment to establish some context.

At some point in the early 1980s, I attended a radical police training program for the first time. The program was called "Street Survival" and was sponsored by a company called Caliber Press. It was the first of its kind that endeavored to teach rank and file police officers real survival tactics and ideas. I called it radical because many police administrations were none too happy about the course.

They studied old failures and promulgated "new" wiser and safer strategies. Suddenly all across the USA, officers were demanding backup to questionable and dangerous-feeling calls and the implementation of strategic responses, thereby taxing manpower and invoking discredit upon that solo "John Wayne" image.

Or as in Texas lore, our "One Riot-One Ranger" attitude. I even overheard one upper-management desk rider complain that those new survival seminars "turned the officers to cowards always needing help and backup for every little thing."

Up to that point, such survival training was hit or miss and usually quite incomplete. You could find some people with experience to show you those tactical ropes, but it was like Russian roulette that you'd find one competent enough to explain and teach you and that you would also have the time to learn. I and some others relied a lot on our military training. Probably the most covered subject back then was traffic stops. And they were and still are very mean and dangerous events. But what about everything and everywhere else?

Meanwhile, people like Chuck Remsberg and Dave Smith were organizing to change the face of police training through an outreach series of seminars by Caliber Press. True pioneers.

I know I paid my own way to that first 1980's Dallas regional survival seminar, and so did many other officers. We had to. I think it was about $100 for two days. Frankly, attending that seminar back then was inspiring and life-changing for me. It made me rethink a lot of things I did or didn't do in dangerous situations.

And within two weeks after attending their survival school, I was looking down the gun barrel of an armed robber; and the ideas and concepts of that Street Survival seminar, within two weeks mind you, no doubt saved my life.

So, this was not merely some tawdry, action-misadventure tale of gunplay and death, but rather a tribute to training, tactics, and to Remsberg, Smith, and the others at Caliber Press for the movement they created. Since we have covered that, our tawdry story begins...

"Armed Robbery. Winston's Auto Parts. Tall white male. Short brown hair, bare-chested. Jeans. Handgun."

THAT'S interesting. Bare-chested? Different anyway, unless he's crazy, I thought. But it was a warm Indian summer in north Texas. The police dispatcher read off the litany of facts about the suspect. I was about 10 miles away, a detective in an unmarked sedan. The passenger-seat side of my car was full of case files I was working on. It was near 5 p.m., and the dispatcher asked for an evening-shift detective to respond to the scene. They reached Mike "Limey" Leverton, who was on evening shift and, therefore, subject to official call. I toyed with the idea of going, too.

"Suspect fled on foot..."

THAT'S not too interesting. He fled on foot probably to a nearby hidden car, so we have no suspect vehicle. Plenty of cops in cars responding to that scene and searching, all for a mystery vehicle. The guy would probably put on a hat and a shirt and drive off by himself or with a getaway driver...

"Suspect ran to a pickup truck at McDonald's while it was in line at the drive-thru. He jumped in the bed of the truck..."

THAT'S interesting, a suspect vehicle getting food at Mac's? I toyed even more with the idea of going.

"The white female driver left the food line and drove away westbound at a high rate of speed. Armed suspect still in the bed of the truck."

THAT's kinda' interesting. I pictured a bare-chested armed robber bouncing about in the bed of a truck. A small, maroon, older truck, in fact, as the dispatcher updated that info. I guessed I'd drive over there to the auto parts store and see if I could help Leverton do something. I was still pretty far away.

When I got there, Limey (yes, he was from Liverpool, England, ergo the nickname) was in the lot, his famous writing pad in hand (he was a meticulous note taker), speaking with a store manager. I pulled over, got out, and listened in on the last half of the story. It was a clean case of quick armed robbery at the counter with a few more personal details such as "he stuck a gun in my face" recollections. Which always added a little spice to a dry report, you know? We were standing in the parking lot; and my Dodge Diplomat with the engine running was right beside us.

"I see the suspect!" came an excited voice over my car radio. My window was down and the door open. Limey and I stepped over to my car to listen in.

"The suspect vehicle has just turned northbound on Interstate I-35. Exceeding speed limits."

THAT'S interesting. Limey and I exchanged glances. I looked down at my wristwatch. Five minutes after 5 p.m. I was technically off duty for the day. I had some of those so-called "mandatory" plans with the wife and kids that night.

"Alerting all agencies up north!" the dispatcher reported. That meant the Texas DPS (the Highway Patrol) and all cities bordering the interstate would send units to the highway. If the suspects made it to Oklahoma? Well, then, God help them; they'd likely be killed by Tommy Gun and shotgun fire by the State troopers, if they tried to run the north border. That's what they did back then.

Limey finished up the interview. I watched a patrolman leave the business across the street, clipboard in hand. Another one jogged from the shoe store in the next building over. All hunting for witnesses and information. The drill.

"I guess I'll run up the highway in case somebody gets him," Limey told me.

"Man, I am damn tempted to go with ya.' But it sounds like you've got plenty of help."

"Okay."

"Okay … might change my mind, though. Don't be surprised if you see me later," I added as I got into my sedan to drive off to the house.

On the drive home, the tension on the radio traffic increased. I could feel the electricity. The suspect truck had been seen again and tracked northbound. It busted through one city's attempt to stop it, but it was a small city for sure with little time and crew to prepare. But the next city, Gainesville in Cooke County and their highway patrolmen, would have plenty of time to prepare; and they had some real tough ol' boys working up there who would shoot you full of holes if you messed with them or their roadblocks. Like the aforementioned Captain Bone. Anyway, no way I would get to the action in time.

I was miles and miles away. There would probably be a traffic stop in a few moments. Arrest, shootout, or whatever. I'd be driving like a bat out of hell and still be 25 minutes late.

I walked into my house with my portable radio in hand and still trying to discern the latest news inside the tinny static. The kids were playing in the yard. Wife weeding a garden. I heard some garbled, shouting voices crackling from the speaker. I ran back out to the car hoping my bigger car radio system would pick up the transmissions. It did.

"The suspect vehicle pulled over when in sight of the Gainesville roadblock," an officer reported. "The suspect bailed out of the truck bed and ran into a tree line." The officer gasped for some breaths. "Female driver in custody. Suspect armed and afoot east of the interstate in Gainesville."

THAT'S shit-fire interesting. The downtown areas. Not too rural, kind of citified. No way would they have enough officers to search for that bad guy.

"Shit-fire," I barked aloud to myself, "late or not, I'm going up there."

I slammed the car door shut, backed out of my driveway, and headed for points north, way north and out of the city. Today a detective suddenly leaving the confines of his or her city would require something like a permission slip from the United Nations, but this was the 1980s, and in Texas we went where we had to go, especially in a fandango like this. Actually, my hard-charging Detective Sgt. Howard Kelly would be a little disappointed in me if I didn't go north at a time like that. He would go. Different times. Different people.

So, under the classic, general, broad, loose theory of "hot pursuit," I drove the 30-some odd miles to Gains, Texas. I swore to myself I was not going to speed, drive recklessly, kill me, or kill somebody else; and if I got up there in time to help in the manhunt, then I would. If not? I'd just help Limey with some wrap-up chores and paperwork and then drive calmly back home. My "war bag" was already in the trunk, and I was good to go.

On the drive north, I hoped to link up with my old friend, Detective Captain David Bone of the Creeks County Sheriff's Office, who I overheard was already in the search. As I said, if I were to ever build a Dirty Dozen Police Department, ol' Bone would take up two of those slots. Maybe even three. He was a former Texas Tech football lineman, a powerlifter, dedicated lawman, crack shot, and a budding computer expert even way back in the 1980s! He was so big, in fact, he had to dismantle the interior of his detective car and reweld the front seat into a more comfortable position so he could properly stretch out and blast hard-rock music as he made his daily rounds harassing and picking at the criminal populace of his domain. Bone and I'd worked on several major cases together and we became each other's "go-to" guy in each other's turf.

Half the fun of going up there was that night was maybe seeing ol' Bone and maybe squeezing in a catfish dinner when the smoke settled.

I kept track of events as best I could on my car radio, which wavered in and out with each hill and valley on the interstate. (That was why Sgt. Howard Kelly kept a CB radio in his car!) The suspect fled into the downtown area and was spotted heading north.

Numerous law officials were searching, and more were gathering to help. I asked our dispatcher to inform both the police and county that I too was in route to help Limey and see if we could set up a rendezvous somewhere. I drummed the dashboard with my fingers and tried to stay calm and keep within the speed limit. No sense killing myself in a wreck.

Shortly, our dispatcher got through to tell me to meet up with "Detective Leverton and Captain Bone" at an intersection on a main street not far from the highway. I knew right where that was. Within 10 or so minutes, I exited the highway and turned for the meet.

I guess news traveled fast back then. It was about 6 p.m. The streets were deserted. Like a Sunday morning. Like somebody had seen a ghost. I saw a few police cars up ahead and three men. One was Limey,

Mike became Sheriff for many a year.

one was Bone, and the third was State Trooper Mike Compton. Compton was a bit of police legend in the county. He and Bone were best buds; and Mike was known for his no-nonsense law enforcement and great respected instincts. In fact, we were about to see a sample of some of those great instincts at work.

I parked, and we got right down to business. Everybody was checking his or her guns and getting ready to roll, but I wondered why we were doing all this downtown? Hadn't the suspect fled north from downtown some time ago? Hadn't the search gravitated well away from downtown?

As we locked and loaded, Limey and Bone told me that the captured woman was the suspect's wife. His name was Chester Whiley. She admitted that her husband was a two-time ex-con who would rather die than face the "big bitch," the three-conviction life sentence in the Texas Penitentiary that this brazen armed robbery would produce. She hadn't expected him to *rob* the store. She claimed it was a surprise.

Compton, in his DPS uniform, rested the butt of his pump shotgun on his hip.

"I got a feeling," Mike said, "that this ol' boy didn't get too far. I think he is still hunkered down around here somewhere. Any everybody else assumed he took off way, way north."

He pointed to the north side of the main street with businesses, some homes, and a big, decaying lumberyard.

And I got a feeling that when Compton got a feeling, his fellow law enforcement comrades listened. Okay. I'm game. I usually have an idea that fleeing suspects travel OUTSIDE the range of the established search perimeters. I had advised and suggested establishing a search area and then immediately expanded it because adrenalized suspects tended to travel farther and faster than common police officers predicted. Police officers or soldiers who jog, run, or wind sprint had a better idea of how far and fast a desperado could and would travel in just a few minutes' time. But the big picture here was out of my control, and this was a good hunch from a good huncher. Let's do it! Somebody's gotta' clear the area, no matter what.

As Compton suggested, we fanned out. I took the far-left side armed with a 1911 .45 semi-auto pistol, four magazines, a snubby .38 revolver in my sport coat pocket, plus a big-assed knife. My portable radio was worthless up there, so I left it in the car. About 30 or so yards to my right was Bone with his pistol, shotgun and Sgt. Rock ammo belt. To the right again some 40 yards was Leverton with a shotgun, magnum revolver, and some speed loaders. And to the far-right end was Compton with his duty rig and shotgun. No doubt those guys had their extra weapons and gear that I was not privy to at the time.

We lined up on the sidewalk of the street. Me, Bone, Leverton and Compton. Looked like a western movie poster. When in position, we looked to each other in the distance; and Compton gave the big "go" hand-flick, move-forward finger sign. Guns at the ready, we advanced into the city at our perspective positions. We instantly lost sight of each other. But an off-beat advance might flush out your quarry, as any hunter would tell you. Only this wasn't any dumb animal business.

My area was the abandoned lumberyard (yuk) that I will call here "Jacksberg Lumber." Bone shared the east end of that turf and some business buildings. Limey and Compton had some stretches of buildings and houses, some vacant and some not; and, as I recall, parts of this lumberyard stretched around back of those areas. This lumberyard had the look of a bombed-out one with buildings, stacks and piles of construction materials, and one-and two-story sheds of wood and metal. Basically, your tactical-search nightmare, an irregular, unpredictable, rotting landscape chock full of many places to duck, hide, and snipe.

So. we four men found ourselves stalking in an area about the size of a football field. Well, make that five men. You see, Trooper Compton's hunch was dead on. That desperate, armed son of a bitch was right in there stalking for us.

On TV, in the movies, and on target-shooting ranges, there was much ado about how police officers or even citizens moved about when searching places with their guns out. Mandatory it seemed was the two-handed grip with both arms up and usually extended out. The knees were bent, and people glided smoothly about. You saw a lot of massive two-handed arm swinging, especially among the TV and movie actors coached by the stuntmen, all trying to look like the common perception of the police searching places. Veteran consultants consistently reported that their practical-tactical, poster-boy suggestions were often used for the sake of cool action and art, yet nixed after a real live, prolonged search over unique terrain that nagged on for a bit. Besides, you were moving things around with your hands, etc. Lifting, climbing, etcetera. Searching was always dangerous, and the ambusher always had the advantage. You were an invisible trigger pull away from a bullet.

I had searched for people in huge houses, giant buildings, massive factories, and in rural and city areas in manhunts for hours at some times, even the length of a day. Replaced and back for more the next day!

No matter how you defined "extensive," be it 10 minutes or 10 hours, those movie-poster, target-range, poster-boy image positions could not be maintained because of sheer exhaustion and practicality; and at times they were even somewhat unsafe! A veteran learned pacing and a multitude of gun arm positions to best facilitate the landscape he was operating in. The gun was transitioned from double-hand to single-arm, extended, and retracted as a professional traversed the search area. You might even have had to climb or move something; and that was why God made holsters, pockets, and even armpits. Always having your arms extended and gun out in front of you and your chest could also actually limit your vision on the immediate ground in front and around you. You might miss things that tripped you up and places where bad guys could hide.

Such was the case as I searched that abandoned lumberyard. Out of sight from Leverton, Bone, and Compton, I made my way through the cluttered mess with my pistol in various ready positions, most of them one-handed grips, to step and look everywhere I could and lift cover items. I even switched hands at times to throw some things around to see what reactions I might get from hidden corners.

About 10 long minutes into the search, I had to cross a bit of clearing that was interrupted by piles of rubble. In doing so, I also had to pass several one-and two-story, three-walled, open sheds with old rusty metal and stale wood inside. And to do that, I had to rapidly look over quite an open area. Or I could spend 50 or more minutes tiptoeing into it and "slicing the pie" around every conceivable corner. I didn't have an hour to do this. And I would have been further exposing myself to other unchecked corners at the same time. Real world terrain just simply sucked sometimes.

My eyes scanned as much as I could. And son of a bitch, there he was! He was flat down on his chest in a two-story shed, head up looking at me, and his pistol pointed right at me about 12 feet away. I was in his line of fire and dead meat! Should I move toward him? Just acknowledge him, and he could just pull the trigger.

But I had made no eye contact with him! You see, I had spied him in my peripheral vision in one second's passing glance as my eyes actually scanned a line about six feet tall over him. I did not change my pace and was able to pretend I had not seen him at all. I just had an instinctive inspiration that to suddenly stop, confront him at that very second, point my gun at him, and make some John Wayne command was an invitation to a few quick bullets. His gun was already aimed at me.

Never changing my pace, never stopping my eyes and head scanning, I kept moving across the clearing. I got within a few feet of a tall pile of rubble and dove for it! Rolled up to a single-leg knee (not as cool as it reads here) and backed off from the pile so I could see both sides of the shed. "Don't crowd cover" was the old school rule.

"Give it up, Chester!" I shouted. "Give it up and throw your gun out!"

Gun barrel first, I peeked around a corner of my pile. I saw him again. I saw the left side of his face while he was still prone on the ground. He saw me. He only saw my gun barrel and my right eye. We made this eye contact with each other. All from about 20 feet away.

"Give it UP!" I shouted again, trying to gain an inch more vision. I still couldn't see his right side or his pistol hand. If I saw the pistol, and it was aimed my way? I'd have taken a shot at his head.

I'd shouted that really loud, hoping Limey or Bone, the next two in line, might hear me. Bone did. He came charging across the yard. He must have heard my shouts. He was talking into his hand-held radio. I motioned dramatically to him with my left hand that our man was in the shed before me. He cut left, then turned right behind me, and took a position that somewhat flanked our bad guy. Not enough yet, but he needed to see the scene for a few seconds before he changed positions.

When I'd looked at Bone for an instant as he ran up, just a second, and then back at Chester? Chester was gone, having retreated inside the rotted wood rubble of that big shed! But I could see both sides of the shed and felt that Chester had escaped back deep into it and in among the hundreds of pieces of old wood. The shed was about 15 feet deep or so.

Limey ran up and then came Compton. They could obviously figure out where Chester was holed up by looking at us, and they fanned out accordingly. I heard car engines racing our way. I popped up, head and gun together, and took another good look at the shed. Our man was not to be seen. Was there a hole in the back wall? Could he crawl out? But Limey seemed to be able to see one side and much of the back from what I could tell.

I stayed up, maintaining a steady vigil on the shed, ready to duck and/or shoot. Two or three cars drove across the yard, over the rubble and parked with headlights beaming into the shed as dusk was approaching. The cars ran over broken boards and litter and made very large cracking and popping noises.

Someone shouted, "Duck, he's fired a shot!" I could not tell with all the units rumbling our way. The guy had a small pistol.

Bone ran up to my pile. The officers piled out of their cars. I'd say it was a who's who of county law enforcement. Deputies, city cops. DAs, investigators, and then even Texas Ranger Weldon Lucas showed up, all of whom had been searching well north of us and were drawn back south by my sighting. Then several of us made a cautious advance into the shed.

On the approach, we spotted Chester in the far, left corner of the shed. He'd crawled under a lot of wood to get over there.

"Chester!" I and others called out. "Throw out your gun!"

Chester's face was now face down. His pistol was still in his right hand, his finger on the trigger. The tension in the finger eased off and expanded. We were all zeroed in, intent on that damn finger.

Then it tightened! We all ducked lower; and my trigger finger tightened in conjunction, as I am sure all the other trigger fingers did. He was still not looking at us, but a single shot into our line of encroaching officers would hit somebody.

"Give it up!" we shouted.

Then it loosened. Then it tightened, and we all loosened and tightened, still yelling commands to surrender and still stepping in. Then I realized something just wasn't right.

Lucas, Bone, and I slipped off to the sides of him. Deputies went to the back wall and shoved away the big planks of wood that were half on him and in our way. Chester lay still.

Bone put a big boot on Chester's pistol hand. Weldon Lucas turned him over as I, a foot away, readied to shoot Chester in the head. Too late. We saw...a head wound already!

"The boy's dead," Ranger Lucas said solemnly.

"He's dead," the report echoed through the troops behind us.

I looked over the shed and the body. Chester crawled under tens of planks and two-by-fours. His bare chest and back were scratched open and red. Was he moving wood over his head and accidentally shot himself? Then wounded, crawled to this point and died? Or, facing that "Big Bitch" in the pen and completely surrounded by a dozen guns, did he just do himself in? He must have fired under all the noise of the cars pulling up and cracking wood and popping over junk after all. All that on-and-off, trigger-finger tension we saw was either his death throes or last-ditch efforts of a wounded man to shoot us.
Lucas stood up, and Bone picked up the pistol.

Limey and I quick searched his pockets. Got his wallet. In one pocket was a wad of cash rolled up. I was betting it was the exact amount missing from the auto parts store robbery. EMTs showed up and did a once-over on the body as Bone, Limey, and I converged with the investigators from the DA's office. It was obvious to me that Chester had shot himself, but not so to the others who arrived late.

There were some rumblings from the county officials that I'd shot Chester in the head. Or Bone did. Or that Bone and I both killed him.

"Man, if I shot him?" I said, "if we'd shot him? We'd just tell you,"

Bone nodded. "What's to hide?" He said.

I felt we showed great restraint under the circumstances. Bone and I could have shot the whole shed up like a target gallery with 50 or more .45 caliber and shotgun rounds, but we had tried to bring him in alive.

"You're gonna' find that the bullet in his head came from his own gun," I told them.

Bone, Compton, Limey, and I ... none of us shot or heard each other's guns go off.

"Yeah, okay," one D.A. investigator said, thinking it over. "But before you leave town tonight, would you write us a statement?"

"Sure." Of course, I would. Of course, I knew I had to because the paperwork never ended.

I went to the Gainesville Police Department, sat at an old typewriter, and hacked out a short statement of a few brief paragraphs. Not much to report. "Went to Gainesville to help a search. Found and surrounded suspect. Suspect took his own life. If they needed more? They could ask later. I left the report with Bone. I checked in with Limey and then got into the Dodge and headed south.

Funny thing was all this had taken about two and a half hours, which was what I thought about on the drive back. Just two and a half hours since the robbery and dead ending. And when I started out, I never dreamed I would even get up there in time, never dreamed I'd be searching in the key area, never thought I'd almost be shot by the robber, and never thought I'd find him and pin him down. And how about that Compton with his gut instincts?

But I was a bit haunted, too, by a close escape. By how I played the scene. How I pretended not to see the suspect until I got behind cover. It was a smart play and one that I was not sure I would have done had I not been to the *Caliber Press*, Police Street Survival School, just two weeks earlier.

Otherwise, it would have been probable for me to "John Wayne" my way into the shootout and have stood out there in the wide open, even though Chester had the first drop-and-stop, dead aim on me. Chester was desperate enough to shoot me on first eye contact rather than be caught.

That was the haunting part, the "what if" part. But I had done something smart, not stupid. Something ... tactical.

Maybe that school had burned a concept indelibly into my brain? Maybe haunted was not a good word for how I felt. Relieved? No. Ironic? Maybe. (Oh, and just for the record, I experienced no major adrenaline rush or dump, nor pooped in my pants as all the lab-rat tester experts like to proclaim always happened, just a low grade of necessary excitement throughout. Been that way my whole life.)

Anyway, that was the ugly story with a side lesson about playing it smart. Y'all had better take it to heart. Leverton would clear the armed robbery case "by arrest," as our CID books defined. Always a good notch. "Cleared by arrest." I had arrested a lot of people in my life, and I was not sure if that was technically an arrest or not? I mean, nobody got cuffed. Well, then, maybe ... arrest by death.

Chapter 18: I Caught the Hitman

We hunted the hitman-killer for days.
Late tips.
"Ohhh, man! You just missed him!"
Bad karma.
That voodoo that he do.
"Come back tomorrow!"
Missed mojo.
Where in hell is he?

While we'd only hunted the killer for several days, it took a full three months for Jeff Wawro and me to get the professional killer's name.

We were the two city police detectives tagged with some 20-and-counting felonies that included a drug gang war, and a hit man murder. It had been about 60 days of a wheels-off ride in the middle of drive-bys, drug raids, angry girlfriends, death threats, shootings, beatings, cuttings, and murder that stretched from central Oklahoma to north Texas. Drugs.

We put several "gangstas" in jail. One, we will call here "Lincoln," was a teenager, an official "minor" and once in a while, drive-by shooter. We were convinced that this kid could crack the whole case open for us. If only the Lincoln would talk. He was a weak link or the weakest link we had in jail.

There were even more obstacles thrown in our way. Smack in the middle of all this, Wawro was "on rotation call-out" for a week, a time when each detective was on call for patrol to roust out when needed. It was routine for the on-call detective to get tagged with the case. He was tagged with a wire-hanger, strangulation murder, a female found dead in her apartment.

"I got the case," Jeff told me the next morning.

"NO!" I said. "No way. Don't they know how busy we are, how close we are?"

"No," he said with a horizontal headshake. Our detective management team at work - a new sergeant, promoted from patrol traffic division with zero detective squad savvy. Your government at work. There was no way I was going to let Jeff get bogged down in yet an- other murder while we had this hit man murder case and all these organized crime cases ticking away like time bombs.

So, I jumped in and we both tackled the strangulation case hard and fast. In two days, we arrested that killer, a married man killed his girlfriend the day his wife gave birth. We arrested the cheater at the newborn wing of a hospital. Apparently, the girlfriend was going to cause too much trouble. But that's yet another story.

At one point we realized we needed to visit the Okla- homa city where one of the gangs headquartered. We drove up there and walked into the country sheriff's office to find all the city and county narcotics investiga- tors in a big meeting room. It was a collective raid day!

They had numerous search and arrest warrants to serve that very day! And one warrant was for one of the guys we needed to talk to. Some other names on the list were interesting. This was like Christmas for us.

Despite the legal fact that all our *PO*-lice authority was in Texas, not Oklahoma, they told us to come along anyway and help. This trip to Oklahoma, kicking doors, chasing fleeing suspects, arresting, seizing drugs could be a small book in and of itself. And we interrogated the man we needed to. We collected more supportive intelligence. He'd heard from his friends about some killer name "Moss," or "Mossman," was hired in Texas to "off" another gang boss.

Meanwhile, among this and other distractions, we continued to squeeze in visits with our jailed juvenile shooter, Lincoln. Jeff Wawro took full point of this. He would eat fast food lunches with Lincoln at the juvenile jail almost every day. Maybe for a month, and after all these trips, conversations, and cajoling talks, one afternoon, this young jailbird broke open. He admitted he was at, and saw the killing.

He confessed. He named names. The hit man was "Jessie Lee Moss," an ex-con, karate expert (not his real name by the way, no way I'd give this skunk any publicity because he would actually enjoy it). Moss was a crack and heroin dealer and a shooter for hire with a gang of his own. Known to torture.

I knew of this guy! And another one of our detectives and a good friend in the Division, Benny Parkey, had arrested Moss several times before, and you might say they had a bit of a personal vendetta toward each other. Benny, like me and like Moss were into "karate." There was no way I was going to hunt down Moss without Benny's insider knowledge and help on Moss.

I got Benny in on the manhunt as soon as possible. The three of us went to work to hunt him down. We looked for days all over the Dallas-Fort Worth Metroplex.

Finally, late one morning, Benny got a call from an informant that our man was visiting a certain house in the so-called "bad part" of town. We raced to it in our sedans. It was a large and rambling old home and we parked down the street to approach by foot.

We split up. Benny and Jeff went to the rear of the house, and I walked up to the front door. I guess I was supposed to knock? Instead, when I got up to the door and delayed a little to let Benny and Jeff have time to get around back. Instead of knocking, I touched the doorknob and gave it a turn. It opened. I instantly pulled my .45 but kept it down at my side in what we use to call a "bootleg" carry in the business.

I stepped in and looked around. The living room was
big, old, and cold; and I could already hear Benny talking to the residents, a man and a woman, way back in the kitchen. His voice was muffled and garbled, but I knew what he was saying to them,

"Look now, someone told us Moss was here. We gotta' look around." That old speech.

They denied any knowledge. That old speech too. I was alone in the front half of the big house, and I walked quietly down the hall and saw a bathroom door open less than an inch. I stepped up, lifted my gun, and peered in. I saw something move.

I shoved the door wide open, and there was our man. I held my pistol, rib high and pointed it at his guts. His eyes darted around the room like he was looking to es- cape, and then into a big, open black duffle bag on the floor beside him. I saw at least a gun and a shotgun in there. He looked like he was going to….

"Don't even think about it," I told him. "Or, you're dead right there."

I gave him the evil eye along with it. And I would've shot that bastard down if I needed to. I think he could tell.

"Turn around. put your hands behind your back," I told him. "Fuck around and I'll drop you right here."

With my left hand, I took the handcuffs that were hooked over the belt at the small of my back and cuffed his wrists. Then I hooked his captured arm, tucked the gun back in my holster, and walked him through the house to find Wawro and Benny in the kitchen, still talking to the couple.

"Yeah, he ain't here…RIGHT!" was all I said to the couple.

Captured! After this big break. With the killer in jail and no bond, and we pretty well cracked open all the related cases. I filed 12 organized crime cases. Wawro filed the hit man murder case.

Police Detective Notebook...

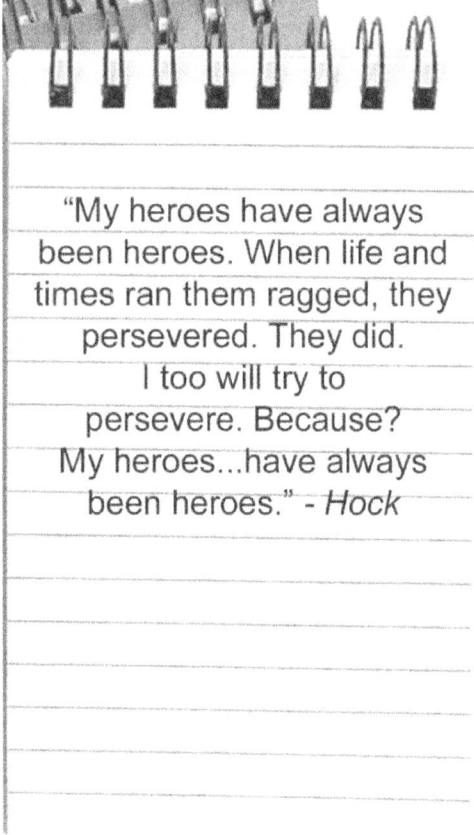

"My heroes have always been heroes. When life and times ran them ragged, they persevered. They did.
I too will try to persevere. Because?
My heroes...have always been heroes." - *Hock*

Chapter 19: Benny Parkey. Adios Amigo

Part 1: Slipped the Veil

I just mentioned Benny Parkey in the previous chapter. Years later he ran for Sheriff of our county. Years after I retired. He called me to say he was going to do it. He and I were never rank seekers and never took promotional tests at the P.D. Yet...this was the ultimate law-boss job. A sheriff!

He told me, that " I want more out of my life, my career. I don't want this detective job to be the sole mark of my life."

"Okay," I said. Who could argue more about that? I retired from the PD to run my training company. He knew my other secret, that I always wanted to be a CID Captain and run a whole division. That and win the lottery.

I helped him out with some writing, some letters and appearances.

He won and ran unopposed next term. But a charismatic guy appeared and ran against him. Benny lost that one. Long story on that one.

Then Benny's wife died. She'd been sickly. Then one day I got another phone call from Benny a few years later. He was going to die at some point from lung cancer. There was nothing to be done about it. Even though he never smoked!

He lasted quite a while. And then poor Benny passed. A lot of people wrote wonderful things about him on his obituary page and on the internet. I could add many more things because we "go back." Too much to say. Lots of people sharing photos of them with Benny. Here is a picture of us in the 1990s. I feel like I need to vent here over his passage.

Me and Benny. We did karate together and chased a lot of bad guys together.

Some people say if Benny was your friend he always had your back. "Regular" people have certain definitions of "having your back," but Benny really has had my back many times.

Benny is one of the few people I could list on one hand that if I was in real trouble, or if my family was in real trouble, I could call him, day or night and he would show up with a gun. And I mean that, and I am also sure he would have still shown up if I called him the very last week of his life. Yeah. Somebody would have driven him - but he'd a come.

I saw him for lunch a few times those last years, knowing full well that underneath, he was bad sick, but it just didn't show, and many of us never fully realizing how soon things would end. I mean, not long ago, like two weeks before he died, he was walking around like his old self, laughing and joking and saying he would soon need a cane.

He wrote to me near the end that "his days were numbered," and he would very soon, "slip the veil," as he put it and he said "you have always been a good friend and supported me. Goodbye, old friend."

I am pretty inept about such things and I didn't really know what to say to that, except to talk about another future lunch. A lunch that never came.

He died while I was teaching several weeks in Europe. Benny was a class act all the way, Texas style. Special. And he did indeed leave his mark as a great Texas Sheriff.

To me though, personally, he will always be a real bloodhound investigator and friend. In the Lonesome Dove book and TV show, Gus complimented a feller once, "he sure was good company at suppertime." That symbolizes a mighty high complement. Benny was all that and more.

Part 2 - View from the Balcony

I was thinking about Benny Parkey again the other day. Thinking about some of the last photos of him, on a balcony in South Padre, way down in South Texas, over- looking the Gulf of Mexico just weeks before he died. He knew then he was going to die very soon. One photo below kind of haunts me. His then girlfriend sent it to me - Benny taking a short vacation with her in Galveston, Texas. Him sitting on a balcony overlooking the Gulf. I still stare at that picture and wonder what he was thinking about, looking over those waves, with life's clock ticking off.

Then - Thanksgiving, 2016 after Benny died - this came in my email. (I have deleted/altered some info as we have to keep sex crime victims protected.)

"Subject: You and Det. Parkey solved my case.
Dear Detective Hochheim, My name is _____.
My maiden name is_____. Back in October 1990, I was followed home from the Kroger on Dallas Drive to my apartment. He followed me there and abducted me at knife point, kidnapped me in my own car and drove me to the outskirts of town where I was sexually assaulted. He planned to dismember me. I remember begging and pleading for my life at the beginning and quickly saw that added fuel to the fire.

So I pretty much surrendered to the situation. I accepted the fact I would be murdered. The turning point came when I asked him for the switchblade he was holding. I asked for him to let me have the dignity of killing myself. I meant it. He let me go.

Anyway, you and Benny were the detectives, and I remember you so clearly sitting in your office that cold, fall day at your typewriter taking my statement. I'll never forget, the next afternoon you all called me, to tell me a State Trooper had pulled over a Brown Datsun with heavy front-end damage that matched the description of the suspect (as he was) leaving a trailer park.

You (got his picture) called me in for a photo lineup and when I identified him, you and Benny high-fived and I'll never, ever forget how excited you both were, including myself, to capture that creep. You too arrested him. It was one of the best days of my life in so many ways!!

Y'all two together hunted him down and arrested him and you saw my mom's old super 8 film camera he stole on the suspect's couch, but I had stupidly forgotten to mention that I had it (in my car). Anyway, y'all drove me to the crime scene too where we found more evidence way out in the middle of nowhere.

Had you both not worked so damn hard, he would not have gotten that 85-year sentence or even had gone to trial. I'll never forget your dynamic personality and Benny's sweetness. You were too!! You took me and my best friend for a coke that next morning after the
assault.

I know this thank you has come years too late. I'm heart-broken over Benny's death when I heard. I think of y'all often and wish I could have thanked you both much earlier. I owe you my life in many ways.

I went on to earn 2 bachelor degrees. I'm married now for 14 years to a great guy who is sensitive to the debilitating PTSD I have. I'm grateful to be here!! I mainly want to thank you with every fiber of my being and from the depths of my heart and soul. I thank you. I'm so grateful. I'm sending Benny my thanks and keep him alive in my spirit. I'm so proud of you both and I treasure you both!!!!

                        Happy Thanksgiving & Love,
"
_____

Now sadly, sadly, I don't remember this case at all. Isn't that terrible that I can't? I mean, it's obviously so important to any person that has experienced this. But it is hard to remember things when you have about some 22 new cases a month for about 18 years in CID. It's a rat race, chasing rats. All the rats in your brain. And...all that pain. The pain. It all melts together as your brain melts. Benny and I "worked on many crimes together (by choice) and for a period of time, were officially assigned together, working in a Crimes Against Persons section within the division, along with a Detective Margaret Yarbrough. Now Benny and Margaret are both dead from cancers. Only I, somehow, remain.

But I hope Benny did remember this one case among so many while sitting on that balcony overlooking the Gulf, remembering things like this, our victories, the times that we "won," and he won, what we affected and effected in that…that "sole mark," he mentioned. when thinking about…life. Maybe on that balcony by the gulf.

Adios. Adios, amigo.

Chapter 20: The "Hockford Files." Private Investigator and the Last Murder Case

Upon retiring, I still had a itch for investigation and for 3 years worked a P.I. while running my training company. My then wife got a job in Georgia, and we moved which ended all of that P.I. business too. I started out this book with an Army story and near the end of this book, I will finish with a P.I. story.

"What happened in Vegas stays in Vegas." We were once all familiar with that ad line. To turn that phrase a bit, "what happened in private investigation stays in private investigation." And as a result, I would publicly discuss only the barest bones of my years as a P.I. as a service to inquiring and ambitious minds. After all, the public was fascinated with private investigators from books, movies, and TV. Lots of people thought they wanted to be one or thought they had what it took to be one.

People would ask me, was being one as exciting as the Rockford Files or Magnum, PI. I would say "Yes, except there were no shoot-outs, car chases or rampant sex."

Each of the 50 USA states had its own state board controlling the rules and regulations of private investigation as well as related security and bodyguard work. Armed and unarmed. In Texas back in the 1990s, such a wannabe P.I. applicant had to have a minimum of two years' experience in law enforcement or some years working under and vouched for by an established, licensed Texas investigator. So, I qualified instantly.

I applied for all the test books and required reading from the Texas State Licensing Board, which translated to dishing out money to Uncle Sam or more precisely, Uncle Sam Houston in Austin, Texas - a.k.a. - you know it as - the "government." One studied the required material that covered a multitude of security-related subjects, even how often to feed your K-9 guard dogs and how to clean the kennels (as if!).

About one month later, I drove to the State Capital; and, with a handful of other applicants, I paid the government the significant testing fee, sat down, and took the test. I drove back to Dallas and within a few days was notified I passed the test. I could hang out a shingle as a licensed private investigator.

But wait now. Wait just a minute. The shingle cost more money than that test fee and a piece of wood-shingle with lettering on it.

- Ka-ching $$$! There was also fee to own a private investigation company.
- Ka-ching $$$$. There was another fee to be a private investigator inside that (and your's even) company.
- Ka-ching $$$. If you carried a gun, there was a special week-long, expensive gun course and a written test fee and yet another license.
- Ka-ching $$$: Annual training and licensing fees. Ka-ching $$$: If you did personal protection, there was another course and even more dollars.
- Ka-ching $$$: Then there were mandatory insurance-bonding fees.
- Ka-ching $$$. If memory serves, there was another fee for something else.
- ALL TO BE RENEWED ANNUALLY!

The "hang-the-shingle" idea started looking like a highway billboard worth of expenses. So, before the shingle was hung by the doorframe with care, you were already out a steady stream of dollars, all raining in the coffers of Texas. And as underlined above, these fees were annual but spread out over several months a piece in such a manner that it seemed like you were constantly sending money to Austin!

I never actually hung an actual physical shingle out or even enrolled in the telephone book ads. Today P.I.s use webpages. I simply told a handful of north Texas lawyers I was available for duty by mailing them a letter. I had worked with or rather against many of them as a detective for almost two decades and developed a decent reputation. Some people hated lawyers, but I always liked hanging out with lawyers. They are usually a smart, fun bunch…out of court. Many are good critical thinkers.

I paid these seemingly never-ending fees. But I quit the licensing drain after a while. I created a hack that not many of you can use. Most of my work came from lawyers. When a lawyer hired me, I requested to become a firm's "paralegal" for a "duration." This job title allowed me to be paid (through the firm's paperwork) and gather information for a case, which is what they do, and I skipped all those fees. Being paid this internal way thwarts the state P.I. licensing rules. Furthermore, when I did bodyguard protection work, I supplied a contract identifying me as a security consultant-organizer, _NOT_ a bodyguard. Was I at the events-scenes-transports? Often with a gun? Yes. Different hacking umbrella.

I am not here to give you hacking advice here. I was just lucky to be connected to attorneys and publicity companies and continued working without blood money to the state. Look, it's a gray area as to what citizens can do and look up information for a variety of legal things and with the web, now more than ever. People can look up almost any information now and offer it to help folks, help police and lawyers. It's tricky. Were they paid or not?

It was not quite what I had expected at first. Because, you see, the ugly truth was that a private investigator was little more than just another citizen who was paying a lot of fees to the State. As a P.I., I discovered that I was essentially powerless to do so so many of the things I had done so routinely as a police detective. That was a gap I instantly noticed.

Let's face it; no one really had to cooperate with me! lash a PI badge? When push really came to shove, it was a skinny piece of tin. It was a bit of a bluff. I was spoiled by officially manipulating people around when I once had the ugly monster of "police or law enforcement" with a open cage door behind me. Suddenly the cage was gone, and the bluff was lame. It was a culture shock for me, and I had to invent new, charming ways to get things done.

At least when I was officially court-appointed to many criminal cases, via the defense attorney's request for an investigator. One new way to influence and "win over" people was my introduction to all involved:

"I have been court-appointed by Judge Johnson of the 380th District Court to help in this investigation."

Now, that sounded like I had a District Judge standing right behind me, not a cop cage. In fact, this was technically true. It helped a little, but I was forced to become increasingly clever and seductive about getting that new job done with a skinnier badge.

I could write another book about all this, but I will just offer for your entertainment, my last PI case.

My Last Murder Case
Late 1990s. I was hired in what I thought at the time would be my last official Texican P.I. case because I was moving to Georgia and would be a total stranger there to the Georgia judicial system. I thought it foolish to pay to take the Georgia test and pay for all the previously explained fees, insurance, etc. over there. So, I would just quit the business. Done! While packing, I got the last, "can you help us" phone call from an attorney.

This case concerned a somewhat famous, former Big 10 college football player from another state arrested for a murder in North Texas. A law office I worked against for years when a police detective and later worked for them as a P.I. called for help. I got in my truck and drove over.

The attorney ushered me into the conference room. At the table sat a large man in his mid-20s.

"This is Willie Tilton," (we'll call him that here as you might recognize him.) You might recognize him. Former quarterback for _____ university and soon to be drafted for the pros."

"Hi, Willie," I said and sat at the table. I didn't recognize him. I don't care much for college football. He was wearing his oversized college bowl championship ring. Willie introduced me to someone else with him at the table, but as of today, I cannot remember the name of the woman. Just someone he knew. And Willie sure needed moral support for his predicament.

You see, Willie was soon to appear in court for a murder. And his story, as many of them are, was a strange one.

"Go ahead and tell Hock what happened," the lawyer kick-started the conversation because he knew the meter was running.

"I met this woman in Texas," he started. "She was wild. Crazy. I never should have picked up with her. I had some business here and when I would come, I would see her. I would, you know…date her. And she was trouble from the start. I realize that now.

"She the dead one?" I asked.

"She's the dead one. She was over-emotional. Snorted coke…"

"That'll help the craziness." I said.

A lot of guys like that sort of "temporary bad girl" in their lives.

"She had all kinds of health problems too. From booze and drugs. We were out on the lake in a boat. The big one south of here, Lake Lewsiville. It was a weekend when I was about to call this whole thing off. We got out in a boat. It was a rented boat. A nice big one. We did some coke and drank on the boat. I mean, I did it too.

She wanted to swim. I said okay. I stopped the boat and she jumped right into the water. She swam around out there. Talking to me. Normal. I didn't jump in right away. You know, doing stuff on the boat. Next thing I know, it started to look like she was swimming or "floating" pretty far from the boat. It was very windy out there. There were some tides and some chop. I shouted to her, and…something wasn't right. She looked sick or something? Like…mentally out of it?

Her jaw hanging down. She started to look like she was drowning or something."

I nodded.

"Yeah. I jumped in the water and swam to her, and she was not right! Sick, or like she was going to faint or something and she couldn't talk. Babbled. She made no sense. Mumbling. I grabbed her with one arm and started to swim back to the boat. But the boat was floating further away with the wind. The more I swam, the further it seemed to get away."

"Was she fighting you like a drowning person would?" I asked.

"No! She did not. But she was moving around. I decided to turn with her and swim for the shore. I was about in the middle at this point. Between the boat and the shore and at least the shore wouldn't moving away from me like the boat was bobbing away from me. It was like a nightmare."

"How were you holding her?" I asked. "Can you show me?"

He stood up. "Like this. I had one arm free to swim and the other wrapped around her. It was hard."

"You ever take any life-saving lessons? Ever been a lifeguard at a pool?"

"No, sir."

"The arm you had wrapped around this woman… wrapped around what exactly?"

"Her arm and her body, then her neck. Chest. She was slipping free and I was changing the grip to get to the shore. I was yelling for help, and some people saw me and heard me. When I got to the shore, I pulled her on land and she was limp. Like dead person. I started some kind of CPR. I mean, I didn't know how to do it. I just did my best."

His eyes wandered all over the tabletop before he put both palms on the table. "She was dead."

Then he looked at all our faces at the table and continued.

"These people walking around the shore. Around us. I called to them for help, as I had got closer to the shore, so they were there when we got there. When we got on the beach, I asked for an ambulance."

"They called? They waited around? You have their names?"

"Yes, sir. The police came first before the ambulance. They took the names of everyone that was still around. The ambulance got there, and it was just too late."

"And you eventually got arrested for murder? Right then? Or when? Did they get an arrest warrant?"

"Well, right then. That afternoon. I mean, I was arrested right there on the beach. I was in handcuffs. For drowning her and killing her."

"Right...then? Who arrested you?"

"Well, the police did! A county deputy."

"I mean, did a detective, an investigator show up, look around, question you and then arrest you?"

"No, sir. The uniformed officers there did it. One of them arrested me for murder."

"City or county?" I asked.

"County." I drummed my fingers on this big table.

This was all out of whack. Out of sync. No protocol. Sounds like the 50s, 60s, or 70s. Not the 1990s. For a quick civilian translation, this was a questionable death at best with strong signs of a simple drowning, or a botched rescue. It required more investigation before an arrest.

I turned to the attorney, "Autopsy?"

He slid me a file. I looked it over. Very standard simplistic report, like the many I'd seen from this very Medical Examiner's office through the years. Water was found in the lungs. There was a toxicology report.

"Significant cocaine found," I mumbled.

"Ever get the boat back? I asked Willie.

"Yes, the police asked for help and some people there with boats got my boat and brought it to a dock."

"Impounded? Searched?"

"Taken? No. It was rented. It wasn't mine. But they looked it over. Took some Polaroids. They said they would call the dock where we got the boat."

"Polaroids. And what are in these Polaroids?

The attorney slid over some very bad photocopies of these pictures to me.

"Beer cans. Whiskey. Towels. Some food," Willie said.

"No coke?"

"They…didn't find the coke. They really didn't search the boat too well. They could have found the coke we had left, but they didn't. Just took photos. Moved stuff around and took pictures."

"Where was the coke?"

"I can't remember for sure. In a jacket pocket?"

"Whose jacket?"

" I don't…" he stammered.

"Hey man, it doesn't matter to me. I am here to help you."

"It was my coke. In my jacket pocket. A windbreaker."

"And the jacket?"

"I don't know. I never saw it again. Went back to the rental place with the boat I guess?"

"They got your wallet, though? From the boat?"

"Yes, sir."

"You're really lucky they didn't find the cocaine, "I said. "You'd probably be plea-bargained into some kind of hand-slapped, manslaughter conviction, Willie. A sweet deal with possession and manslaughter tied up like a box. The cocaine giving you the most punishment you can't dodge. An offer, one you simply could not refuse, to wash all this mess away and still get a conviction."

"I know I'm lucky, but that girl died of drugs. Drowning. I did not kill her. I tried to rescue her."

"You said health problems. What kind of health problems did this woman have. Exactly."

"I know she'd been to a heart doctor. Heart problems. She's been in rehab twice for drugs. I called her brother right away. He and his wife, or girlfriend, I don't know what she is. They showed up at the police station, and he told the cops all about her bad health and bad heart. From drugs. The cops heard all about it."

"Any of it in these conversations in any report?" I asked the lawyer.

"No," the lawyer said.

"I heard about them from the deputies, the way they questioned me that day. Then the brother accused me of wanting to break up with her and even killing her. After I got arrested, at the county, a detective spoke with me. He told what the brother said."

"And the detective just let the arrest, let everything stand."

"Uh-huh."

"We've tried to talk with the brother and he will not cooperate," the lawyer said. "I think they want to see Willie in jail for murder and maybe even sue Willie."

"Lawsuit. Yeah." I said.

" I think the police officers recognized they had a dead body and a famous football player and they thought they'd caught a big fish for murder," The lawyer declared. Lawyers like to make such declarations and arguments, but you know, way stranger things have happened than this mess.

"You got any idea, any possible idea that someone would think you'd have a motive to kill this girl?" I asked Willie.

"A few people knew I wanted to break up with her. She knew I was engaged. She must have told her brother. He was angry at me. He blames me for the whole thing."

"You married at home? Engaged?" I asked.

"I was engaged. At the time."

"And...that's not you?" I asked the lady at the table with him.

She shook her head, no.

"Was she going to interfere with that? The marriage?" I asked

"She said she might. The drugs talking I think."

"And again. When you were pulling her to the shore, ever have your arm wrapped around her neck?"

"Several times I imagine. Her neck and arm. Upper chest. Neck, Yeah. She was slippery. Squirming. It was hard."

"Okay," I said. "We need a subpoena for the hospital records and any medical records for the woman. A bad heart and cocaine make for easy positional asphyxia argument."

"Posi....what's that?" Willie asked. The blank expressions on the lawyer's face and Willie's face told me they both needed an explanation for that term. The term was a bit unpopular in the 1990s, but police and martial arts ground fighters were familiar with it. P.A. means semi-containing and/or squeezing the torso and/or neck of a person enough to restrict breathing. It means being stuck in a position causing breathing problems.

I explained, and for the readers here, an official definition:

"Positional asphyxia (PA) is a form of asphyxia which occurs when someone's position prevents them from breathing adequately. A small but significant number of people die suddenly and without apparent reason during restraint by police, prison (corrections) officers and health care staff. Positional asphyxia may be a factor in some of these deaths. Positional asphyxia is a potential danger of some physical restraint techniques. People may die from positional asphyxia by simply getting themselves into a breathing-restricted position they cannot get out of, either through carelessness or as a consequence of another accident."

All the desperate neck pulling and the chest squeezing, combined with drugs and a pre-existing heart condition could be easily explained as P.A. And it's a very believable defense. I will get the girl's background. I will find a national expert on this subject. And it will cost you more for a medical expert or two."

He flipped his hand over and side-to-side with a smirk, signaling money was no problem at this point.

"My guess is," I continued, "if this case actually goes any further, because it is a lame case on many points, you'll have to take the stand and explain what happened. We usually hate that. But you might have to. A lot will be brought up, but the arm positioning is case-hanger. Your defense hangs on that and positional Asphyxia. Without your testimony on the stand describing it, I don't see now how else to get it introduced."

The lawyer nodded. I asked a few more questions that I cannot discuss here. I stood. The lawyer directed Willie to write a check to the firm for me, once again the paralegal. It was hefty one, for several thousands of dollars. Goodbyes to all.

And then goodbye…to my job too! Yup. On the parking lot, walking to my car, I decided to finish this job and quit the P.I. business then and there. I got in my truck and drove away. We already had a home picked in Georgia and leaving a house in Dallas at the time, one full of cardboard boxes ready to move east. As I drove to the house, I looked at my watch.

I hadn't been in that law office for longer than 40 minutes and I had just seriously sliced and diced up a murder case. Would I miss this job? Am I wasting an accumulated amount of lifetime experience? At that time in my life, I could effectively game plan any case laid before me. Like a lawyer. It was like an instinct by then. No brag. Just fact. You can just ask anyone I worked with or against.

But I will tell you something else. That very day something else happened to me? I guess with the momentum of me moving away, I felt a big change coming? I felt like I didn't want to do this anymore. I was sick of people's problems. Decades and decades of nothing but people's problems.

Within 48 hours I'd found and interviewed the best expert on positional asphyxia in the country, a doctor (coincidentally also in Georgia), and we shipped him all the medical reports and the case file.

He assured me that this had all the signs of a medically enhanced, drug-enhanced, asphyxia case, beyond a reasonable doubt. Barring no other surprise circumstances, that is. As always.

I also met the brother at a restaurant under the friendly guise of "getting to the bottom of all this," which I was. And I suggested that maybe if I were him, I'd be seeking a quick lawsuit settlement for him of some kind. He told me everything. I deduced he had no claim. He had no claim and no testimony that would affect a criminal or civil case.

Within a month, the prosecution knew we had this renown P.A. expert ready to testify and actually chomping at the bit to testify. The entire case against the football player suddenly dropped.

A note...
I thought I was done. I have since worked on a cold case or two (helped solve a 1981 murder 40 years later) since and some civil and even criminal case consulting

when asked by the police chief at the time. And I have been hired by a few police departments once in a while, and some attorneys to review things. Mostly now, I just train people for hand, stick, knife and gun fighting, except for these occasional things that pop up. I don't seek them out.

But if you have something you'd like to talk about? Or a problem with someone, somewhere or something? I'll probably at least listen. If it's interesting or weird enough? I may saddle up.

```
Police Detective Notebook
```

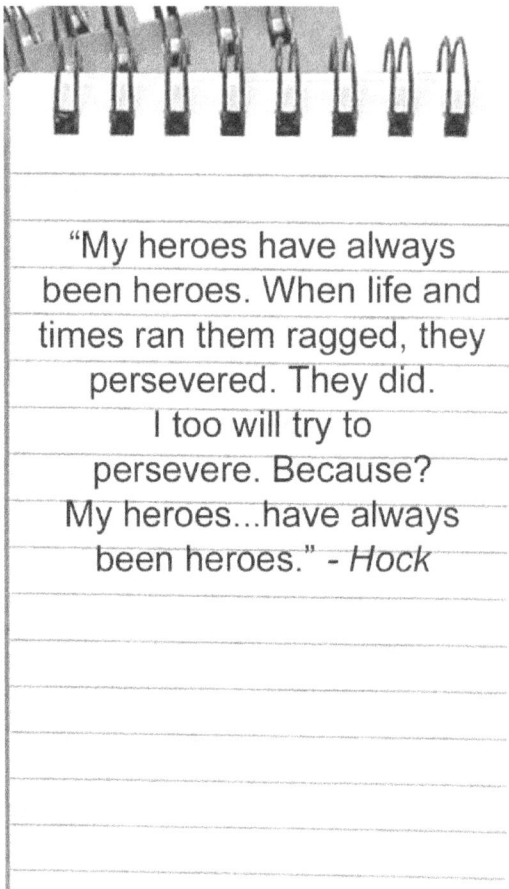

"My heroes have always been heroes. When life and times ran them ragged, they persevered. They did.
  I too will try to persevere. Because?
My heroes...have always been heroes." - *Hock*

Chapter 21: Back to Lynch's Hunch

Well, it looks like this memoir-manuscript has hit 300-plus pages and 73,000 words already, more than the suggested publisher's limit. Still, there's no way I'm going to be able to write about all my interesting felony cases, nor the interesting years I put in later as a private investigator (another book?), so I'd better shut this one down.

I started out this book with my old police chief Hugh Lunch's hunch about me, to come full circle. About a decade after that "you want to be a detective" question he asked me while I was booking in a prisoner. Well many years after Lynch had retired, I'd busted a pretty big armed robbery gang. It was in all the local newspapers.

I was shopping in a large video-tape rental store like the old Blockbuster Video (remember them?), and who walked in but the retired ol' Hugh Lynch himself.

I was glad to see him, because, boy, he was a character let me tell you. We caught up just a bit, and then he said,

"You in on that big gang bust in the newspaper?"

"Yup. That was my case."

"I *knew* it," he said with a big smile. "You are the best detective this city ever had."

Well…wow. I smiled when I first typed this and smiled again when I re-read those words. I never tell people this story because it sounded like, you know, I was bragging. There were many detectives in my city, he was even one once. Some were damn good. Some threw cases right in the trash like the incorrigible Skeens.

Maybe I am bragging just a bit right now, but I thought it was a good way to start off and to end this book. Start with Lynch. End with Lynch. Lynch and his…hunch.

THE END

Me, from what I must call…my better, most useful professional days.

It's Texas in the 1980s and 90s, and his world is full of corrupt police, bad judges, seedy bail bondsmen, conniving complicit lawyers, the Cowboy Mafia, violent career criminals, cartels, desperate drug addicts, rapists, weaselly thieves and frightened snitches. He smells them out, stomps on them, puts them away or sometimes? Sometimes he has to kill them.

Some say that Jack Kellog is a "Texas Dirty Harry," or maybe call him a "rogue," but Jack is more complicated than that. He's a former Houston street cop, a Harris County city detective who almost died in the field and was resurrected as a special agent in the Texas State Police Intelligence Division. There, he might work as a "lone wolf" or command a whole task force. The Governor knows him. The CIA knows him. Mexican generals, the Cosa Nostra and the Cowboy Mafia know him. How about you? Do you know Jumpin' Jack Kellog?

The early 1900s. A time just after the American gunfighter, and right before the noir detective. A time when men with a certain experience were called upon to solve difficult problems. Men like Johann Gunther, former military officer and war vet, ex-Texas lawman, spy and owner of a special firm called Remedies in Fort Worth, Texas. Due to Gunther's worldly experiences, he is often tasked with international adventures, bringing his special "code of the west," western hero ethics into the life and death of international war and crime.

    Book 1: Gunther! The Law West of Medieval
      Book 2: Guns of the China Alamo
      Book 3: Last of the Gunslingers
      Book 4: Riders of the Khyber Pass
      Book 5: Rio Grande Black Magic
      Book 6: The Horse Killers

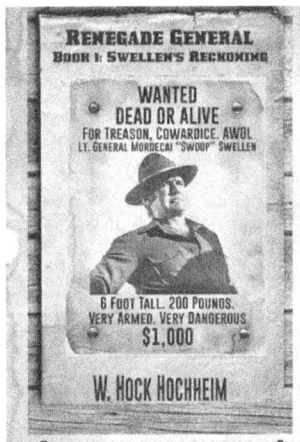

Falsely accused of treason, Swoop is back "on the run" in this new Ebook and paperback series, thanks to a passel of worldwide distributors such as Barnes and Nobles. If you like the classic westerns of old, like "Josey Wales," "Branded" and "One-Eyed-Jacks," you will saddle up with Swoop Swellen as he travels the world to stay ahead of the U.S. Army, Wells Fargo and vicious bounty hunters, all the while falling into dangerous adventures and misadventures.

They Killed the Chinese Ambassador's wife. To cover it up, they had to kill an N.Y.P.D. detective. They shot him in the head. But he didn't die. They just made him...crazy.

Really crazy.

Search for all of Hock's fiction and non-fiction books on Amazon, and Barnes and Nobles

www.ingramcontent.com/pod-product-compliance
Lightning Source LLC
Chambersburg PA
CBHW071726080526
44588CB00013B/1909